西安外国语大学著作出版专项出版资助

教师角色与身份建构：
中学英语教师专业发展研究

ROLES AND IDENTITY:

Researching Secondary School EFL Teachers' Professional Development

徐 斌 著

重庆大学出版社

图书在版编目（CIP）数据

教师角色与身份建构：中学英语教师专业发展研究 /
徐斌著.--重庆：重庆大学出版社，2023.2
ISBN 978-7-5689-3637-8

Ⅰ.①教… Ⅱ.①徐… Ⅲ.①英语—中学教师—师资
培养—研究 Ⅳ.①G633.412

中国版本图书馆CIP数据核字（2022）第223350号

教师角色与身份建构：
中学英语教师专业发展研究
JIAOSHI JUESE YU SHENFEN JIANGOU：
ZHONGXUE YINGYU JIAOSHI ZHUANYE FAZHAN YANJIU

徐 斌 著

责任编辑：杨 琪　　版式设计：品木文化
责任校对：谢 芳　　责任印制：赵 晟

*

重庆大学出版社出版发行
出版人：饶帮华
社址：重庆市沙坪坝区大学城西路21号
邮编：401331
电话：（023）88617190　88617185（中小学）
传真：（023）88617186　88617166
网址：http://www.cqup.com.cn
邮箱：fxk@cqup.com.cn（营销中心）
全国新华书店经销
重庆升光电力印务有限公司印刷

*

开本：720mm×1020mm　1/16　印张：16.75　字数：380千
2023年2月第1版　　2023年2月第1次印刷
ISBN 978-7-5689-3637-8　定价：98.00元

本书如有印刷、装订等质量问题，本社负责调换

Forward

Language teachers' identity research has grown exponentially over the past decade. Existing scholarship has proved that the construction of language teachers' identity is a multifaceted and constantly shifting process which has been influenced by a wide range of personal, professional and contextual factors. Notwithstanding the copious research on language teachers' identity, fewer studies have been conducted to examine secondary EFL teachers' professional identity construction, and little is known about professional identity development of teachers in rural elementary or secondary schools in regions of multiethnic groups in China. In order to fill the gaps in literature, this study aims to explore secondary school EFL teachers' professional identity development, and to examine the factors that might influence the process of teachers' professional identity construction.

This study selects three English teachers from rural secondary schools in Xishuangbanna Dai Autonomous Prefecture as research participants. Guided by an integrated theoretical framework (the Identity Formation Theory, the History-in-Person Theory, Identity-in-Discourse and Identity-in-Practice), this qualitative case study adopts stimulated-recall interview, non-participant observation, documents and field notes as research instruments to generate data.

Findings from case studies reveal that for the rural secondary school EFL teachers, their professional identity is an intricate, dynamic and formative process, which has been formed, developed, reshaped and enhanced in teachers' personal and professional experiences. As for the personal dimension, teachers' personal biographies, including critical events, significant others, teacher role models, personal hobbies, and earlier language learning experiences have direct connection with the formation of teachers' professional identity. Teachers' professional experiences, including their practicum, reflective classroom practices, school-based peer coaching activities and their attempts in conducting action research have been discovered as powerful forces in shaping EFL teachers' professional selves.

This study also identifies three major tires of influencing factors that affect the participant teachers' construction of professional identity: the local socioeconomic situation and multiethnic cultural context as the macro-level; institutional environment, professional training programs and courses as the meso-level; teachers' personal qualities including their linguistic competences, teaching beliefs and agentive quality micro-level of influencing factors. This study argues that these influencing factors act as both formative elements and powerful variables in creating and shaping the teachers' professional identity. Findings of this study contribute to the understanding of the complexity of teachers' professional identity development, and provide valuable information for language teaching and language teacher education research.

Contents

Chapter 1 │ Introduction

This introduction chapter first describes the researcher's personal motivation for carrying out this study. Next, it identifies the problem and introduces the aims of the study. Then it provides a synopsis of research methodology. Finally, it suggests the potential significance and outlines the structure of the study.

1.1 Personal motivation

Before the researcher went to Shanghai International Studies University (SISU) to pursue further academic development in 2015, he had been living, learning and teaching in Kunming, Yunnan province, for 11 years. In 2003, the researcher enrolled in a Master Program of English Language and Literature in Yunnan University (YNU). Three years later, he graduated and became a faculty member in the School of Foreign Languages and taught English courses to university students in YNU. In 2010, he was invited to lecture on the second language acquisition courses for rural secondary school teachers in a training project organized by Yunnan Normal University. The training courses he taught were parts of the training courses structured by the National Teacher Training Project for Primary and Secondary School Teachers (*zhong xiao xue jiao shi guo jia pei xun ji hua*, hereafter the NTTP) [中小学教师国家培训计划]. The NTTP is a nationwide and long-term teacher education program aiming to improve pedagogical competences of primary and secondary school teachers in midwestern and southwestern rural regions. From 2010 to 2014, the researcher instructed pedagogy course in every summer and winter vacation for teachers from rural schools. His experience as a teacher trainer allowed him to establish rapport with many secondary school English teachers from rural schools.

The influence from colleagues in YNU is another encouraging reason for the researcher to embark on this research. Dr. Wang, who is the researcher's former colleague and friend, offered substantial help when the researcher was a novice teacher in the School of Foreign Languages. Dr. Wang generously shared his teaching experience and coached the researcher in teaching methods as a mentor. Moreover, Dr. Wang is a professional in language teaching, and a scholar with international vision and research literacy. He was a Fulbright Fellow (2014—2015) and an active enthusiast for the promotion of education equality and trilingual education. In 2012, the researcher joined Dr. Wang's research team on the study of trilingual education in multiethnic regions in Yunnan province. Since then, the researcher worked with Dr. Wang and conducted many rounds of fieldwork collecting data in the rural schools in remote multiethnic regions.

In 2016, when the researcher chose his research topic and he began to look for appropriate informants for the research, professor Hou, another researcher friend of his from Yunnan Normal University offered him great help to select desirable participants. Professor Hou is one of the leading experts in charge of implementing the NTTP in Yunnan province. Meanwhile, she is a teacher trainer herself and the director of the trainer team. Because of many years of training experience, she has a close connection with many rural teachers and local government officials. The researcher talked to Professor Hou about his research proposal and she kindly introduced him to a Teaching and Research Coordinator (*jiao yan yuan*) [教研员] from the Municipal Education Bureau of Jinghong city. Later, the researcher established relationship with more local stakeholders including the director of Municipal Education Bureau (*shi jiao yu ju*) [市教育局], the principal of Teachers' Training School (*jiao shi jin xiu xue xiao*) [教师进修学校] and several school headmasters. With their generous help, the researcher successfully conducted two rounds of pilot studies.

The researcher's own experience as an English learner, college EFL teacher, part-time teacher trainer, together with his rigorous doctoral training and rapport with different levels of stakeholders and teacher participants enabled him to carry out a qualified research on the topic of teachers' professional identity formation. In addition, when the researcher was doing fieldwork in many rural schools, he was encouraged by those rural secondary school teachers' commitment and devotion to their teaching career, and witnessed their endeavor and painstaking effort in the professional growth. Much doctoral research, teacher professional development research in particular, centered on language teachers in tertiary level. The value of their research cannot be denied, however, they seem to ignore that in this vast country, while urban teachers are taking advantage of substantial educational resources, many rural teachers are lacking in sufficient resources for professional development. In this sense, the researcher perceives that he has the responsibility to reveal the professional life status quo of this cohort of secondary EFL teachers by taking teachers' identity as a lens and research framework.

1.2   Statement of the problem

Identity has been conceptualized as an analytical tool for understanding the relationship between school and society (Gee, 2000). Central to educational research on identity is teachers' identity which has emerged as a separate area (Beijaard et al., 2004). As one of the sub-categories of teachers' identity research, language teachers' identity (hereafter as LTI), has attracted increasing attention from researchers and theorists in the field of language teaching and language teacher education, and the number of research has grown exponentially in the past decade (Martel & Wang, 2014).

As can be seen from the research literature, great efforts have been made to explore the definitions, constituents, characteristics and influencing factors about LTI. In terms of definition, many studies (Barkhuizen, 2017a; Varghese et al., 2005; Xu, 2017) have defined LTI as an "interaction of how we see ourselves as language teachers (English language, bilingual, or foreign/ world language teachers) and how others see us" (Varghese et al., p.21). In addition, Xu (2017) posits that LTI contains three layers of meaning: firstly, it is a combination of a language teacher's self-positioning of who he/ she is and others' collective conceptions of who he/she is; secondly, LTI is a continuous process of becoming, which is constantly negotiated with various resources available within certain social, cultural, historical and political context; thirdly, LTI is the pursuit of membership in a community (p.122).

Pennington and Richards (2016) argue that LTI is comprised of two types of competences: *Foundational Competences* and *Advanced Competences*. The Foundational Competences contain five sub-identities: language-related identity, disciplinary identity, context-related identity, self-knowledge and awareness, and student-related identity; while the Advanced Competences of language teachers' identity comprise two different teaching skills (Practiced and Responsive Teaching Skills and Skills of Theorizing from Practice) and teachers' membership in communities of practice and profession. Pennington and Richards's (2016) identification of elements of LTI provides the literature with a solid foundation in understanding the intricate notion.

A thorough review of existing studies indicates that researchers have investigated LTI from multiple perspectives and yielded fruitful findings. According to the literature, researchers find that personal factors, generally including teachers' biographies and prior experience, significant others, linguistic positions and cultural status, play a considerable part in shaping their professional identity (Bukor, 2015; Duff & Uchida, 1997; Izadinia, 2013; Trent & Gao, 2009; Tsui, 2007). Moreover, the literature suggests that teachers' education programs, teachers' reflexive practices in applying new pedagogies and experience to teachers' community of practices affect language teachers in building up professional identity (Block, 2015; Martel, 2015; Park, 2012; Yazan, 2017; Yuan & Lee, 2015). Another strain of literature focuses on the contextual influence on the formation of LTI (Han, 2016; Nguyen, 2017; Salinas, 2017). This strain of studies argues that curriculum reforms, workplace environment, local community cultures, relationship with colleagues all have been evidenced by the literature as important factors that exert an impact on the development of LTI.

Although there is a copious list of studies in literature, gaps still exist:

Firstly, in terms of participants, great concern was paid reporting how student teachers' professional identity has been shaped or reshaped during practicum, and in-service teachers' professional identity change seemed to be ignored; secondly, a large majority of studies chose urban cities as research sites, very few of them were conducted in rural areas, and even fewer works examined secondary school EFL teachers' professional life in remote, rural, multiethnic and multilingual regions; and thirdly, previous research has discovered that teachers' education programs and courses play important roles in shaping language teachers' professional identity. However, this line of studies has its limits. For one thing, most of the studies concentrated on student teachers' or teacher candidates' professional identity construction in teachers' education programs or practicums, and relatively little attention was paid to in-service teachers' professional identity transformation happened in these programs; for the other, many of these studies usually observed how education programs affected the teachers' identity construction, but failed to examine how their experiences and reflections were internalized and manifested through classroom practices.

In order to fill the research gaps, the present study sets out to investigate the complicated professional identity construction of three secondary school EFL teachers who are teaching in remote, rural and multiethnic regions in southwest China. In order to achieve this goal, the following questions are raised:

1) How is secondary school EFL teachers' professional identity formed and developed by their personal and professional experiences?

2) What are the possible factors that shape teachers' professional identity construction in different phases of their professional development?

1.3   Aims of the study

Previous studies have explored the process of professional identity construction from multiple perspectives. According to Lasky (2005), teachers' identity refers to "a construct of professional self that evolves over career stages" (p.901). Cooper and Olson (1996) described the development of teachers' identity as being continually informed, formed and reformed. Knowles (1992) identified that teachers' self-conception might be impacted by four sources: role models, prior teaching experience, remembered education classes, and informal, personal experiences of learning and activities. Franzak (2002) added that from childhood to their present state of adulthood, these multiple factors gradually shape a teacher's identity until it manifests and becomes explicit. He pointed out two types of competences, namely, "foundational competence" (e.g., language-related identity, disciplinary identity, context-related identity, self-knowledge and awareness, and student-related identity) and "advanced competence" (e.g., practiced and responsive teaching skills, theorizing from practice, and membership in communities of practice and profession) as core competences that language teachers should possess in creating their professional identity.

In light of the previous research, the present study aims to examine the professional identity development of three rural secondary school language teachers and how their professional identity is affected by personal, professional, and contextual factors. It sets the English teaching in secondary school as the research context and selects language teachers from the schools in rural and multiethnic regions as focal participants. This study is guided by an integrated theoretical framework including *History-in-Person, Identity-in-Discourse,* and *Identity-in-Practice and Identity Formation Theory* as a theoretical base, seeking to shed light on the professional identity formation of rural school EFL teachers in a specific sociocultural and institutional context. It sets out to explore how personal factors such as past language learning activities, teacher role models, significant events, language and disciplinary related knowledge affect teachers' sense-making process. This study also seeks to elaborate on how external learning experiences, for instance, school-based peer-coaching and national teacher training programs like the NTTP help to reshape their professional identity. In addition, the study makes efforts to reveal how school environment, multiethnic culture and parents' investment might form teachers' professional identity construction. It is also the researcher's expectation that the exploration of teachers' professional identity formation process would offer implications for teacher educators and front-line teachers, especially EFL teachers in rural and border regions with insufficient resources in China, a novel perspective to teachers' professional development.

1.4　Research design

To answer these research questions, the present study employs qualitative case study to elicit information from the participants through semi-structured, stimulated-recall interviews, participant observation and document analysis. All the research methods used in this study are interconnected.

The major objective of this case study is to explore the ongoing formation process of three case teachers' professional identity. The semi-structured and stimulated recall interview comprised four major aspects: 1) past learning experiences; 2) past classroom practice before attending the NTTP; 3) teachers' experiences in different training modules in the NTTP; 4) teachers' reflections on doing classroom-based teacher action research.

Yin (2014) defines three types of observation: non-participant, participant, and unobtrusive. Non-participant observation means merely watching what is happening and recording events on the spot (Patton, 1990). This study looks into teachers' identity development by using on-site and non-participant observation of participants' instructional practices such as teaching procedures, teacher-student interactions and classroom activities. The observation method is also conducted outside the classroom, and some teaching-related activities outside school are also observed, such as interactions between colleagues, and teachers' discussions in the Teaching and Research Groups (hereafter TRGs) (*jiao yan zu*) [教研组].

The classroom video allows the researcher to present complex classroom settings in an authentic way. According to Burns (1999), video recording is a technique for capturing in detail naturalistic interactions and verbatim utterances. The classroom video recording used in this study provides indispensable sources of reliable information on teachers' past teaching practices. By observing the videotaped classroom, comparison can be made between teachers' past and present instructional practices, which offers the researcher an invaluable window to explore and apprehend teachers' professional identity formation and negotiation.

Document analysis can complement other research instruments to obtain information that cannot be observed or interviewed directly (Merriam, 1998; Patton, 1990). In this study, three types of documents are collected for analysis—textbooks, teachers' lesson plans and official documents. The textbooks, including students' books and teachers' reference books, are the most fundamental documents of instructional material. The lesson plans normally represent teachers' understanding of material, pedagogical strategies and implementation of beliefs. The lesson plans generally include teaching objectives (what the students are supposed to learn), how the objectives will be reached (the method, tasks or activities) and the way of measuring how well the objectives are reached (homework or test, etc.). The official documents provided the present study with another window to gain a holistic picture of educational settings and backgrounds of teacher development and curriculum reform.

In order to answer the research questions, the present study adopts a grounded approach to analyze the qualitative data. Interview transcriptions, observation notes, and classroom video data are analyzed through open, axial and selective coding techniques. In addition, different personal, professional and contextual factors are subsequently identified.

Purposeful and snowball sampling techniques are adopted by the present study in screening research participants. The choice of participants is purposeful (Merriam, 1998; Patton, 1987; Stake, 1995) and the selection of three case teachers is also based on the following criteria: 1) teachers who can provide sufficient and valuable data for the study; 2) teachers who have experienced the NTTP and can provide data about the influence on their beliefs and practices; 3) teachers who are accessible and willing to provide information for the study. Based on the above considerations, the chosen teacher participants are supposed to provide rich information for the study. As a result, three qualified participant teachers, Jenifer, Amy and Kelvin (pseudonyms) were selected as focal participants for this study. The three teachers were all experienced teachers and "backbone teachers" (*gu gan jiao shi*) [骨干教师] in their schools who had been selected as trainees in the NTTP. The three teachers were well informed and aware of the research purpose and procedures of the present study and kindly agreed to participate and became the research participants of the study.

1.5 Significance of the study

Significance of this study lies in the abundant and valuable information about how secondary school language teachers develop their professional identity in a rural, multiethnic sociocultural context in Yunnan province, China. This empirical research helps front-line teachers, school leadership, government policymakers, teacher educators and researchers to get access to the real situation of Chinese rural EFL teachers about their classroom practice and professional development.

Firstly, the present study is significant for rural secondary school EFL teachers. This study examines the professional identity formation of three rural secondary school EFL teachers, whose personal biographies, language learning and teaching beliefs and experience gained from professional training programs are valuable for front-line teachers.

Secondly, detailed comparison of teachers' classroom practice before and after their participation in the NTTP offers the teacher educators and school leaders a useful reminder to understand teachers' true response to the curriculum reform and professional training program. The present study is particularly vital for educational researchers, for it offers a new perspective to explore language teachers' professional identity.

Thirdly, the present study is important for educational policymakers. This study selects rural EFL teachers working in multiethnic regions as focal participants, and describes how local socioeconomic situation and multiethnic cultural characters indirectly affect teachers' teaching beliefs and pedagogical practices in the classroom. These data are particularly pragmatic for the policymakers.

Taking teachers' identity as an analytical tool, this research is one of the pioneering studies that explore professional development of Chinese rural EFL teachers in multiethnic regions. The significance of the present study also lies in the implementation of an integrated theoretical framework for exploration of the multilayered, multifaceted professional identity construction process. The study adopts the Identity Formation Theory (Wenger, 1998), History-in-Person Theory (Holland & Lave, 2001), and Identity-in-Discourse and Identity-in-Discourse (Varghese et al., 2005) as an integrated theoretical framework to support the exploration of teachers' professional identity development. The combination of integrated theoretical framework and qualitative case study research approach builds up a new and powerful interpretive framework, which can be taken as an example for other research.

1.6   Organization of the study

The study contains nine chapters. The first introductory chapter outlines the general information of this research, including personal and theoretical rationale of the research, motivation, statement of problems, solutions to the problems, overall description of methodology, and significance of the present study.

Chapter 2 portrays the contextual background in which the present study is situated. The description of the research context includes the brief history of English language teaching in China, the status quo of English education in secondary schools, the landscape of secondary school EFL teacher training and a summary of the NTTP.

Chapter 3 aims to build up the theoretical foundation for the present study. It reviews the existing literature about key concepts, definitions, theoretical as well as methodological approaches in language teachers' identity studies. In the end, a conceptual framework that guides the study will be established.

Chapter 4 explains the methodology adopted by the present study, including brief introduction of research sites, rationale for choosing the qualitative paradigm, data collection instruments and analysis procedures.

Chapters 5—7 present the research findings. Detailed description of participants' personal biography, teaching context, classroom practice before and after attending the NTTP, reflections on participating the NTTP and doing classroom-based teacher research. These three chapters provide direct evidence for the formation, development and reconstruction of secondary school EFL teachers' professional identity.

Based on the analyzed data and guided by the integrated theoretical framework established in Chapter 3, an overall summary and in-depth discussion of findings are provided in Chapter 8. Commonalities and discrepancies in the construction of professional identity between the participant teachers are discussed in detail. At the end of this chapter, a tentative model of secondary school language teachers' identity formation is proposed.

The last chapter summarizes the findings, draws conclusions and highlights the contribution of this study. It closes with implications and recommendations for future research.

Chapter 2 | Research Background

The objective of this chapter is to delineate the general research background in which the present study is situated. The description of the research context includes a brief history of English language teaching in China, the status quo of English education in secondary schools, the landscape of secondary school EFL teacher training and a summary of the NTTP.

2.1   A brief history of English language teaching and learning in China

English has been taught in China for over 300 years and English language learning has a long and fascinating history in China (Adamson, 2002; Gil & Adamson, 2011). Foreign language learning had existed in imperial China since late 1289, when languages were learnt by aristocrats to enhance commerce with countries in Southeast Asia (Gu, 1996). In the 17th century, because of burgeoning international trade, pidgin variety of English was used between Chinese compradors and businessmen from European countries. Since her humiliating encounter with the West in the 19th century, China has displayed ambiguous and shifting attitudes towards the English language (Adamson, 2002; Bolton, 2003; Gao, 2014). In the late Qing Dynasty, in response to external aggression and the technological inferiority exposed in the Opium War (1840—1860), a strategy of synthesis was provided by scholars in the Westernization Movement (*yang wu yun dong*) [洋务运动]: the principle was "study China for essence, study the West for utility" (*zhong xue wei ti, xi xue wei yong*) [中学为体，西学为用]. Influenced by such a strategy, foreign languages were learnt to gain access to Western technology and English became one of the subjects in the mainstream curricula in secondary schools. The study of English came to be a conduit for the introduction of new philosophies, religions and social theories at the time when the Qing Dynasty was overthrown and the Republic of China was established. When the government of the Republic shifted to reform its education system by following the U.S., English assumed greater proportion in China's education system (Adamson, 2002).

After the foundation of the People's Republic of China in 1949, English had long been regarded as a language associated with "military aggressors" and "a threat to national integrity"; it had also been seen as a strategic language that helped the nation learn advanced technology and essential knowledge from the West for her modernization (Adamson, 2002, p.231). Thanks to the reform and opening-up policy, the 1980s witnessed rapid economic growth and tremendous sociocultural changes. During this period of time, English was regarded as "barometer of modernization" (Ross, 1992) and was progressively associated with promoting international exchange, learning technology, fostering economic progress, and participating in international competition.

In the new millennium, English is still deemed vital for modernization, but it has taken on another role: "English for international stature" (Lam, 2002, p.246). The Chinese nation has embraced English as an index of global identity and Chinese learners have embraced English learning as central to their future careers and professional lives (Graddol, 2006). The significance of English can be seen from a macro-policy perspective that the new language policy and curriculum reform (MOE, 2001) officially required Chinese students to learn English from the third grade in elementary school through college to graduate school. Chinese English learners view English as a key to a vast range of opportunities: to enter and graduate from university, to study abroad, to secure jobs, especially in international companies, or to get promoted in professional or higher education institutions (Liu et al., 2016).

However, because of a vast territory and regional economic unbalanced development, English language teaching in China is facing diverse problems. In spite of being long criticized as not efficient enough and wasting time, a variety of factors have been identified that constrain the implementation of English teaching and learning, for example, class size, limited teacher proficiency, insufficient resources and instructional time, examination pressure, and cultural resistance (Hu, 2002; Nunan, 2003; Trang &

Baldauf, 2007). Based on the interviews with English teachers from various primary and secondary schools in urban and rural areas in three different Chinese cities. Li and Baldauf (2011) identified five constraining factors of English teaching, namely, teaching materials, teachers, educational system, teaching methodology, and assessment (p.795). Additionally, some large-scale cross-sectional surveys discovered that, though Chinese students (in secondary schools and in universities) in general are favorably disposed towards studying English as a foreign language (You & Dörnyei, 2016), they reported reading and writing as strengths and speaking and listening as areas of weakness. Additionally, learner characteristics such as gender, major, hometown, home dialect, extramural studies, and parents' level of education were statistically significant (Liu. et al., 2016).

In order to present a holistic background for the present study, a brief history as well as problems and tensions of English language teaching are delineated. In the next section, the rural-urban gap in basic education in China will be described.

2.2   The urban-rural gap in basic education

Since the 1980s, China has achieved tremendous success and established herself as the second largest power in the world economy. However, when the country is advancing at the full speed towards modernization, diverse problems in education were caused by the unbalanced distribution of economic, social and educational resources.

Taking the basic education sector for example, government financial input, student enrollment and teacher quantity and quality help to create a big gap between rural and urban schools and accordingly hamper education equity. It is evidenced in public financial budget report in 2015 (see Figure 1.1).

As illustrated in the figure, the amount of average funds from government investment for students in schools (ranging from primary school to university) is quite different between the first-tier cities like Beijing and Shanghai, and cities in western regions like Yunnan and Guizhou.

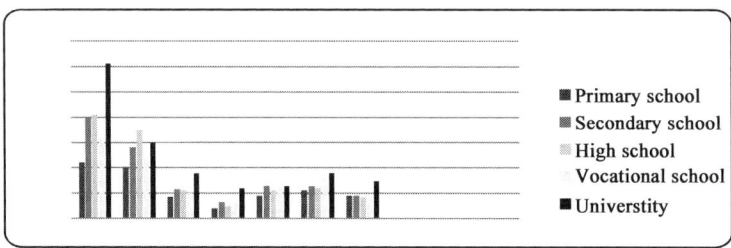

Figure 1.1   Average funds in the public budget for students in 2015 (Data retrieved from www.eol.cn)

Statistics also reveal that about 40% of the rural school-age population don't participate in the College Entrance Examination (MOE, 2015) because of the poor quality of high school education in rural areas. More serious problem lies in the enrollment in higher education. The gross enrollment ratio of Beijing higher education for local students is 49%, while only 8.64% in Yunnan province. In addition, the enrollment number of rural students for top universities is decreasing year on year (Meng & Mai, 2007).

The quality and quantity of teachers have been another noteworthy problem. In Zhou and Xiong's (2017) report, the ratio of teachers with associate's degrees or above is 78.01% in Chinese urban primary schools, 31% higher than in rural areas; the ratio of that in urban secondary schools is 62.44%, 38% higher than rural areas (p.2). Additionally, geographic distance, limited resources and lack of professional support make the efforts in improving teacher quality a challenging job. Moreover, in spite of relatively lower teacher quality, many rural schools suffer from a serious shortage of teachers. It is a common scenario to see a rural teacher stand in different classrooms teaching multiple subjects. In many rural schools, especially in primary schools, there are a considerable number of post-transfer teachers (*zhuan gang jiao shi*) [转岗教师] (teachers who are not the major in some school subjects are transferred to teach that subject. For instance, the school accountant may teach music or math). Li (2012) found that post-transfer English teachers accounted for 57% of all the English teachers in Liaocheng city in Shandong province; and the study of You (2016) showed that the post-transfer English teachers still account for 32.5% of the whole group of primary school English teachers of Heyuan city in Guangdong province.

2.3   Sociocultural context in multiethnic regions

In the vast rural areas in China, there exist five autonomous regions, 30 autonomous prefectures and 117 autonomous counties. There are 56 officially recognized ethnic groups living in these regions. Alongside the Han population, which constitutes approximately 91.6% of the total population, the other ethnic groups have a total population around 106 million and are diverse in terms of history, culture and language (Adamson & Feng, 2014). Not only facing challenges that other rural schools and teachers have, such as insufficient financial investment, shortage of competent teachers or lack of professional support, schools and teachers in multiethnic regions have also been encountered with particular complications such as multilingualism and multiethnic culture.

According to the statistics of 2001, nearly a third of the multiethnic regions were officially defined as poverty-stricken areas (Yang, 2005). Many schools in multiethnic regions, therefore, lack basic resources. Without access to modern facilities and qualified teachers, most of ethnic students are usually found to be poorer performers than their Han peers (Hu, 2007; Jiang et al., 2007; Tsung, 2009) and their dropout rate is usually high (Adamson & Feng, 2014). Besides economic and geographical factors, some scholars believe that educational failure for many ethnic students often arises from the inappropriate use of languages in education (Adamson & Feng, 2014). In addition to their mother tongue (language used by a specific ethnic group), ethnic students in primary school need to learn another two different languages: Standard Chinese (*pu tong hua*) [普通话] and English, both are linguistically-distant from their mother tongue in terms of pronunciation, written form, vocabulary and syntax. Under these circumstances, ethnic students tend to have a high drop-out rate, while those who stay in school often perform worse than their Han peers (Adamson & Feng, 2014; Hu, 2007; Tsung, 2010).

The ethnic groups usually inhabit in some geographically remote regions. Far from Confucius culture centers, the ethnic groups have developed unique ethnic cultures, costumes, traditions, religions or ideology of their own. These indigenous cultures and ideology, mingling with particular local socioeconomic situation, have a great impact on formal school education. Taking Xishuangbanna Dai Autonomous Prefecture in southwestern China as an example, thanks to the tropical climate, fertile land, large scale deforestation and fueled by favorite agricultural policies, local farmers have been growing rubber trees, banana trees and various tropical plants on an unprecedented scale. The tropical economic plants yield not only abundant produce but large seasonal cash income. However, cash income usually would not be advisably deposited in banks or used to enlarge the production, instead most of the income as a custom would go for excessive or conspicuous consumption, with only a meager part spent on education.

The Dai people believe in Theravāda Buddhism and pursue harmony with nature. Influenced by such a religious ideology, most Dai parents maintain a naturalistic belief in educating their children. They consider that children should grow up in a natural environment and should not be forced to learn anything that they would not like. If the child hates going to school, for example, the parents would have a more tolerable attitude towards their children. Nevertheless, if the child demonstrates capability and interest in learning at school, they would be willing to provide their children with available financial and mental support. The unique regional socioeconomic situation and the particular ethnic culture exert significant influence on school education.

2.4   Rural teachers' professional development and the NTTP

As aforementioned, rural areas make up a large proportion of the country's territory. Many of these regions are on the inland or border part of the country and in areas where diverse ethnic groups reside. Because of the vastness or geographic remoteness, most of the multiethnic regions are less resourced and lagging behind in sociocultural development. It is not surprising that before the millennium, there were not many professional development programs for primary and secondary school English teachers in multiethnic regions like Xishuangbanna.

In order to improve the quality of teaching, especially to enhance the pedagogical competence of primary or secondary school teachers in the not well-resourced rural areas, the NTTP, a national-level teacher training program was implemented in 2010 (MOE, 2010, 2011). From 2010 to 2013, the central government invested about RMB

4.3 billion to support the training activities across the country (Yan et al., 2013). The training contents of the NTTP mainly focus on the enhancement of teaching ethics, subject knowledge and pedagogical competence. Teachers' ethics are firstly stressed in order to help teachers become more aware of their social values and responsibility; training courses on subject knowledge are designed to broaden and improve teachers' knowledge about the specific subject they teach in school; and lessons on pedagogy aim to strengthen teachers' ability in teaching skills and methods. Pawan et al. (2017) summarize three major approaches implemented in the NTTP. The first approach is to utilize theoretical or conceptual models that are developed and then applied across programs. The second one is a field-based approach of "teacher replacement" programs in which undergraduates from universities in urban centers temporarily exchange places with in-service teachers in rural areas. The third one is a blended (face-to-face and online) approach to providing instruction.

In 2009, the Ministry of Education (MOE) formulated the overarching framework of this nationwide teacher training project. The MOE stated that:

> Depending on the key normal universities and teachers' colleges, teams of training experts, high quality training resources will be established and developed and then will be sent to teachers and schools in rural areas. Backbone teachers will be selected and be trained in this project. In terms of the high-quality training resources, training resources outside provinces, within the province and in local regions will take up 1/3 respectively. Front-line master teachers and outstanding backbone teachers from primary and secondary schools across the country will make up no less than 50% within expert teams.
>
> (MOE, 2009)

As can be seen from the government document by the MOE, the normal universities in each province played their part in implementing the project. The teams of training experts basically formed by lecturers or professors from universities are the major force to fulfil the project.

In order to strengthen the educational quality of the primary and secondary schools in border and multiethnic regions, the Ministry of Education assigns Northeastern Normal

University and other MOE affiliated normal universities to provide no less than 50 class-hour training for 3,000 primary and secondary school backbone teachers from Inner Mongolia and other autonomous regions or provinces alike. Universities will provide collective training in the form of "sending training programs to each province" (*song pei dao sheng*) [送培到省] and "sending training courses to schools" (*song jiao shang men*) [送教上门]. For example, Northeastern Normal University to Inner Mongolia Autonomous Region, Shaanxi Normal University to Ningxia Hui Ethnic Autonomous Region, Southwestern University to Guizhou province respectively. About 1,000 primary and secondary school backbone teachers from each of the above regions or provinces will receive training, among whom 70% trainees should be teachers working at county levels and below (MOE, 2009).

As for Yunnan province, Yunnan Normal University (YNNU) and other three teachers' colleges are assigned to be in charge of providing training courses for teachers in autonomous prefectures like Xishuangbanna and Dehong. Based on the reality of local educational context, training professionals from YNNU developed three major modules tailored to training teachers from multiethnic regions, namely, Trainer-Training Module (*pei xun zhe pei xun*) [培训者培训], Demonstration Module (*song jiao xia xiang*, sending demonstration class to countryside schools) [送教下乡], and Distance Education Module (*wang luo yan xiu*, taking training courses on the Internet) [网络研修].

2.5　Summary

This chapter provides the contextual background of this research. It first traces the history of English language teaching and learning in China. It then describes the gap that exists in basic education between urban and rural regions. Next, it introduces the sociocultural context of multiethnic regions in China, with a focus on the current situation in basic education status quo in Xishuangbanna Dai Autonomous Prefecture. This chapter concludes with an introduction to China's national-level teacher training project which is tailored to improve rural teachers' professional competences. In the coming chapter, existing scholarship on current study of identity, teachers' identity, and then language teachers' identity will be reviewed.

Chapter 3 | Literature Review

This chapter aims to present a solid theoretical rationale and a conceptual framework for the present study. Based on the previous scholarship, sections 3.1, 3.2 and 3.3 introduce definitions of identity, teachers' identity and then language teachers' identity respectively. Language teachers' identity is delineated, including definitions, core components and shaping factors. Then, section 3.4 presents the results of holistic review of current literature on language teachers' identity research. Following the literature review, section 3.5 critiques the existing studies and points out the research gap which necessitates this research. Finally, in section 3.6, a conceptual framework and working definition that guide the present study are reviewed.

3.1 Identity

"Identity" has long been a subject of study in fields as varied as psychology, anthropology, sociology, philosophy, theology, and literature (Holland & Lanchicotte, 2007; Kumaravadivelu, 2012). However, scholars' opinions have diverged widely in defining "identity" and there is very little consensus about what it constitutes, or how it is actually constructed. As Elliott and Gay (2009) complain that defining "identity" "has proved to be one of the most vexing and vexed topics in the social sciences and humanities" (p.viii).

Researchers used many terminologies such as *social identity, ethnic identity, cultural identity, linguistic identity, subjectivity, the self* and *voice*, which refer to approximately the same notion. The first tricky problem in defining "identity" is to distinguish "identity" from these perplexing terms, especially from the notion between "identity" and "self", as Beauchamp and Thomas (2009) point out, "one must struggle to comprehend the close connection between identity and the self" (p.176).

According to Mead (1934), "self" can arise only in a social setting where there is social communication; in communicating we learn to assume the roles of others and monitor our actions accordingly. Mccormick and Pressley (1997) argue that the concept of "self" can be defined as an organized representation of our theories, attitudes, and beliefs about ourselves. Oyserman et al. (2012) simply put that "self" often refers to a warm sense or a warm feeling that something is "about me" or "about us" (p.71) while "identities" are the traits and characteristics, social relations, roles, and social group memberships that define who one is (p.69). However, the authors also note that while "self" and "identity" are often used interchangeably, some clarity can be attained by considering them as a series of nested constructs, with "self" as the most encompassing term, self-concepts being embedded within the self, and identities being embedded within self-concepts (Oyserman et al. 2012, p.69). The concept of "identity" has rich meanings in the literature, but these various meanings share a common idea that identity is not a fixed attribute of a person, but a relational phenomenon (Beijaard et al. 2004). Gee (2000) identifies four interrelated perspectives on "identity": the *nature perspective* (N-identity, or those parts of who we are that have their source in nature rather than society, e.g. a tall person); the *institutional perspective* (I-identity, or those parts of who we are that have their source in institutional authority, e.g. a school teacher); the *discourse perspective* (D-identity, or those parts of who we are that have their source in the discourse or dialogue of other people, e.g. someone who is deemed by others to be a "charismatic" person); and the *affinity perspective* (A-identity, or those parts of who I am that have their source in a "distinctive set of practices", e.g. a Red Sox fan).

The notion of "identity" is difficult to understand in terms of its nature. Mead and Ericson might be the predecessors who tried to define "identity" in early literature. "Identity" had been long considered as one of the physical characteristics of human beings in the middle 20th century (Holland and Lachicotte, 2007) until Mead (1934) connects "identity" with "the self" and an individual's self-concept. In Mead's book *Mind, Self and Society*, the author argues that people's identity is shaped and reshaped rather than perceived as being certain features and common characteristics. Mead's argument is the first to expand the concept of "identity" from the inner sense of self to much wider social context. Later on, psychologist Erikson (1968) adds that "identity" is something that develops during one's whole life, but not something one possesses. Holland and Lachicotte (2007) summarize these lines of theorizing identity that:

> *An Eriksonian identity is overarching. It weaves together an individual's answer to questions about who he or she is as a member of the cultural and social group(s) that make up his or her society. A Meadian identity, on the other hand, is a sense of oneself as a participant in the social roles and positions defined by a specific, historically constituted set of social activities.* (p.104)

Thus, based on the comparison made by Holland and Lachicotte, it can be seen that Mead's definition stresses the social nature of "identity" while Erikson's conception of "identity" focuses on the ongoing and coherent characteristic of "identity". Beijaard et al. (2004) develop this notion and determine that "identity" is an ongoing process, dynamic rather than stable, a constantly evolving phenomenon. Although scholars' opinions vary to a great extent and a clear definition of "identity" is not easily reached, a review of literature converges on the idea that the notion of "identity" is multi-faceted and dynamic in nature, as Rodgers and Scott (2008) summarize:

> *Contemporary conceptions of "identity" share four basic assumptions: (1) that identity is dependent upon and formed within multiple contexts which bring social, cultural, political, and historical forces to bear upon that formation; (2) that identity is formed in relationship with others and involves emotions; (3) that identity is shifting, unstable, and multiple; and, (4) that identity involves the construction and reconstruction of meaning through stories over time.* (p.733)

In this starting section, multiple definitions of "identity" as well as the relationship between "identity" and "self" are reviewed from historical perspective. In the next section, the notion of teachers' identity will be analyzed from multiple perspectives, as a basis for understanding language teachers' identity.

3.2 Teachers' identity

The notion of professional identity, emerging from research on "identity", is used in different ways in the area of teaching and teacher education. During the last decade, researchers have increasingly acknowledged that "identity" could be used as an analytical tool to understanding teachers' professional development (Beauchamp & Thomas, 2011; Varghese et al., 2005). The notion of teachers' identity gradually became central to the teaching profession and a popular topic in teaching and teacher education in recent years (Beauchamp & Thomas, 2009; Lee, 2013; Rodgers & Scott, 2008; Trent, 2010; Tsui, 2007). Akkerman and Meijer (2011) summarize three recurring characterizations of teachers' identity: the multiplicity, discontinuity and social nature. Multiplicity refers that the teachers' identity is not a fixed and stable entity but contains various facets, or "sub-identities" (Beijaard et al., 2000). The discontinuity feature of teachers' identity describes "identity" as fluid and shifting from moment to moment and context to context. Social nature of "identity" is explained as acknowledging the social environment that exerts influence on the formation of teachers' identity. Akkerman and Meijer's (2011) idea of three characterizations lays a foundation for the present study to analyze the literature from two lines: the identity per se, and the nature of teachers' identity.

3.2.1 Defining teachers' identity

A review of literature shows that researchers have studied the professional identity from multiple perspectives and defined it in various ways, and no unanimous agreement has been achieved about what teachers' identity means. Although defining teachers' identity is one of the main challenges for understanding of the concept (Beauchamp & Thomas, 2009), many researchers try to propose their understanding of this complex notion and some major definitions are summarized in a sequence of time in Table 3.1:

Table 3.1   Overview of major definitions of teachers' identity

Authors and Years	Definitions
Block (2015)	How individuals, who both self-position and are positioned by others as teachers, affiliated to different aspects of teaching in their lives. Teacher (s') identity is related to factors such as one's ongoing contacts with fellow teachers and students as well as the tasks that one engages in, which can be said to constitute teaching (p.13).

continued

Authors and Years	Definitions
Farrell (2011)	Teacher (s') role identity includes teachers' beliefs, values, and emotions about many aspects of teaching and being a teacher (p.54).
Sutherland et al. (2010)	A teacher's voice develops when preservice teachers interpret and reinterpret their experiences through the processes of reflection. A teacher's voice is articulated as part of the persons' self-image (p.455).
Olsen (2008)	Teacher (s') identity is the collection of influences and effects from immediate contexts, prior constructs of self, social positioning, and meaning systems (p.139).
Hoffman-Kipp (2008)	Teacher (s') identity is "the intersection of personal, pedagogical, and political participation and reflection within a larger sociopolitical context" (p.153).
Varghese (2006)	Teacher (s') professional identities defined here in terms of the influences on teachers, how individuals see themselves, and how they enact their profession in their settings (p.212).
Lasky (2005)	Teacher (s') professional identity as a construct of professional self that evolves over career stages (p.901).
Beijaard et al. (2004)	Teacher (s') identity is an ongoing process of interpretation and re-interpretation of experiences (p.108).
Danielewicz (2001)	Teacher (s') identity is composed of multiple, often conflicting, identities, which exist in volatile states of construction or reconstruction, reformation or erosion, addition, or expansion (p.10).
Beijaard et al. (2000)	Teacher (s') identity as consisting of three sub-identities: the teacher as a subject matter expert, pedagogical expert, and didactical expert (p.751).
Palmer (1998)	Identity is a moving intersection of the inner and outer forces that make me who I am (p.13).
Volkmann & Anderson (1998)	Identity as a dynamic and complex equilibrium between personal self-image and teachers' roles one has to play (p.20).
Cooper & Olson (1996)	Teacher (s') identity is continually being informed, formed, and reformed. It can be understood and shaped by various experiences, events, environments, or influences as individuals develop over time and through interaction with others (p.35)
Dworet (1996)	Teacher (s') "identities" refer to the different views that individuals have about themselves as teachers in general, and how this view changes over time and in different contexts (p.67).
Weedon (1987)	Teachers' sense of identity—which is multifaceted and contingent on time and location (p.8).

As shown in Table 3.1, previous researches have studied the concept of teachers' identity per se from various angles, focusing on different aspects and defining it in different ways. The discussion about what teachers' identity means began to appear in Dworet's (1996) earlier review of teachers' identity research. The author regards teachers' identity as different views that teachers have about themselves and how that view changes over time and in different contexts. Cooper and Olson (1996) argue that teachers' identity is continually being informed, formed, and reformed. Teachers' identity can be understood and shaped by various experiences, events, environments, or influences as individuals develop over time and through interaction with others. Samuel and Stephens (2000) define teachers' identity as a "perlocated understanding" and acceptance of a series of competing and sometimes contradictory values, behaviors, and attitudes grounded in the life experience of the self in formation (p.476). Inspired by Bromme's (1991) work about different types of knowledge and professional self-concept, Beijaard et al. (2000) argue that teachers derive their professional identity from (mostly combinations of) the ways they see themselves and describe teachers' identity as subject matter experts, pedagogical experts, and didactical experts (p.751). In the authors' later work, Beijaard et al. (2004) conclude generally from their literature review that a teacher's professional identity consists of sub-identities relating to teachers' different contexts and relationships. Other research also makes a contribution in the attempts to define the concept of teachers' identity, for example Sutherland et al. (2010) distinguish professional identity as one component of multiple perspectives of a person's identity and Day et al. (2007) identify three "dimensions of identity" (p.106): professional identity, situated identity, and personal identity.

Review of existing literature indicates that though it appears that there is no clear definition of teachers' identity (Beijaard et al., 2004), there is a general agreement on its significance in teacher education and professional development. Literature suggests that teachers' identity is not stable or predetermined (Beauchamp & Thomas, 2009; Beijaard et al., 2004; Maclean & White, 2007), but dynamic, and it is created and recreated during an active process of learning to teach (Trent, 2010). The concept of teachers' identity is often considered elusive, probably because of the much-debated nature of identity itself. As Beijaard et al (2004) summarize that professional identity is *an ongoing process* of interpreting experience that connects "*person and context*", consists of "*sub-identities*" and needs the exercise of "*agency*" (p.122). These features are consolidated in Sachs's (2005) often-cited conceptualization of teachers' identity, which is worth quoting again here:

> It [teachers' professional identity] provides a framework for teachers to construct their own ideas of "how to be", "how to act" and "how to understand" their work and their place in society. Importantly, teacher (s') identity is not something that is fixed nor is it imposed; rather it is negotiated through experience and the sense that is made of that experience.   (p.15)

Different definitions provided by the literature are informative in understanding the complex notion of teachers' identity. In addition to various definitions, a literature review of research on teachers' identity also shows postmodernist features which will be elaborated in the next section.

3.2.2   Major issues in teachers' identity research

Besides the definition of teachers' identity, how teachers develop professional identity and what factors influence their professional identity construction are other two fundamental issues in the research of teachers' identity. Review of previous studies suggests that previous studies have largely focused on two areas of teachers' identity: characteristics of teachers' identity and factors contributing to teachers' identity development.

Varghese et al. (2005) maintain that teachers' identity is a profoundly individual and psychological matter as it relates to the self-image and other-image of particular teachers; at the same time, "It is a social matter because the formation, negotiation, and growth of teachers' identity is a fundamentally social process taking place in institutional settings such as teacher education programs and schools" (p.39). In terms of characteristics of teachers' identity, scholars in the field of teacher research basically agree that teachers' identity is fluid and shifting from moment to moment and context to context (Akkerman & Meijer, 2011, p.310). From biographical perspective, Kelchtermans (1994) clarifies professional self as a complex, multidimensional and dynamic system of representations and meanings which develops over time as the result of interactions between the person and an environment. Volkmann and Anderson (1998) believe professional identity as a dynamic and complex equilibrium between personal self-image and teachers' roles one has to play. Coldron and Smith (1999) state that professional identity is not a stable entity that people have, but a way to make sense of themselves in relation to other people and contexts, and thus it cannot be interpreted as fixed or unitary. Beijaard et al. (2004) argue that identity is an ongoing process of interpretation and re-interpretation of experiences, and identity can be seen as an answer to the recurrent question "Who am I at this moment?" (p.108). In a similar vein, Rodgers and Scott (2008) add that identity is constructed in a social context and that rather than being stable and fixed, it is shifting and dynamic (p.736).

Regarding the factors that exert an impact on the development of teachers' identity, review of literature suggests that previous studies have examined individual and social dimensions as two lines of inquiry. Many studies address the individual dimension of teachers' identity and argue that teachers' personal biography, significant others, earlier learning experiences, pre-service teacher education and in-service teacher education programs (Bullough, 1997; Flores & Day, 2006; Jackson, 2006; Kagan et al., 1993; Kelchtermans, 1994; Knowles, 1992; Kwo & Intrator, 2004; Lamote & Engels, 2010; Samuel & Stephens, 2000; Sugrue, 1997; Tsui, 2007; Varghese, 2006) have a great influence on the construction of teachers' identity. Knowles's (1992) comprehensive study discovers that teachers' past experiences including childhood experiences, early teacher role models, previous teaching experiences, and significant people impact their beliefs about teaching and teacher images, and subsequently their classroom practices. Varghese (2006) and Jackson (2006) discuss how difficult, even traumatic, experiences in the participants' own schooling shape their teacher identities. Jackson (2006) examines how the personal history relates to the development of teachers' identity. Samuel and Stephen (2000) reveal that teachers' early role models may also shape teachers' positive and negative responses to what it means to be a teacher. Holt-Reynolds (1992) and Tsui (2007) report that teachers' past experiences affect their teaching beliefs in the classroom and consequently shape teachers' professional identity. Previous research also attach importance to the impact of different levels of pre-service teacher education, in-service teacher training courses to the development of teachers' identity (Flores & Day, 2006; Kagan et al., 1993; Knowles, 1992).

In addition to the individual facets of teachers' identity, previous research also discusses the social dimension of teachers' professional identity. Social dimension of teachers' identity refers to the influence of contextual factors to the teachers' identity development. The foregoing studies have found that social culture, school culture, relationship with colleagues, students have either positive or negative impact on teachers' professional identity (Beauchamp & Thomas, 2009; Day, Christopher & Kington, 2008; Day et al., 2007; Lee et al., 2013; Zeichner & Gore, 1990). Zeichner and Gore (1990) have observed that the influence of students is important in the process of teachers' socialization and the influence ranges from the general teaching approach, patterns of language used by teachers to the type and frequency of specific teaching methods used by teachers. Jackson (2006) examines how sociocultural influences and social interactions construct the participants' teacher identity. Day et al. (2006) find that school culture enables or constrains the achievement of satisfaction, commitment, and motivation. Tsui (2007) claims the complex relationships between membership, competence and legitimacy of access to practice constitute the formation of teachers' identity and highlights the central role of participation in certain communities and practice in teachers' identity construction and reconstruction. Day and Kington (2008) discover that the school-level factors such as teamwork, pupil behavior, support from leadership, parental support, and in-school communication are closely related to teachers' professional identitiy. Three key factors, namely, school/departmental leadership, supportive colleagues, and family, positively contribute to a positive sense of agency, resilience, and commitment in many teachers. Miller (2009) summarizes that:

> *The negotiation of teachers' professional identities is…powerfully influenced by contextual factors outside of the teachers themselves and their preservice education… [T]he identity resources of the teachers may be tested against conditions that challenge and conflict with their backgrounds, skills, social memberships, use of language, beliefs, values, knowledge, attitudes, and so on. Negotiating those challenges forms part of the dynamic of professional identity development.*   (p.175)

To sum up, teachers' identity can be outlined as being unitary and multiple, continuous and discontinuous, personal and social. The construction of teachers' identity is an ongoing process, and the development of teachers' identity is influenced by a range of personal and contextual factors. Conceptualization of teachers' identity in general teacher education paves the way for understanding language teachers' identity research.

3.2.3　Teachers' identity and teachers' knowledge

Teachers' knowledge, or teachers' cognition, has been highly valued and considered as an important component of a teacher's makeup. In teachers' identity research, however, scholars process some conflicting views on the relationship between knowledge and identity. Some researchers view knowledge holistically without setting clear boundaries between knowledge and identity, e.g., Olsen (2003) claims that "each is part of the other" (p.4). The in-depth research on teachers' knowledge and beliefs has been an essential precursor of research on teachers' identity since they are inextricably connected with who we are as teachers. Other researchers view knowledge as "external to the individual and fixed" (Smith, 2007, p.379). The interaction between the development of teachers' knowledge and professional identity has been investigated particularly with pre-service teachers. Smith (2007) concludes that pre-service teachers' professional identity formation is complementary and connected to the development of teachers' knowledge in teacher education programs. According to Kincheloe (2003), "Mainstream teacher education provides little insight into the forces that shape identity and consciousness. Becoming educated, becoming a critical teacher-as-researcher/teacher-as-scholar necessitates personal transformation based on an understanding and critique of these forces…" (p.47). Smith (2007) also argues along the same lines claiming that teacher education programs should focus both on pre-service teachers' identity work and knowledge growth. Alsup (2006) claims that pre-service teachers would more likely leave the profession if the discrepancy between the personal and the professional aspects of their identitiy is too big. Johnston et al. (2005) portray teachers' knowledge linked to teachers' identity and professional development. In their words, "teacher (s') knowledge is seen in relation to teachers' lives and the contexts in which they work" (Johnston et al., 2005, p.54). While Richards and Farrell (2011) identify "disciplinary knowledge" and "pedagogical content knowledge" as two broad types of content knowledge relevant to language teachers. Such dichotomy of teachers' knowledge will be denoted in the coming section of 3.3.2.

3.2.4   Teachers' identity and teachers' beliefs

Pajares (1992) argues that teachers' teaching behavior such as making lesson plans and instructional decisions and classroom practice is strongly associated with teachers' beliefs. As professional identity manifests teachers' language learning and teaching beliefs, it is worth examining how teachers' different beliefs work in the formation process of teachers' professional identity.

Richards (1998) summarizes "information, attitudes, values, expectations, theories and assumptions about teaching and learning (which) teachers build up over time and bring with to the classroom" (p.66) as the content of the belief system. Borg (2001) posits that the main features of teachers' beliefs based on view of literature are context-specific, personally-accepted, teaching-related, guiding teachers' thinking and actions as well as re-constructible due to personal interpretations and reinterpretations of learning and teaching experiences. In this sense, teachers' beliefs are mainly associated with teachers' teaching and learning process, and may be categorized according to multiple aspects in this process. Richards and Lockhart (1994) categorize teachers' beliefs into five categories—beliefs about English, about teaching, about learning, about the program and the curriculum, and about language teaching as a profession.

Beliefs about English

Richards and Lockhart (1994) point out that it is important to explore EFL teachers' beliefs about English because English might be endowed with different meanings by different people. They further explain that English could be thought of as representing English literature for some people whereas for others, it might be the carrier of cultures of English-speaking countries. As English education is traditionally valued for its instrumental purpose in China, teachers' beliefs about English might directly influence their teaching approach of English in the classroom, which reflects their beliefs about teaching and learning.

Beliefs about teaching

Johnson (1992) states that ESL teachers conduct teaching in accordance with their beliefs, resulting in differences in the nature of instruction. Through investigating thirty ESL teachers' beliefs about teaching, Johnson (1992) discovers three approaches they hold towards teaching: a skills-based approach (focusing on discrete skills of listening, speaking, reading and writing), a rule-based approach (highlighting grammatical rules and understanding of the form of language), and a function-based approach (emphasizing the interactive communication and cooperative learning, as well as the language use in authentic social situations). Similarly, Richardson et al. (1991) find that English teachers' beliefs about their roles in teaching are to facilitate students in finding out effective learning approaches, to transmit language knowledge and skills to students as well as to adapt their teaching approaches to meet students' needs. In addition, Glasersfeld (1995) claims that teachers view teaching as a two-fold activity. The primary level is about teachers' transmission of what they expect students to know through speaking and acting, and the second level is to convey their beliefs about teaching and learning in speech and act.

Beliefs about learning

As teaching and learning are closely connected in the classroom, teachers' beliefs about learning also contribute to teachers' belief system as a major element. Teachers' beliefs about learning might be based on their training experience, teaching experience as well as their own learning experience as language learners (Freeman, 1992). Studies on teachers' beliefs about learning exemplify a great variety of teachers' understanding of learning.

Marton et al. (1993) propose a continuum ranging from a surface approach to learning which interprets learning as a process of memorizing and reproducing learned materials to a deeper approach viewing learning as a constructive process of meaning making. The continuum shows teachers' diversified views of learning. Furthermore, Glasersfeld (1995) classifies teachers' beliefs about learning into four categories and terms them more theoretically by referring to psychology—behaviorist orientation, cognitive orientation, social constructivism and radical constructivism. The four categories are in accordance with those of Marton's et al. (1993) continuum, ranging from a surface approach (behaviorist orientation viewing that learning brings immediate changes to learners' behaviors) to a deeper approach (social constructivism viewing learning as co-construction of meaning in social events and relating learning to time and place; radical constructivism emphasizing the importance of context in the learning process and the goal-oriented nature of learning).

Beliefs about learners

Teachers might hold various beliefs about those whom they teach, reflecting individual teacher's view of learners. These views have a profound impact on their classroom teaching practices with Meighan and Meighan (1990) suggesting that learners could be interpreted metaphorically as resisters, receptacles, raw materials, clients, partners, individual explorers and democratic explorers. These metaphors indicate the role of teacher and student as well as their relationship in the process of learning.

Viewing students as resisters, teachers might emphasize the weight of punishment or force in the process of learning since this is the most appropriate way in dealing with students' resistance to learning. The metaphors of receptacles and raw materials indicate teachers' leading roles in the process of teaching and learning since knowledge delivery and teachers' constructive work are underlined respectively.

These metaphors imply an unbalanced teacher-student relationship in which teachers hold the dominating position. In contrast, the relationship between teachers and students is to be altered by viewing learners as clients because it highlights learners' educational needs and teachers' actions to meet these needs. Teachers begin to take learners' needs into consideration instead of dominating everything in the process of teaching and learning. The conception of viewing learners as partners stresses the cooperative relationship between teachers and students, proposing negotiation as the major mode of teacher-student interaction. The notions of learners as individual explorers as well as democratic explorers both see the teacher's role entirely as a facilitator of learners' learning.

3.2.5   Teachers' identity and teachers' agency

A teacher's professional identity consists of multiple sub-identities and involves personal and social or contextual dimensions in the formation process, thus a teacher's active role, or teachers' agency becomes an important issue (Beijaard, et al., 2004). Day et al. (2006) explain that in relation to each form of identity, agency is to fulfil these identities and their reconstruction where necessary, and to manage critical incidents and trends which may threaten the identities or which need to be managed. That is, teachers need to perform their multiple identities, and at the same time they need to respond to and manage any critical incidents in their identity formation in order to construct and reconstruct their identities. Moreover, agency also indicates to what extent people can live with contradictions and tensions within various identities (Day et al., 2006). In this way, teachers' agency means that teachers are active in the process of professional identity construction (Coldron & Smith, 1999), and teachers strive to make sense and act as agents in their world (Beauchamp & Thomas, 2009). Researchers agree that teachers' agency is important in professional identity formation (Beauchamp & Thomas, 2009; Beijaard et al., 2004; Parkison, 2008; Sfard & Prusak, 2005; Zembylas, 2003). Since teachers are active agents in their professional identity construction, and at the same time their professional identity is to a certain extent subject to their professional contexts, the relationship between agency and structure emerges as an important variable in teachers' professional identity formation (Coldron & Smith, 1999; Day, et al., 2006; Tsui, 2007). Coldron and Smith (1999) use structure to "denote relatively intractable social constructs, including cognitive frameworks and affective templates as well as institutional practices" (p.715). There are different views about the relationship: some researchers hold that teachers can exert their agency over structure (Coldron & Smith, 1999; Samuel & Stephens, 2000), while others argue that teachers' active location in their professional contexts can be undermined by policies or institutions (Moore et al., 2002), which is illustrated below.

Coldron and Smith (1999) emphasize the importance of agency over social structure. They contend that from the beginning and in their teaching career teachers are actually engaged in creating themselves as teachers in the landscape in which they are located and the choices which teachers make constitute their professional identity. They believe that teachers' identity is partly given and partly achieved by teachers' active location in social space which involves an array of possible relationships that one person can have to others. Teachers locate themselves by expressions of both affirmation and rejection, and form their practices in unique ways. Teachers' active location displays that "teachers are to some extent empowered" in their teaching practices (Ibid., p.717).

3.3   Language teachers' identity

In line with the "sociocultural turn" in the second language teacher education (Johnson, 2009), a new line of research on language teachers' identity emerged in the past few years (Clarke, 2008; Tsui, 2007). Previous studies on teachers' identity in general education provide rich soil for research on LTI. In the last fifteen years, researchers and theorists in TESOL as well as language teacher educators have explored LTI from diverse perspectives. Based on the results of previous scholarship, this section first presents some key definitions of LTI. Next, it explains the constituents of LTI. Lastly, relevant studies on LTI are reviewed and critiqued in order to find the research gap and establish a conceptual framework.

3.3.1   Definitions of LTI

To understand language teachers' identity, knowledge of what has been documented in the existing literature is required. Rich definitions have been formulated by previous studies on LTI, and some of the major notions are shown in Table 3.2:

Table 3.2   Definitions of LTI in literature

Authors and Years	Definitions
Martel (2017)	LTI is an internalized set of meanings associated with the role of language teacher that is negotiated and constructed in interaction with others and /or generated and maintained by oneself (p.89).
Xu (2017)	LTI has three layers of meaning: first, it is a combination of a language teacher's self-positioning of who he/she is and othes' collective conceptions of who he/she is; second, LTI is a continuous process of becoming, which is constantly negotiated with various resources available within certain social, cultural, historical and political context; third, LTI is the pursuit of membership in a community (p.122).

continued

Authors and Years	Definitions
Oda (2017)	LTI is a teacher's perception and understanding of what resources he or she has accumulated through past experience inside and outside of the classroom in order to respond by taking action in teaching at the present time in the future (p.225).
Donato & Richard (2016)	LTI, or any professional identity for that matter, is defined as the simultaneous enactment of an agent's subjectivity in real-time discursive (semiotic) process situated in local, social, and historical circumstances (p.26).
Varghese et al. (2005)	LTI is an interaction of how we see ourselves as language teachers (English language, bilingual, or foreign/ world language teachers) and how others see us—a claimed and assigned identity (p.21).
Duff & Uchida (1997)	Language teachers and students in any setting naturally represent a wide array of social and cultural roles and identities: as teachers or students, as gendered and cultured individuals, as expatriates or nationals, as native speakers or nonnative speakers, as content-area or TESL/English language specialists, as individuals with political convictions, and as members of families, organizations, and society at large (p.451).

Published studies have defined the concept of LTI, which is largely based on the conceptualization of teachers' identity. This is reasonable because language teachers' identity sets its root in identity and teachers' identity. Since language teacher is one of the categories of teacher profession, and teachers' identity is one of the sub-categories of teachers' professional identity, the two notions share a lot in common. Among the limited works that provide explicit definitions on language teachers' identity, Barkhuizen (2017b) proposes a comprehensive explanation of what language teachers' identity means:

Language teacher identities (LTIs) are cognitive, social, emotional, ideological, and historical—they are both inside the teachers and outside in the social, material, and technological world. LTIs are being and doing, feeling and imaging, and storying. They are struggle and harmony: they are contested and resisted, by self and others, and they are also accepted, acknowledged, and valued, by self and others. They are core and peripheral, personal and professional, they are dynamic, multiple, and hybrid, and they are foregrounded and backgrounded. And LTIs change, short-term and over time—discursively in social interaction with teacher educators, learners, teachers, administrators, and the wider community, and in material interaction with spaces, places and

objects in classrooms, institutions, and online.   (p.4)

Barkhuizen's (2017) definition of language teachers' identity is a complete synthesis of thinking and reflection of 41 language teaching professionals and language teacher educators. Barkhuizen interprets the meaning of language teachers' identity from a variety of theoretical perspectives as well as from different contextual realities. His definition contains multiple layers: firstly, LTI is cognitive because it concerns teachers' beliefs, theories, and philosophies about language teaching and it is related to both content and pedagogical knowledge; secondly, LTI is a two-folded concept in nature which contains both intrinsic and extrinsic sides of a particular teacher. Intrinsic nature refers to teachers' personal aspects including their biographical experiences, knowledge base, teaching beliefs, emotions or agentive behaviors; while extrinsic nature refers to the external world that teacher lives in broadly includes interactions with people, institutional context and sociocultural norms. In addition, LTI lies in what teachers do or perform. It is formed, developed, shaped and reconstructed when they teach in the classroom, grade homework, and attend professional development courses. De Costa (2017) also stresses this point that teachers' identity is not merely something that exists in the mind or explained elegantly on a piece of paper in the form of a well-crafted teaching philosophy statement. Rather, teachers' identity needs to be performed and manifested through a good instruction (p.160). At last, LTI is a continuous process of becoming, which is constantly developed over time and constructed discursively in social interaction. Language connects people to the society, and it is through the language choices they make that they negotiate a sense of self (Barkhuizen, 2017, p.9).

3.3.2   Components of LTI

Review of literature shows that a majority of scholars focus on exploring definitions or features of LTI but seem to neglect to explain what elements constitute LTI. Only a few studies (Bukor, 2015; Pennington & Richards, 2016; Richards, 2012; Smith, 2007) have explicitly interpreted what LTI comprises. Richards (2012) identifies ten professional identity-related dimensions of teachers' knowledge and skills as the "core of expert teaching competence and performance in language teaching" (p.46) The ten competences are: 1) language proficiency; 2) content knowledge; 3) teaching skills; 4) contextual knowledge; 5) language teachers' identity; 6) learner-focused teaching; 7) pedagogical reasoning skills; 8) theorizing from practice; 9) membership in a community of practice and 10) professionalism (Ibid). In her empirical exploration of language teachers' identity construction, Bukor (2015) concludes that teachers' knowledge, beliefs, professional development and emotions are essential components of LIT and important aspects that may influence the development of teachers' identity construction and professional development. Based on a systematic review of literature, Pennington and Richards (2016) recognize a number of critical elements that create teachers' identity in language teaching profession. These elements are summarized in Figure 3.1:

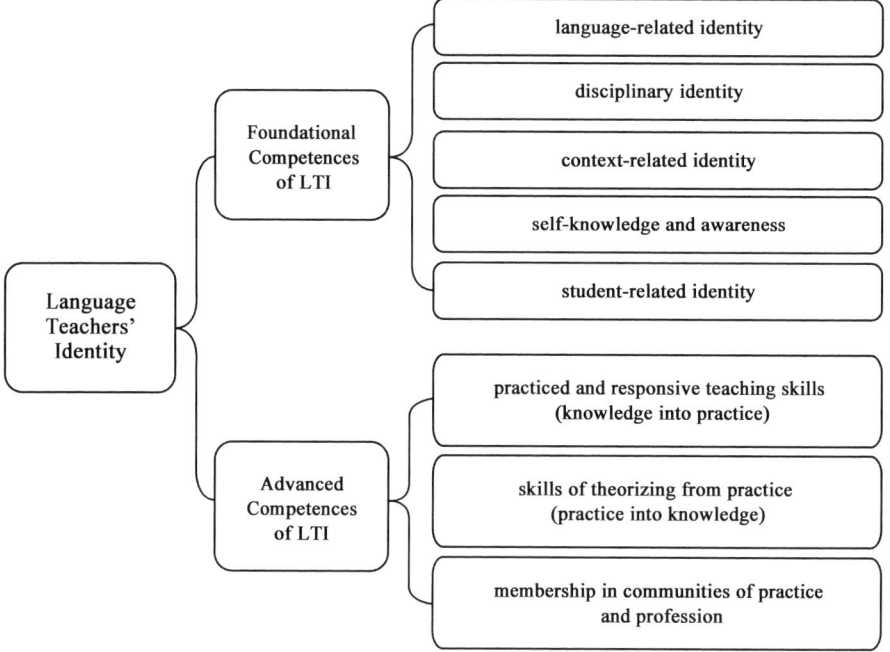

Figure 3.1   Elements of language teachers' identity (Summarized from Pennington & Richards, 2016)

Pennington and Richards (2016) categorize the elements that make LTI into two types of competences: *Foundational Competences* and *Advanced Competences*. As shown in Figure 3.1, the foundational competences are then divided into five sub-identities: language-related identity, disciplinary identity, context-related identity, self-knowledge and awareness, and student-related identity. Language-related identity stands for the individual teacher's language background and proficiency; the disciplinary represents a language teacher's specific knowledge of the content of the filed which is obtained not only from teaching experience but also from previous formal education. The disciplinary knowledge contains two types of specific knowledge relevant to language teaching: *disciplinary knowledge* and *pedagogical content knowledge*. The *disciplinary knowledge*, like the history of English teaching methods, linguistic theories, psycholinguistics or sociolinguistics, is a body of linguistic knowledge that a teacher should process essential knowledge to gaining membership of the profession. The *pedagogical content knowledge* means another line of knowledge that a teacher draws from language teaching and learning practices and theories, and the knowledge can be applied to solve practical problems in the classroom. The *context-related identity* refers to the favoring or disfavoring conditions that provide teachers with different kinds of constrains and opportunities for teachers' practices (Richards, 2012, cited in Pennington & Richards, 2016, p.14). The *context-related identity* is one of the critical elements in shaping LTI, having "a strong impact on the evolution of a teacher identity" (Pennington & Richards, 2016, p.14). Pennington (1989) maintains that being aware of one's strength and weakness and optimizing teaching on the basis of such awareness are important elements of the competence of a language teacher. In this sense, Pennington and Richards (2016) suggest that language teachers should develop experience and image of self that is built on self-awareness in relation to acts of teaching and that incorporates one's personal qualities, values, and ideals into effective teaching performance. A focus on the learner is characteristic of skilled teacher behavior (Borg, S., 2006). Therefore, the *student-related identity* is a significant aspect of LTI as a language teacher evolves over time to incorporate collaborative performances that are linked to students' identities and that show concern for their welfare (Pennington & Richards, 2016).

Advanced competences of language teachers' identity comprise of two different teaching skills (*practiced and responsive teaching skills* and *skills of theorizing from practice*) and membership in communities of practice and profession. In language teaching, teaches will use pedagogical knowledge and skills to instruct learners, their ready set of skills specific to language teaching are also required to be increasingly and responsively practiced to apply in different circumstances of teaching and learning, and will have a degree of reflexibility in being able to customize as needed. At the same time, language teachers are suggested possessing not only the ability to get familiar with the theoretical orientations of the field of language teaching but also the awareness and ability to produce and generate theories from teaching practices, in another word, as Sharkey (2004) puts, "They should be active readers, users, and producers of theory" (p.281). According to Pennington and Richards (2016), the last aspect of a language teacher's identity is the teacher's connection with one or more communities of practice, such as teachers at the school where one teaches, teachers in other school and communities in other parts of the country or the world (p.20). Teachers participate in such communities of practice through sharing knowledge, perspectives, and values; reflecting on those of others; and acquiring new knowledge and then shifting perspectives and values accordingly (Ibid).

In summary, Pennington and Richards (2016) make a significant contribution to the literature by providing an explicit categorization of constituents of LTI. Their original outline of the components of LIT greatly deepens the understanding of the repertoire of the formation and development of LTI.

3.3.3　Previous studies on LTI

Studies of teachers' identity began to emerge in the 1980s. Having been influenced by the surge of teachers' identity research and globalization of language contact, studies which specifically focus on language teachers started to arise at the end of the 1990s. Since then, researchers and theorists began to turn their eyes to the professional development of language teachers and then used identity as an effective lens for inquiry. In the last fifteen years, research on LTI has grown exponentially (Martel & Wang, 2014, p.289) and has become a separate research area in the field of language education. The goals of this section are two-fold: firstly, through a holistic review of existing literature, the research gap can be filled; secondly, the present study will benefit from such a review in order to establish the conceptual framework by recognizing the general foci, current methodologies and major findings of the current scholarship on LTI. The selection criteria for inclusion and exclusion of studies are:

1) Studies specifically focus on language teachers' identity related topics;

2) The participant(s) must be language teacher(s), regardless of their linguistic position or stage of professional development. They may be student teacher/pre-service teacher, novice teacher/in-service teacher, NES/NNES teacher or FL/ESL/EFL teacher from education institutions of different levels;

3) The language being taught is not limited to English but any languages used by considerable population;

4) No preference for gender of participants and geographical places where research was conducted;

5) Studies reviewed include published journal papers, monograph or book sections but not cover unpublished theses or dissertations.

An initial search was carried out using a key word-based procedure available for some major online database at home and abroad like Web of Knowledge, ERIC, ScienceDirect, Jastor, ProQuest, SAGE, Taylor & Francis Online, and CNKI. An article was selected to match the topic tentatively if it had any one key word like "teacher (s') identity", "teacher (s') professional identity" or "language teacher (s') identity" in its title. As a result, 1371 articles published between 1999 and 2017 were identified as relevant. Given the limit of word number and time, some of the most significant work (most cited) and latest articles (published in recent 10 years) were selected for the review to analyze the studies by reading them, looking for key words, and focusing on how teachers' identity was being investigated. A table was created to record the theoretical frame-work, research questions, methods, and findings. Using this table as an analytic tool, the researcher followed a process of emergent coding (Miles & Huberman, 1994) to identify recurring ideas across the studies. From these initial codes, the researcher has generated three categories of themes: 1) empirical studies that explore LTI from personal perspectives; 2) studies explore LTI development from professional dimension, and 3) studies examine the contextual factors on LTI construction. Findings are shown in Table 3.3:

Table 3.3   Summary of review articles and empirical studies on LTI

Studies	Focus	Context	Approach
	Review article		
Barkhuizen (2017b)	Definitions of LIT	/	Literature review
Pennington & Richards (2016)	Elements of LTI	/	Literature review
Martin & Strom (2016)	Linguistically Responsive Teacher Identity		Literature review
Cheung et al. (2016)	Narrative approach	/	Literature review
Xun & Zheng (2014)	Overview	/	Literature review
Martel & Wang (2014)	Overview	/	Literature review
Izadinia (2013)	Student teachers	/	Literature review
Liu (2012)	Narrative approach	/	Literature review
Miller (2009)	Overview	/	Literature review
Varghese et al. (2005)	Theorizing LTI	/	Literature review
Empirical studies on personal dimensions of LTI			
Ubaque & Castaneda-Pena (2017)	Life histories affect LTI	3 EFL teacher-researchers in a private but non-profit institution	Narrative Inquiry
Martel (2015)	Significant others	A Spanish student teacher	Symbolic interactionism; interviews, observations, and documents

Zhang & Zhang (2015)	Linguistic positions NNES teachers' professional identity	2 NNESTs at a university in Singapore	ethnographic case study approach
Reis (2011)	How do NNESTs establish their legitimacy as credible, qualified instructors	An ESL writing teacher	classroom observations, interviews, and a dialogic journal
Liu (2009)	How Chinese college English teachers construct LTI	2 Chinese college English teachers	Interview
Motha (2006)	Native speaker status	Public school teachers	Feminist ethnography
Pavlenko (2003)	Personal autobiographies influence LTI	44 student teachers in a TESO program	Narratives
Empirical studies on professional dimensions of LTI			
Torresrocha (2017)	Influence of language policy	University EFL teachers in Columbia	Narrative inquiry
Yuan & Burns (2017)	LIT construction in community of practice	2 ELTs in secondary schools in Beijing	In-depth interviews, field observation
Chesnut (2015)	Policy implementation	2 dual immersion teachers	Participant observation, interviews
Cammarata & Tedick (2012)	Immersion teacher preparation and professional development	3 language teachers in immersion schools	Interviews and classroom observations
Park (2012)	Professional identity change before and during their TESOL programs	5 East Asian students	E-Auto; E-Journal; Interviews

continued

Studies	Focus	Context	Approach
	Review articles		
Kanno & Stuart (2011)	Identity shapes practices	2 student teachers in TESOL program in a U.S. university	Interviews, journals, stimulated recalls, classroom observations, videotaping
Empirical studies on contextual dimensions of LIT			
Salinas (2017)	how macro and micro contextual factors have influenced (EFL) teachers' identity in education reform contexts in Chile	12 EFL teachers in Chilean elementary schools	Grounded theory, semi-structured and focus group interviews
Nguyen (2017)	How ELT of young learners created LTI in their local contexts	4 EFT from primary schools in Vietnam	narrative interviews
del Rosal et al. (2017)	LTI in the online context	11 high school language teachers in the U.S.	Case study
Qi & Wang (2017)	Using WeChat as online context	5 Chinese language teachers	Content analysis
Gayton (2016)	Societal and school-level influence on LTI	11 teachers of French, German, English	Narrative interview
Han (2016)	Investigating Korean English teachers' LTI construction in responses to their national English curriculum	5 Korean English teachers working in different state academic high schools	socio-psychological framework
Kim & Kim (2016)	Instructional focuses and practices shape LTI	3 Korean heritage language (HL) teachers	Interviews and classroom observations
Jimenez-Silva & Olson (2012)	LTI constructed in Teacher-Learner Community	26 pre-service teachers	Mixed methods

Study	Focus	Participants/Context	Theoretical/Methodological Approach
Liu & Xu (2011)	Complexity of teachers' identity in the context of a curriculum reform	A university EFL teacher in China	Narrative inquiry
Menard-Warwick (2011)	Popular culture and teachers' identity	3 English instructors in a Chilean university	Bakhtinian dialogism
Empirical studies using diverse theoretical and methodological approaches			
Donato & Davin (2017)	Novice teachers LTI were influenced by history-in-person processes	2 language teachers from a primary school in the U.S.	History-in-Person Theory
Yuan (2016)	Language teacher educators' professional identities	2 language teacher educators in Hong Kong universities	Sociocultural Linguistic Perspective
Darvin & Norton (2015)	Relationship between identity, investment, and language learning	A student in Uganda and a student in Canada	Investment Theory
Martel (2015)	How teacher preparation programs affect LTI	A Spanish student teacher	Symbolic Interactionism and Teacher Socialization
Trent (2012)	Educational reform affects LTI	2 language teachers from primary schools in Hong Kong, China	Positioning Theory
Akkerman & Meijer (2011)	Introducing the Dialogical Self Theory	/	Dialogical Self Theory
Reis (2011)	How do NNESTs establish and professional identity	An ESL writing teacher	Vygotskian Sociocultural Theory
Menard-Warwick (2011)	Popular culture and teachers' identity	3 English instructors in a Chilean university	Bakhtinian Dialogism

As depicted in Table 3.3, the literature review demonstrates some distinctive features of previous studies on LTI. Firstly, the review articles are either comprehensive and specific. Barkhuizen (2017b), Martel and Wang (2014) and Miller (2009) make comprehensive and holistic review of research on LTI, while other review articles focus on specific aspect or teacher group. For example, Izadinia (2013) reviews 29 empirical studies on LTI construction of student teachers; Cheung (2015) and Liu (2012) show the importance of narrative as a lens to explore teachers' identity.

Secondly, literature reveals that researchers have explored LTI from a wide range of aspects, and the themes have been roughly categorized into three major types: studies on personal dimensions, studies on professional dimensions and studies from contextual dimensions. The core themes of current studies on LTI will be summarized and discussed in the next section (section 3.3.4).

Thirdly, diverse theoretical and methodological approaches have been drawn upon to explore professional identity development in language teachers. The majority of studies use theories foregrounding the importance of social settings and social interactions in understanding identity such as Socio-cultural Theory (Reis, 2011), History-in-Person (Donato & Davin, 2017), Positioning Theory (Trent, 2013) and Investment Theory (Darvin & Norton, 2015). Having been affected by poststructural thoughts, scholars adopt a wide range of methodological approaches like ethnography (Duff & Uchida, 1997), narrative inquiry (Higgins & Sandhu, 2014), symbolic interactionism (Martel, 2015) or sociocultural linguistics (Yuan, 2016).

In this section, some key literature on LTI is presented and general features of the existing literature are briefly summarized. In the next section, core themes that emerge from the literature review will be elaborated.

3.3.4 Themes in LTI research

As shown in Table 3.3, such plurality in LTI research makes it impossible to review all the literature, only highly relevant studies can be selected and reviewed. However, the previous literature can be grouped by themes. For instance, some studies specifically choose pre-service teachers as participants, while some other studies investigate how personal biographies affect the formation of LTI; therefore, those distinctive features of literature make it possible for this study to categorize previous scholarship into groups according to the themes. In this section, more empirical studies will be discussed and critiqued. It has been found that three prominent themes emerge from the review of empirical studies on language teachers' identity. Researchers have investigated the formation, development and construction of language teachers' identity from personal, professional and contextual dimensions.

Theme 1: Empirical studies that explore LTI from personal perspectives

Literature review suggests that personal factors, generally including teachers' biographies and prior experiences, significant others, linguistic positions and cultural status, play considerable part in shaping their professional identity (Bukor, 2015; Duff & Uchida, 1997; Izadinia, 2013; Trent & Gao, 2009; Tsui, 2007). Bergner and Holmes (2000) argue that early childhood experiences and the assertions of significant others (e.g., parents) involve in the development of teachers' self-concept. Tsui's (2007) study reports that teachers' personal learning experiences form their beliefs about English teaching and learning and shape their professional identity. Trent and Gao (2009) observe the lived experiences of second-career teachers as they form identities as English language teachers in Hong Kong secondary schools. The second-career teachers drew upon their past experiences as students in secondary- and tertiary-level classrooms, as well as from the various career trajectories they pursued prior to their entry into teaching. From a "holistic" perspective, Bukor's (2015) study confirms the influence of personal experiences on three language teachers' development of teachers' identity. Her study proves that participant teachers have explored their beliefs and perceptions, and interpretations originating from their personal, educational, and professional experiences have affected their teachers' identity. Researchers notice that significant others and critical life events would exert either positive or negative influence on teachers' professional identity construction (Liu, 2009; Martel, 2015; Park, 2012; Yuan, 2016). Liu (2009) demonstrates an example of how prior experiences, like critical incidents influence teachers' formation of professional identity. Teacher Ying, one of the participants in the study, regarded herself as a "product of the times" (p.258) and reflected by her decision to major in

English despite the fact that she disliked it, by working in Tibet as an interpreter, and by beginning teaching in her late 40s as a "late entrant" (p.259). Martel and Wang (2015) hold that important others with whom teachers associate shift throughout their careers; during teacher education, common significant others include mentor teachers, classmates, and teacher educators, while in the workforce, they could be colleagues, administrators, and students (p.290). Following this vein, Martel's (2015) study on a Spanish student teacher finds that Anna whose experiences demonstrate the extent to which becoming a teacher is an ever-shifting, complex process involving an interplay between significant others' messages and personal goals. However, significant others do not always have a positive effect on shaping language teachers' professional identity. They may also harm the identity formation process. Yuan (2016) reports the identity construction of two pre-service language teachers through their interactions with school mentors and university supervisors during their teaching practicum. His findings demonstrate how negative mentoring dismantles the student teachers' ideal identities and create different "ought" and "feared" identities, which impinges on their professional learning and growth.

Review of literature manifests that teachers' linguistic positions and cultural statues emerge as important influencing factors on the formation of LTI. The majority of the studies about teachers' linguistic positions have focused on the dichotomy of Native English-Speaking Teachers (NESTs) and Non-Native English-Speaking Teachers (NNESTs). A strain of latest research has discovered that the NNESTs, faced with challenges in the English language teaching profession, have experienced being marginalized and have comparatively low self-esteem (Aneja, 2016; Kim, 2011; Wang & Lin, 2014; Wolff & De Costa, 2017; Zhang & Zhang, 2015). Kim (2011) investigates how non-native English-speaking teachers' identity is affected by the native-speaker ideology within the intersections of power, language, culture, and race. Wang and Lin's (2014) study examines 258 pre-service non-native English-speaking teachers' professional identity from the micro and macro social context. The result of their study indicates that in the micro-social context, the participants encounter contradictory discourses brought by the presence of NNESTs in terms of what the participants can offer as opposed to what ideal English teachers should possess. In the macro-social context, the participants face competing discourses caused by the presence of NNESTs, in terms of what constitutes good teaching practice, as opposed to what is valued by the government and the major stakeholders in the society. Wolff and De Costa's (2017) research focuses on how emotional factors might affect the identity construction of NNESTs. Puja, the focal participant of their study was confronted with numerous emotional challenges in her first year in a U.S. MATESOL program. The research examines the impact that emotion has on her overall teachers' identity development. The other line of inquiry of LTI underlines to the cultural status of language teachers (Fichtner & Chapman, 2011; Menard-Warwick, 2008, 2011). Fichtner and Chapman (2011) investigate how far foreign language teachers affiliate with more than one culture and how this cultural identity affects their classroom practice. Results show that foreign language instructors engage with their cultural affiliations intellectually, by embracing but not embodying "the other" culture. Menard-Warwick (2008) provides a long-term case study of a Brazilian and a Chilean native who worked as English language teachers in a Californian school. From the teachers' perspective, the study examines the connections between their transnational life experiences and development of intercultural competences. The author appeals that the profession needs to put more value on the pedagogical resources that transnational and intercultural teachers bring to English language teaching. Based on life history interviews with Chilean English teachers, Menard-Warwick (2011) compares the similarities and contrasts differences between generations of Chilean university teachers in their appropriation of English language popular culture. The author states that the connections between teachers' investments and their English teachers' identity outline teachers' perspectives on popular culture and English language pedagogies.

Theme 2: Empirical studies explore professional dimensions of LTI

Professional dimensions refer to teachers' language teaching related practices such as attending teacher education programs, teachers' reflexive practices in applying new pedagogies and experiences in teachers' community of practices. For both pre-service and in-service language teachers, it is claimed that different teacher education courses and programs modify their professional identity (Block, 2015; Martel, 2015; Park, 2012; Yazan, 2017; Yuan & Lee, 2015). Park (2012) examines the experiences of five East Asian women before and during their TESOL programs. The result highlights the disconnectedness between participants' experiences in home country, TESOL programs, and their mentored student teaching experience. Block (2015) examines how two Spanish nationals develop Spanish language teachers' identity while attending a Postgraduate Certificate of Education (PGCE) course at a university in London. Yuan and Lee (2016) investigate how three government-funded student teachers construct and reconstruct their identities in a pre-service teacher education program in China. The findings of the study suggest that pre-service language teachers develop and modify their identities through engaging in cognitive learning, interacting with different socializing factors and experiencing various emotions in university coursework and teaching practicum. Yazan (2017) explores a cohort of preservice teachers' identity development during teacher education coursework. The findings show that three preservice ESOL teacher candidates subjectively negotiate their teachers' identity as they position themselves as an ESOL teacher through online and face-to-face course discussions, professional interaction with teacher educators and in the teacher-learning community. Grounded in the concept of Community of Practice (CoP) proposed by Lave and Wenger (1991), studies (Herrero, 2016; Jiang, 2017; Jimenez-Silva & Olson, 2012; Liu & Xu, 2013; Martel, 2015; Qi & Wang, 2017) prove that both the face-to-face and online community of practice promote the development of teachers' cognition, the sharing of teachers' professional knowledge and the cultivation of teachers' professional spirit (Jiang, 2017, p.20).

Theme 3: Empirical studies on contextual factors

The contextual factors, also acknowledged as social dimensions of LTI are powerful in shaping language teachers' professional identity. Previous studies suggest that curriculum reforms, the workplace environment, local community cultures, the relationship with colleagues all have been evidenced by the literature as important factors that influence the development of LTI. As Richards (2012) maintains that different contexts for teaching create different potentials for learning that teachers must come to understand and provide different kinds of constraints and opportunities for teachers' practice (p.48). A number of studies (Han, 2016; Nguyen, 2017; Salinas, 2017) report the contextual influences on LTI construction from different aspects. Based on sociocultural theory and using grounded theory, Salinas (2017) gives an account of how macro and micro contextual factors, such as emotion and national EFL curriculum, exert influence on the construction of English as a foreign language (EFL) teachers' identity in education reform contexts in Chile. Nguyen (2017) reveals how Vietnamese primary school English language teachers to young learners create spaces for developing practice and identity in their local contexts. The study finds that participation in the school community is inadequate for professional development. In order to improve their practice and practice professional identity, the participants crossed the school boundary and joined learning communities, including a separate group of primary English language teachers, English classes for adult learners, an imagined community between local and expatriate teachers and their own families. Han (2016) provides another interesting case about the English language teaching environment that powerfully influences the construction of LTI. His research notices diverse attributes and dynamic of professional identity by investigating Korean English teachers' cognitive, emotional and behavioral responses to their national English curriculum and related policies.

In summary, this section presents the findings that have been achieved by previous research on various personal, professional and contextual factors that would exert influence on the formation and evolution of LTI. A review of the literature suggests that shaping factors of LTI fall into two categories: personal-related and context-related factors. The personal-related influencing factors generally include teachers' individual biographies, learning experiences, influential others and critical events; while the contextual factors are school cultures, teachers' community of practice, classroom practice, education policies, and values of local communities.

3.4 Critiques of previous studies

In the last two decades, researchers in the field of language education have increasingly explored the professional identity development of language teachers from various perspectives and collated fruitful findings. Since the studies on LTI have derived from teacher studies in general education, this line of scholarship naturally has inherited the characteristics of teachers' identity construction, which is well acknowledged as an ongoing, multifaceted, multilayered, complicated and discursive process. Although a copious list of studies in literature have invested the construction of LTI from personal, professional and contextual dimensions, it still has the following limits:

Firstly, in terms of participants, existing literature shows great concern to the teacher candidates without fully being aware of the secondary school in-service EFL teachers.

Secondly, concerning the place of research, the large majority of studies choose urban cities as research sites, very few of them are conducted in rural areas, and even less works choose to examine secondary school EFL teachers' professional life in remote, rural, multiethnic and multilingual regions.

Thirdly, previous researches have discovered that teacher education programs and courses are featured in shaping language teachers' professional identity. However, this line of studies has its limits. For one thing, most of the studies concentrate on student teachers or teacher candidates' professional construction in teacher education program or practicum, relatively little attention has been paid to in-service teachers' professional identity transformation happening in these programs; for another, many of these studies usually observe how education programs have influenced the teachers' identity construction, but fail to examine how their experiences and reflections are internalized and manifested through classroom practices. As De Costa calls, "Teachers' identity is not merely something that exists in the mind or explained elegantly on a piece of paper in the form of a well-crafted teaching philosophy statement. Rather, teachers' identity needs to be performed and manifested through a good instruction" (Barkhuizen, 2017b, p.160).

The previous studies are far from a thorough understanding of the nature and influencing factors of LTI. There is still much room for researchers to investigate LTI from a holistic perspective. Based on the findings from the prior scholarship on teachers' identity research and fruitful results from language teachers' identity studies, the present study fills the research gaps by looking at the complicate professional identity construction of three secondary school EFL teachers who are teaching in remote rural schools in southwestern China.

3.5   An integrated theoretical framework in understanding LTI

The following sections denote three theories which help to understand the dynamic construction of language teachers' identity. The present study utilizes an integrated theoretical framework including "Identity Formation Theory" (Wenger, 1998), "History-in-Person"(Holland & Lave, 2001), and "Identity-in-Discourse and Identity-in-Practice"(Varghese et al., 2005) as theoretical underpinnings.

3.5.1   Wenger's Identity Formation Theory

Wenger (1998) states that "identification takes place in the doing" (p.193). In Wenger's theoretical framework, identity construction is reflected in terms of three modes of belonging: engagement, imagination, and alignment. Through engagement, individuals establish and maintain joint enterprises, negotiate meanings and establish relations with others. As Cohen (2010) points out that teachers' identity has been regarded as being constructed partly through an individual's relations with others, including mentors, school authorities, teacher educators, and other teachers. Imagination is a creative force for identity construction.

Imagination moves beyond the physical limits of engagement by enabling individuals to create images of the world, and their place within it, across time and space. As Wenger (1998) puts, "It is through imagination that we conceive of new developments, explore alternatives, and envision possible futures" (p.178). In language teacher education, membership of imagined communities has been shown to legitimize new identity options by allowing non-native language speaking teachers and their students to position themselves as legitimate L2 users (Pavlenko, 2003).

In terms of alignment, Wenger (1998) contends that it is "the process through which modes of belonging become constitutive of our identities by creating bonds or distinctions in which we become invested" (p.191). Alignment translates into the membership of social communities, which constitutes one's identity formation as a form of competence—the competence of knowing who we are and who we are not. It is participative. For one thing, identity is a participative process of "being identified with something or someone" (Wenger, 1998, p.191). In other words, it is a process of building associations whose experience is constitutive of who we are. For another, it is a process of identifying as or being identified as something or someone, being labeled as the member of a group or a category.

Wenger (1998) also examines identity formation in terms of the negotiation of meanings that matter within a social configuration. Meanings compete "for the definition of certain events, actions, or artifacts" (Wenger, 1998, p.199). However, if negotiability over meanings is absent, an identity of non-participation and marginality can result; the individual's experience "becomes irrelevant because it cannot be asserted and recognized as a form of competence" (Wenger, 1998, p.203).

3.5.2 The Theory of History-in-Person

The notion of History-in-Person is derived from social practice theory and primarily used to explain the processes of social formation and cultural production emerging as a result of complex social, political, and economic struggles (Holland & Lave, 2001). The present study employs the History-in-Person Theory because professional identity is largely manifested through teachers' discursive practices, their instructional talk must be viewed from the perspective of their sociocultural and historical origins, as history-in-person processes. Teachers' history-in-person is "the sediment from past experiences upon which one improvises, using the cultural resources available, in response to the subject positions afforded one in the present" (Holland et al., 1998). History is brought to the present through the minds and bodies of individuals, as they are addressed by external people, forces, and institutions and respond using the words and practices of others, representing history-in-person (Holland & Lave, 2009). History-in-Person Theory represents the generative fashioning of individual identity and self-making through their relationship with local conflictual practice in the past and present (Holland & Lave, 2001). Clearly, the individual and society cannot be separated and are closely intertwined. By teasing apart the dominant perspectives of both of these inter-related theories of identity construction, analytical attention can be focused on how historically produced agents come to a particular perspective and way of participating (Donato & Davin, 2017).

In this study, analytical attention is focused on exploring the trajectory of professional identity formation of three secondary school EFL teachers. Since teachers' identity formation is a continuous process, teachers' past personal and professional experiences and current practices are both pivotal in shaping the professional identity. For instance, teachers' early experiences as language learners sometimes directly affect their language teaching beliefs and instructional practices in the classroom. Therefore, the History-in-Person Theory is functional in supporting the present study in connecting teachers' past and present in the trajectory of professional identity formation. Thus, to understand professional identity construction, one's personal history and the present forces must be included in the interpretive frame.

3.5.3   Identity-in-Discourse and Identity-in-Practice

Varghese et al. (2005) maintain that a comprehensive understanding of teaching and teachers requires attention to both "Identity-in-Discourse" and "Identity-in-Practice" (p.39). According to the theoretical framework of Varghese et al. (2005), Identity-in-Practice denotes an action-orientated approach to understanding identity, stressing the need to investigate identity formation as a social matter, which is operationalised through concrete practices and tasks. While another aspect of comprehensive way in understanding teachers' identity construction, Identity-in-Discourse, posits that identities are discursively constituted, mainly through language. As Varghese et al. (2005) argue that, "Identity is constructed, maintained, and negotiated to a significant extent through language and discourse" (Varghese et al., 2005, p.23).

"Identity-in-Practice" and "Identity-in-Discourse" are the two facets of a coin. Both of the dimensions play a pivotal role in identity development. Identity is discursively constructed, with language being used to represent a specific kind of knowledge and to construct identity—hence Identity-in-Discourse (Block, 2007). Hall et al. (2010) add that "as people learn the characteristics associated with the identities available to them, they can adopt the language and speech patterns connected to them in order to position themselves as a certain type of person" (p.235). In language teacher research, as for teachers in academic growth, they acquire new modes of discourse, i.e., a professional language to talk about their work, carving out new identities for themselves (Freeman, 1993; Richards, 2010). Identity formation can also be operationalised in the daily tasks and practices people engage in, hence Identity-in-Practice (Gee, 1996; Miller, 2009). People perform identity work and enact their identity through what they do; as Gee (1996) contends, identity is "what you are doing while you say it" (p. viii). While Varghese et al. (2005) use Identity-in-Practice to refer to the enactment of identity (as Different from Identity-in-Discourse). Kanno and Stuart (2011) regard relationship between Identity-in-Practice and Identity-in-Discourse as "mutually constitutive" (p.240). Thus Identity-in-Practice can be understood in terms of both "narrated identities" and "enacted identities" (Lee, 2013, p.332).

3.6　Conceptual framework for the study

Drawing on the literature review on teachers' identity formation and language teachers' identity construction, a tentative conceptual framework that guides the present study is established. The conceptual framework not only encompasses the integrated notions and different variables that constitute LTI but denotes the relationship between different variables.

The conceptual framework is firstly built on knowledge about teachers' identity and then language teachers' identity. Research on LTI sets its roots in how identity has been defined and is informed by copious research on teachers' identity. Recent conceptualizations of teachers' identity seem to reflect postmodern views on identity, describing teachers' identity as involving "sub-identities", as being "an ongoing process of construction" and as "relating to various social contexts and relationships" (Akkerman & Meijer, 2011, p.310). In this sense, LTI, as one of the sub-categories of teachers' identity, has been simply put as how teachers see themselves as language teachers (English language, bilingual, or foreign/ world language teachers) and how others see them—a claimed and assigned identity (Varghese et al., 2005, p.21). Researchers argue that LTI contains three layers of meaning: a combination of a language teacher's self-positioning of who he/she is and others' collective conceptions of who he/she is; a continuous process of becoming, which is constantly negotiated with various resources available within certain social, cultural, historical and political context; and the pursuit of membership in a community school environment, but also by changes in their personal lives (Xu, 2017, p.122).

Elements that constitute LTI are the center of the conceptual framework. LTI has been an elusive, vague and implicit notion until Pennington and Richard (2016) explicitly interpret what elements should be included in the LTI. As mentioned in section 2.4.3, LTI consists of four major strains of competences required for teaching: teachers' knowledge base, teachers' belies, teachers' agentive quality and their instructional practice in the classroom.

The conceptual framework shows various shaping factors that impact LTI construction and interplay of different variables. The literature review suggests that empirical studies have explored the LTI from diverse perspectives which can be generally grouped into three categories: personal, professional and contextual. The personal dimension basically includes language teachers' personal biographies, important others, critical life events and so forth; the professional dimension of LTI demonstrates influences of teacher education programs, new pedagogies and teachers' community of practices; the contextual factors acknowledge social dimensions which are powerful in shaping language teachers' professional identity. Previous studies suggest that national curriculum reforms, workplace environment, local community cultures, relationship with colleagues all have been evidenced by the literature as powerful factors that influence the development of LTI.

To summarize, based on the conceptualizations of language teachers' identity, which is constituted by various sub-identities and constantly influenced by a range of personal, professional and contextual factors, a tentative conceptual framework has been established and is mapped in Figure 3.2:

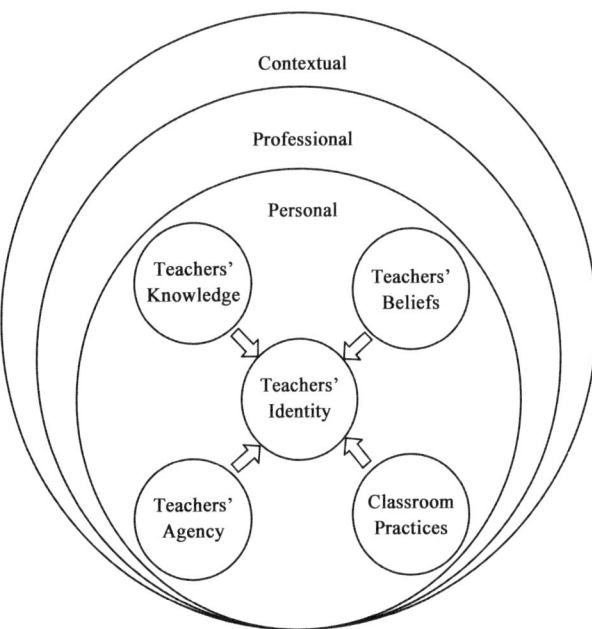

Figure 3.2   A tentative conceptual framework in understanding language teachers' identity

3.7   Summary

By reviewing the existing scholarship related to language teachers' identity studies, this chapter provides the theoretical basis and the conceptual framework for the present study. This chapter starts with the current conceptualization of the notion of identity, then reviews the relevant literature on teachers' identity, focusing on multiple definitions made by scholars and different issues emerging from the current literature. Then this chapter delineates in great detail about the definitions, components, previous studies and core issues in the literature on language teachers' identity. In the end, by critiquing the literature, research gaps are identified and a tentative conceptual framework is established.

Chapter 4 | Research Design

This chapter illuminates the research design for this study. It focuses on presenting information of research sites, justification for choosing qualitative paradigm and rationale for choosing case study approach. It also introduces the sampling strategy, data collection instruments as well as data analysis procedures adopted in the present study. Issues related to research validity and trustworthiness are discussed at the end of this chapter.

4.1　The research sites

This qualitative case study investigates professional identity formation of secondary school EFL teachers who are teaching in rural and multiethnic regions in Yunnan province. The data is collected from teachers in three different schools in the rural areas in Jinghong city, Xishuangbanna Dai Autonomous Prefecture. This section introduces basic geographic and demographic information of Jinghong city, Xishuangbanna Dai Autonomous Prefecture and Yunnan province respectively. This section indicates the geographical and demographical information of the research sites.

4.1.1　Yunnan province

Yunnan province is a frontier province in southwestern China with the largest diversity of language, culture and ethnicity. With a territory of 394,100 square kilometers and a population of 47,209,000 (National Bureau of Statistics of China 2021), Yunnan is home to 26 officially identified ethnic groups, among which 15 are exclusive to China and 16 are cross-border ethnic groups. The largest ethnic group, the Han people, makes up 66.88% of the population, while the other 25 ethnic groups constitute a combined 33.12% of the total population. Now, Yunnan has 8 autonomous prefectures and 29 autonomous counties, which cover 70.2 % of the provincial territory, inhabited by 48.08% of the provincial population. The 26 ethnic groups speak 26 languages and use 22 scripts (Dao, 2005). From 1954 to 1979, supported by the central government, 14 written scripts were created for those ethnic groups who had no written languages. The 14 newly developed written languages include the Jingpo, Buyi, Yi, Naxi, Miao, Li, Hani, Lisu, Dong, Zhuang, Miao, Wa, Bai, and Zaiwa. Furthermore, the central government helped to reform the written languages of the Uygur, Kazakh, Dai, Lahu, and Kirgiz people (Teng and Wen, 2005).

Yunnan is famous for her multiethnic cultures and linguistic diversities. Here, 26 officially identified ethnic groups live together in a pattern of "big dispersion and small concentration" (*da za ju, xiao ju ju*) [大杂居 , 小聚居]. This demographic feature has further encouraged the integration of some ethnic groups with the Han people and other neighboring ethnic groups throughout history. There are 11 ethnic groups living in the cross-border areas where different ethnic people mix, and 22 ethnic groups speak 28 languages (Tsang, 2005) because in some co-inhabited communities, people can usually speak more than one language due to frequent inter-ethnic contact. As mentioned in the literature review chapter, in addition to the economic and geographical factors, studies find that educational failure for many ethnic students often arises from the inappropriate use of languages in education (Adamson & Feng, 2014). Living in such a multicultural and multilingual context, ethnic students need to learn different languages which are linguistically-distant form their mother tongue in terms of pronunciation, written form, vocabulary and syntax. Under these circumstances, many ethnic students tend to have a high drop-out rate, while those who stay in school often don't perform well.

4.1.2   Xishuangbanna Dai Autonomous Prefecture

Xishuangbanna Dai Autonomous Prefecture, located at the extreme southern tip of Yunnan province, China, is about 540 kilometers from Kunming, the capital city of Yunnan province. It occupies an area of some 19,096 square kilometers. There are more than ten ethnic groups like Dai, Hani, Bulang, Jinuo, etc, with a total population of 792,800 according to the statistics of 2021. Among them, the Dai people take up one third in the permanent resident population. Xishuangbanna lies just below the Tropic of Cancer and the land is hilly with some mountains and deep valleys. The Lancang River and its tributaries flow through the area. The Indian Ocean monsoons bring in humid air and it is often windless. The climate is ideal for plants and animals. One quarter of China's faunal species and one sixth of her plant species are living and growing in this rich and fertile area.

Xishuangbanna operates nine years of compulsory education for all children. However, in practice this is not always achieved. According to the government statistics in 2015, between 80% and 100% of under sixteen in this area have some education. This implies an improving trend in education levels across the general population of Xishuangbanna. Of the adult population, about 40% have only primary education, and 25% have junior high school. There are more illiterate people than senior high school graduates in this area.

A comparison of the educational achievement of the household head and the most highly educated household member suggests that the highest educational achievement within the household is usually one level up from the household head's. This again implies an improving trend in education at all elevations.

Even so, a considerable proportion of household heads are illiterate. This should be considered when developing extension or training materials. The highest illiteracy rates are found in the low and medium elevations in Mengla. The lowest average educational achievements are also found at the medium and low elevations of Mengla.

Education achievement by ethnic groups can also be analyzed. Although rapid improvements have been made, 30 percent of ethnic households still lack a literate family member. The Dai people have a surprisingly low education rate compared to the Han, Yi and Hani people. This corresponds to anecdotal evidence that a high proportion of Dai people leave education early to focus on rubber farming, which is relatively lucrative.

4.1.3   Jinghong city

Jinghong, the capital city of the Xishuangbanna Dai Autonomous Prefecture, is the political, economic and cultural center of local people. Its administrative territory covers 6,867 square kilometers and comprises of 7 counties. Jinghong is a boarder city of China sharing 112.39 km demarcation with Myanmar, Laos and Thailand with the Lancang River (Mekong), a trans-boundary river running through the town. Jinghong lies at a latitude range of 21°27'N–22°36' N and a longitude range of 100°25'E–101°31' E (Wikipedia data) and neighboring Pu'er city to the north.

The city has a generally humid climate with strong monsoonal influences. Despite about 3—5 weeks of lower temperature (range from 5℃—10℃) , the summer is long and there is virtually no "winter". The climate can be clearly divided into "dry season (from December to April)" and "wet season" (from May to October) in which the annual rainfall can range from 1,100 to 1,700 millimeters. The subtropical climate and mountainous environment harbor much of the biodiversity of China.

The city is ethnically diverse, there are 13 officially recognized indigenous groups living together. The total population reached 547,700 in 2019, and among other small ethnic groups (Jinuo, Blang, Lahu, Yi, Yao, Zhuang, Hui, Miao, Jingpo, Wa), Dai (144,658, 33.28%) and Hani (78,058, 18.05%) are the major ethnic groups (Data retrieved from Jinghong government website, 2019). Jinghong, the name of the city, is derived from the Dai language which means "The Town of Dawn". Now, the city takes on an urban landscape—in addition to buildings for the government department and agencies, there are various architectures such as the airport, educational and research institutions, tourist resorts, super markets and shopping malls for city life. Buddhist temples and towers can be seen in the park, and traditional costumes are no longer favorite dresses for people living in urban regions.

4.2　Methodology

As mentioned in the literature review chapter, teachers' professional identity is multidimensional and multifaceted, it takes shape in teachers' personal biography, influenced by their professional experiences and significantly influenced by external context. Given the intricate nature of teachers' identity, the current research adopts a qualitative case study approach as the methodology for inquiry.

4.2.1   Qualitative research paradigm

There are several reasons for adopting a qualitative research paradigm. To begin with, qualitative research is generally appropriate when primary purpose of research is to explore, describe, or explain (Leavy, 2017). This research focuses on examining language teachers' professional identity construction, which decides the nature of this research to be explorative.

Yin (2011) points out that qualitative research has five distinctive features: 1) it involves studying the meaning of people's lives under real-world conditions; 2) it differs because of its ability to represent the views and perspectives of the participants in a study; 3) it covers contextual conditions—the social, institutional, and environmental conditions within which people's lives take place; 4) it is not just a diary or chronicle of everyday life; 5) it strives to collect, integrate, and present data from a variety of sources of evidence as part of any given study (p.7). Qualitative research advocates a naturalistic inquiry that focuses on the experience people "lived" or "felt" or "undergone" in their world (Denzin & Lincoln, 2003; Merriam, 1997) and aims at understanding the process of these experiences (Maxwell, 2004). For the current research, a qualitative approach enables the researcher to have a closer examination of secondary school language teachers' different personal and professional experiences. Moreover, the qualitative research approaches empower the researcher to investigate the complex institutional and sociocultural environment in which teachers construct their professional identity in a natural way.

Adler et al. (1995) argue that qualitative approach is responsive to the changing conditions in progress. As an ongoing process, teachers' professional identity has been formed, developed and shaped constantly in different professional stages. Such a long trajectory of professional identity formation is rich in reflections, conflicts and changes. Therefore, enlisting of qualitative research approach allows the researcher to discover and describe the dynamic process of identity formation. At the same time, qualitative research approach can be useful in explaining a wide range of latent and intricate, intrinsic and extrinsic influencing factors that affect the professional identity construction.

4.2.2　Case study approach

Rossman and Rallis (2003) point out that case study seeks to understand a larger phenomenon through intensive examination of one specific instance. Gall et al. (2003) describe case study research as "the in-depth study of instances of a phenomenon in its natural context and from the perspective of the participants involved in the phenomenon" (p.436). By addressing issues of scope, data collection, and analysis strategies, Yin (2003) defines case study as "an empirical inquiry that investigates a contemporary phenomenon within its real-life context, especially when the boundaries between phenomenon and context are not clearly evident" (p.13). Regarding scope and data collection, Yin stresses that "there should be many more variables of interest than data points, and as one result relies on multiple sources of evidence" and "data need to converge in a triangulating fashion, and as another result benefits from the prior development of theoretical propositions to guide data collection and analysis" (p.14). According to Mills et al. (2010), as a research strategy, case study focuses on "the interrelationships that constitute the context of a specific entity (such as an organization, event, phenomenon, or person)" (p.29). Wolcott (1994) continues that exploring the experiences of a small number of individuals, in depth, in real contexts, the case study aims for "concrete and complex illustrations" (p.364). Furthermore, Nunan (1992) states that case study is particularly suitable for clarifying teachers' understandings of their work, and responding to their problems encountered in their professional lives.

In this study, three Chinese EFL teachers are selected as research participants who are epitomes of a large group of secondary school EFL teachers working in not only geographically remote regions but also in ethnically diverse areas. Few previous studies select this cohort of frontier language teachers as informants. This study aims to explore the complex relationship between the intrinsic and extrinsic factors that affect teachers' professional identity construction. In addition, the interplay of different variables of influencing factors are carefully examined. Substantial data which has been collected is displayed in this study in order to present teachers' change in classroom practices and teaching beliefs before and after they participate the NTTP, as well as their problems, conflicts, struggles and reflections on implementing the competing pedagogical models.

Case study approach is reasonable to fulfil the purpose of the present study, as Mills et al. (2010) state "the explicit purpose of using those insights (of the interactions between contextual relationships and the entity in question) to generate theory and/or contribute to extant theory" (p.29). Therefore, case study is particularly appropriate for this research.

4.2.2.1   Case sampling

The present study adopts purposive and snowball sampling techniques in selection of participants. Purposive sampling means that the inquirer selects individuals and sites for study because they can purposefully inform an understanding of the research problem and central phenomenon in the study (Creswell, 2007; Miles & Huberman, 1994). While the snowball, chain, or network sampling is perhaps the most common form of purposive sampling (Merriam, 2009). Snowball sampling involves approaching some key participants who firstly meet the criteria established for participation in the study. As interviewing the key participants, the researcher may ask them to introduce more potential participants. "By asking a number of people who else to talk with, the snowball gets bigger and bigger as you accumulate new information-rich cases" (Patton, 2002, p.237).

Using purposive sampling and snowball sampling as the major case sampling strategies, this study selects three teachers as participants from secondary schools in the rural and suburb multiethnic regions in Jinghong city. The detailed procedure in selection of the case teachers involved in the study will be provided next.

4.2.2.2   Selection of participants

Purposive and snowball sampling strategies are adopted by the present study in screening research participants. The potential research participants are all frontline practitioners working as EFL teachers in rural schools in the multiethnic regions, who meet the following qualifications:

a) Experienced in-service teachers who can provide abundant and valuable data;

b) Teachers who have been selected to attend the NTTP training courses;

c) Teachers who are accessible and willing to participate;

d) No gender preference in the selection of participants.

Based on these considerations, the chosen teacher participants are supposed to provide rich data about the influence on their beliefs and practices as well as professional identity formation.

During the fieldwork, it took a long time in screening appropriate participants. The researcher visited different schools, sat in the classrooms of teacher training courses, and observe the demonstration classes (*gong kai ke*) [公开课]. The researcher met and talked to as many teachers as possible and finally found three qualified participant teachers for this study: Jenifer, Amy and Kelvin (pseudonyms). In the selection of qualified teacher participants, Miss Ling, the Teaching and Research Coordinator (*jiao yan yuan*) [教研员] from the Municipal Education Bureau offered the researcher enormous help. She kindly provided the researcher rich information about the schools and EFL teachers, moreover, she helped the researcher to arrange the visit to different schools and introduced many teachers to the researcher. Finally, during the second phase of fieldwork, three teachers were selected as research participants for the present study. The three teachers were all experienced teachers and "backbone teachers" (*gu gan jiao shi*) [骨干教师] in their schools, and had been trainees of the NTTP. After knowing about the research purpose and procedures, they gladly agreed to participate and became the research participants of the study. The following table (Table 4.1) provides brief information about the three EFL secondary teachers:

Table 4.1　Profiles of three case teachers

Name	Gender	Age	Title	Degree	Years of teaching
Jenifer	Female	55	Senior teacher	Junior college, English major	26
Amy	Female	36	Junior teacher	BA in English	14
Kelvin	Male	28	Junior teacher	BA in Botany	6

As shown in the table, the three teachers were different in professional levels and had taught for many years when they participated in the study in 2016. During the research process, the teachers and the researcher built up close friendship and mutual trust, and with their kind help, the researcher finished the fieldwork of data collection.

4.2.3　Data collection

Aiming at investigating the trajectory of teachers' professional identity formation as well as discovering the potential factors affecting the professional identity development, the present study enlists interviews, observation, documents and ethnographic field notes as methods for data collection. The data collection period lasted roughly a year from early June 2016 to August 2017. This section describes the data collection procedure, instruments and the rationale for selecting them to carry out the study.

4.2.3.1　The data collection procedure

Qualitative case study requires multiple source of data to guarantee the research validity. The most frequently used instruments to collect qualitative data are questionnaires, interviews, observation, videos, documents, archival records and physical artifacts (Cohen et al., 2000). This study uses three types of research tools to collect data, namely, interviews, observations and documents. The data collection procedure constitutes three phases. Table 4.2 below outlines the three phases of data collection:

Table 4.2　Three phases of data collection

Phase	Time	Methods
Phase 1	Jun 20, 2016 — Jun 29, 2016	Interviews, classroom observations
Phase 2	Sept 29, 2016 — Oct 30, 2016	Interviews, ethnographic observation
Phase 3	Nov 1, 2016 — Jun 30, 2017	Online interviews

The first phase of data collection is actually a quasi-pilot study. Since there are over 150 EFL teachers and 12 secondary schools in Jinghong city, it is a great challenge to visit all the 12 schools and approach all the EFL teachers. In addition, in spite of four schools are in town area, all other schools scatter near and far along the borderline. The major task for the first phase of data collection is to conduct a fieldwork with the goal to gather the information as much as possible, acquire knowledge of local ethnic communities, establish rapport with local stakeholders, and make preparation for the second phase of data collection. Luckily, with the substantial help of the Teaching and Research Coordinators (*jiao yan yuan*) [教研员] from Municipal Education Bureau, the fieldwork in the first phase of data collection was complete before the coming summer vacation. The researcher visited nine schools and talked to 32 teachers and was equipped necessary knowledge about the local teachers and schools.

Also with the kind help of officials from education bureaus, school principals, local teachers and parents, the second phase of data collection is fruitful. By using the ethnographic approach, the researcher listened to teachers' discussion in the Teaching and Research Group (hereafter TRG) (*jiao yan zu*) [教研组] meetings, attended two seminars on teachers' professional development, participated teachers' open classes (the demonstration classes), talked to the school principals and visited student families in multiethnic communities. By doing this, the researcher established a panorama picture of the sociocultural and educational context in which rural EFL teachers were working. During the second phase of fieldwork, the researcher interviewed over 30 teachers and finally screened three focal participants. In the later period of the second phase fieldwork, the researcher stayed in three different schools where the case teachers were teaching. The researcher spent two weeks in each school conducting interviews, collecting documents and observing teachers' classroom activities. By positioning himself in the schools, the researcher was able to draw a more detailed picture of each school context, and generate common patterns through a closer observation of teachers' daily life. In addition, a tight schedule of interviews and observations enabled an easy and clear comparison between teachers' claims in interviews and actions in practices.

Because of the tight schedule, the second phase of fieldwork lasted for about two months. At the end of October, 2016, the researcher left the research sites in Jinghong and returned to Shanghai. In view of the ongoing nature of teachers' identity development and the data saturation, the third phase of data collection started from the end of 2016 and was completed in early July, 2017. During this period, face-to-face talk shifted to online interviews. The online interaction with the three case teachers allowed the researcher to ask additional questions about teachers' changed teaching beliefs and reflections on implementing the new teaching models; moreover, in examining the interview and observation data, incongruence between what teachers said and how they did often appear, and then the online interviews enabled the researcher to ask the participants for further explanation.

4.2.3.2   Interviews

Interviews are one of commonly used instruments in eliciting qualitative data. It allows participants to go deeper in exploring the themes that they has reflected on beforehand. It helps researchers to investigate "things we cannot directly observe, such as feelings, thoughts and intentions" (Patton, 2002, p.278). According to Lincoln and Guba (1985), the purposes of interviews include: present constructions of events, feelings, persons, organizations, activities, motivations, concerns, claims; reconstructions of past experiences; projections into the future; verifying, amending and expending data. With different degrees of formality, interviews can be categorized into three types: unstructured interviews, semi-structured interviews and structured interviews. As the intention of the present study is to explore how secondary EFL teachers build up the professional identity through personal and professional experiences, as well as what external factors help to construct the development of the professional identity, interviews with the participants allow the researcher to understand teachers' motivations, feelings or reflections about their experiences in different period of professional development. This study employs two types of interview techniques: semi-structured interviews and stimulated recall interviews with participant teachers for data collection.

Semi-structured interviews

Semi-structured interviews with a guide of several open-ended questions are conducted with the three case teachers, respectively. Semi-structured interviews with teachers are supposed to elicit information about:

1) teachers' personal biographies, mainly including their family and pre-service language learning experiences;

2) past classroom practice before the NTTP;

3) possible influencing factors that affect teachers' classroom instruction;

4) teachers' reflections on the NTTP courses and how they apply the pedagogical knowledge learned from the NTTP;

5) how they negotiate with their old teaching belies and new pedagogies which are advocated by the education authority.

The three participant teachers were offered to choose English or Chinese for the interviews and they all selected their mother tongue since it was more comfortable and easier for them to express their ideas concisely and freely. Because of the busy schedule of secondary school teachers, the interviews were arranged in a flexible way. For instance, 10—15 minutes of interview were conducted when the teacher just finished her/his listening and speaking instruction and went back to the office for rest; a longer interview (about 90 minutes) was carricd out after supper; a formal interview (lasted about 120 minutes) was conducted when the researcher was invited to the teachers' home or in their offices. All the interviews were audio-recorded, translated into English and transcribed for analysis.

Stimulated recall interviews

In spite of in-depth interviews with teachers, stimulated recall interviews were also undertaken to allow the researcher to obtain teachers' interpretations of important events, significant others and classroom practice in preceding period. Stimulated recall interviews were conducted after the lesson observations in order to prompt teachers to recall their intentions and thought while they were teaching particular lessons (Gass & Mackey, 2000). When time permitted, the researcher invited participant teachers to watch the classroom video together. Based on his own observation, the researcher asked the teachers to interpret their motivation or reason for their classroom practices. Usually the stimulated recall interviews lasted about one hour and were conducted during the break time or after the supper when the teacher had relatively longer time for talk. The stimulated recall interviews were conducted in Chinese, which made participant teachers feel more comfortable and freer to express their ideas as explained earlier. All the interviews were audio-recorded, translated into English and transcribed for later analysis.

4.2.3.3 Observation

As aforementioned in section 4.2.2, the qualitative research should take place in the natural settings. Teachers' ways in delivering instructional activities and interactions with students or colleagues should be examined without interruption. Lichtman (2006) defines four types of observation: observing in natural settings; observing written materials; observing images and observing online data. Yin (1994) categories three types of observation: non-participant, participant, and unobtrusive. Since teachers' professional identity is not merely presented from their narratives and stories, but also reflected through their instructional activities and interaction with students, therefore it should be examined in a natural setting without interventions. In this study, the non-participant observation technique was adopted and conducted in natural settings. In this study, the participant teachers' teaching-related activities were closely observed, including their daily classroom instructions, giving the open class (*gong kai ke*) [公开课] and collective lesson preparation meetings (*ji ti bei ke*) [集体备课].

As for the classroom observation, the researcher adopted the non-participant observation technique and observed 26 classes in total. Before the researcher conducted the classroom observation, the participant teachers were well informed and kindly agreed that the researcher sat in a corner at the back of the classroom. Meanwhile, the participant teachers were informed and agreed that any of their instructional practices and teacher-student interaction were video recorded by the researcher. Classroom observation mainly focuses on teaching activities in classroom, with particular attention on observing how teachers' past language learning experiences affect their current classroom practices, as well as examining how teachers translate the knowledge learned from external trainings. In addition, close classroom observation provides evidences for the researcher to discover any possible contextual influencing factors on teachers' classroom instructions. Classroom observation of each participant teacher lasted for two weeks, 26 lessons with each lesson lasting for 45 minutes were observed and video recorded.

Beside observing teachers' classroom activities, the researcher also observed how teachers prepared and gave the demonstration class (*gong kai ge*) [公开课]. All the three participant teachers were celebrated as "backborn teachers" (or model teachers) (*gu gan jiao shi*) [骨干教师] in their schools, and had been selected as trainees to attend the NTTP course in Yunnan Normal University. When they completed learning the NTTP courses and returned to their home school, they were required to give demonstrations for other teachers who were not assign the opportunity to learn. The demonstration was a great challenge for the rural EFL teachers to accomplish, for they were required to not only learn and apply new teaching methods in their own classes, but also demonstrate how to use these new methods in other school and with students they were not familiar with. However, difficult and challenging as the demonstrations would be, it was a great opportunity for the researcher to examine how teachers translated new pedagogical knowledge into their present instructional practices, and how they negotiated and moderated the conflicts between new methods and classroom reality.

In addition, teachers' professional identity has been constructed and reshaped in their interaction with colleagues and in teachers' collective activities such as the TRG meetings or discussion in teachers' learning community. For Chinese secondary school teachers, the most common professional development happens in the TRG meetings and collective lesson preparation meetings (*ji ti bei ke*) [集 体 备 课]. Participant teachers in this study, though they are teaching in different schools, their routine work is to take the 90-minute meeting every week organized by their TRG. The activities in the TRG meetings are diversified, including collective lesson preparation, seminars, textbook analysis, commenting novice teachers' lessons, or observing demonstration classes. The researcher was allowed to participate in eight TRG meetings respectively in three different schools, and observing teachers' activities in such meetings helped the researcher to draw a vivid picture about teachers' professional life outside the classroom.

4.2.3.4 Documents

Document analysis can complement other research instruments to obtain information that cannot be observed or interviewed directly (Merriam, 1998). In this study, different types of documents, including teachers' paper-based and electronic version of teaching plans, textbooks that they currently use for classroom teaching, and printed government documents, are analyzed. The document data also includes the researcher's own filed notes. Besides the classroom observation, the researcher took field notes to record his own feelings and reflections about the multiethnic culture, teachers' working and living environment, or parents' education philosophy. Additionally, field notes are indispensable in this study for the exploration of teachers' thoughts and opinions, feelings, practices, attitudes, body language, behavior, informal talks on teaching among colleagues, so on and so forth. These field notes helped the researcher conduct more effective and deeper fieldwork. The field notes are necessary supplement to interview and observation data.

4.2.4   Data analysis

There are two types of data analysis in this study. One is the analysis of the narratives and stories collected from the teachers' interviews; the other is the analysis of the classroom observation. Both analyses have facilitated the rich appreciation of the teachers' professional identity formation and will be described in the following two sections. The data analysis procedure involves reviewing field notes, annotations, memos and manual coding. The process of data analysis follows the analytic approach provided by Miles and Huberman (2014) to analyze the transcription of the interviews, since it is important to investigate the relationships underlying interactional experiences.

The data analysis procedure consists of three concurrent flows of activity: 1) data condensation, 2) data display, and 3) conclusion drawing/verifying, as is shown in Figure 4.1. As Miles and Huberman (1994) suggest, qualitative analysis needs to be well documented as a process in order to make it more usable by others (p.12).

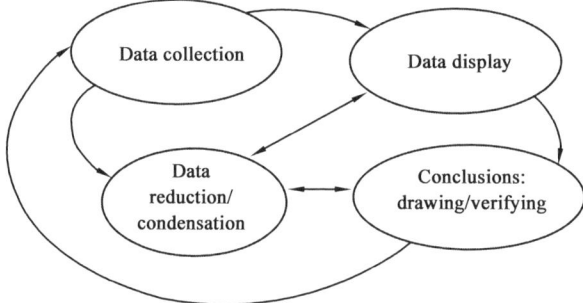

Figure 4.1   Component of data analysis (Miles and Huberman, 1994, p.12)

4.2.4.1   Interview data analysis

The data analysis procedure involves reviewing field notes, annotations, memos and manual coding. The process of data analysis follows Creswell's (2007) *Data Analysis Spiral*. According to Creswell (2007), to analyze qualitative data, "the researcher engages in the process of moving in analytic circles rather than using a fixed linear approach. One enters with data of text or images (e.g., photographs, videotapes) and exits with an account or a narrative. In between, the researcher touches on several facets of analysis and circles around and around" (p.150).

The interview recordings are firstly carefully transcribed. Each teacher's individual interview data is analyzed in turn. The analysis process is triangulated from multiple perspectives: teachers' voice, students' feedback and the researcher's own perceptions based on his fieldwork observing of teachers' school life. In the process of data analysis, field notes, interview transcripts and observational notes undergo an iterative process of data reduction, data display and verification (Miles & Huberman, 1994). Interview data analysis follows a grounded approach that allows for the emergence of patterns directly from the data, instead of testing theories, which follows three stages: open coding, axial coding and selective coding (Strauss & Corbin, 1998).

Coding

The essential idea of coding is to find research concerns from raw data through small steps, each step building on the previous one (Auerbach & Silverstein, 2003). Qualitative data analysis is characterized by its cyclical nature and therefore is a reiterative process because transcripts are carefully read and reread to get immersed in the data, to dialogue with the data and negotiate with the data. The researcher noticed that the three informants often utilized the same or similar words and phrases to express the similar ideas, which is called repeating ideas. Those repeating ideas shed light on the research concern. A group of repeating ideas on an implicit topic forms a theme. Repetition is the most common technique to recognize themes, and is based on the premise that if an idea recurs throughout the transcribed data, it is likely a theme (Bernard & Ryan, 2009).

Coding is essentially a system of classifying data, noting what is related to the research concern and labeling them to organize the information contained in the data. Saldana (2015) defines a code in qualitative inquiry as a word short phrase that symbolically assigns a summative, essence-capturing and evocative attribute for a certain portion of data. Thus, codes are a type of shorthand names or identifiers that are relevant to one's study.

Coding procedures

The coding procedures in this research include "initial coding", "focused coding", "axial coding" and "theoretical coding" (Charmaz, 2006; Creswell, 2014). In this study, the research questions to guide the creation of provisional codes to look for salient factors are relevant to teachers' identity construction. These provisional codes are interpretive "initial codes" which look at broader items. Then more specific categories emerge, for instance, teachers' perceived changes in perception of language teaching, academic development. Those are classified as "thematic codes" or "pattern codes". Table 4.3 shows the examples of this coding procedure:

Table 4.3   Examples of initial codes and thematic codes

Open coding	Categorization	Theme
But things changed like a nightmare when I entered high school. Our English teacher was so harsh with us that students frequently got physical punishment for making mistakes in assignments or for their mischief in class (Interview, P3-1, 2016).	Teachers' identity formation; Significant others;	Personal experience; Personal biography
My colleagues seemed to be very busy. When I had a question in teaching, there wasn't anyone whom I could approach. Though I was confident in my subject matter knowledge and teaching competence, yet I was not sure if I was in the right track and got things right. Among the teachers in our jiao yan zu, there is only one who would offer help and open for discussion. I never forget those days, when I passed her window (the teacher lives in the first floor and we are neighbors in the same apartment building) I tried to catch any possible opportunity consulting her about how to write teaching plans… (Interview, P3-7, 2016) .	School environment; English *jiao yan zu* (Teaching and Research Group); Relationship with colleagues	Professional experience

4.2.4.2   Observation data analysis

The transcribed data and field notes of observation are analyzed to generate interview questions for teachers and students and to triangulate data collected through interviews. The observed interaction between teachers and students, among teachers and among students, helps to gain a deeper understanding of teachers' response to the new curriculum, and the reasons why they do in such a way. In addition, the transcribed observational data are coded and labeled with properties consistent with the codes emerging in the interview data. These codes are constantly compared with codes in the interview data, trying to determine whether there is any commonality or discrepancy between teachers' practical teaching actions and their claimed teaching behavior. Thus, follow-up investigation into the influencing factors contributing to the commonality or discrepancy can be conducted for a deeper understanding of teachers' response to the curriculum. Within-case comparison is conducted to identify the changes of teachers' response to the new curriculum as well as consistency and inconsistency between teachers' beliefs and practical teaching. Cross-case comparison is conducted to identify the commonality and discrepancy of different teachers' response to the new curriculum, generating investigation to the influencing factors contributing to their different responses.

4.3　Validity, reliability and ethical considerations

As far as the credibility of qualitative research is concerned, the conventional criteria widely discussed in literature are reliability and validity (Bogdan & Biklen, 2003; Lincoln & Guba, 1985; Merriam, 1998). The following section will discuss the validity, reliability and ethical considerations of the present study.

Internal validity refers to the interpretability of the research, that is, how findings from the study are valid, accurate and match the reality (Lincoln & Guba, 1985). Several strategies are employed in the present study to establish the internal validity of the research. Firstly, prolonged engagement with each teacher and school helps to minimize distortion, build trust and identify the most salient elements related to the research (Riessman, 2008). Secondly, triangulation from multiple sources of data and multiple perspectives is employed to contribute to the validity overall. The present study has collected data through multiple methods—interviews with teachers, observations of teaching in and out of the classroom, observation of teachers' professional development activities and document analysis. Furthermore, teachers and students have been both asked to voice their ideas regarding the implementation of the new curriculum, affording multiple perspectives in understanding issues studied in this research. Thirdly, the researcher has used the member check to determine whether his interpretation of the data is accurate by sending all transcriptions to the participants for their feedback and confirmation of his accuracy in capturing their opinions and ideas. The researcher has showed his interpretation of the interview data to teachers and students, asking them to check the accuracy of his interpretation and to make comments or changes, if necessary. Also, the researcher has sent the translated version of selected quotes presented in finding chapters to participant teachers to ensure the accuracy of the translations, and to make adjustments if necessary. To ensure confidentiality, the researcher makes sure that all the personal identifiers have been removed during the entire data collection process. Instead, pseudonyms have been used to identify teachers and schools in the current study to protect participants' personal information.

Reliability concerns the consistency and replicability of the research, which is closely related with the internal validity. As reliability may be shored up through the enhancement of internal validity (Lincoln & Guba, 1985), strategies such as triangulation and member check are used as well to establish the reliability of the research. Finally, the present study employs an audit trail, —the records documenting the research process, to establish the reliability. Detailed memos documenting the whole research process afford an opportunity for the researcher to reflect on the research steps. Lincoln and Guba (1985) outline six categories to report in any audit trail, including raw data, data reduction and analysis products, data reconstruction and synthesis products, process notes, materials relating to intentions and dispositions, and instrument development information.

Ethical considerations

In the study involving human participants, the researcher needs to consider whether it is right to conduct a study or investigate a certain question under specific circumstances (Fraenkel & Wallen, 2000). The following considerations are addressed to ensure the ethical acceptability of the study.

Firstly, the researcher understood that ethical considerations were very important as he negotiated his entry to the site of the research, invited teacher participants to join this study, gathered their personal, sometimes emotional data that revealed the details of their lives, and asked them to give considerable time to this study.

Secondly, the researcher understood that the research participants' school, represented by the principal and teachers, should be informed about the nature and consequences of this study with proper respect. This study was supported by the Municipal Education Bureau of Jinghong and approved by the principals of each secondary school the researcher visited. The officials from educational authority and school principals were clear about the research purpose and specific activities in the school (e.g., teacher interviews and classroom observation). Then the researcher visited the teachers in their office and explained the research purposes, concrete research procedures and their rights in the study, and acquired their formal approval. In this way, the problems of deceiving and exploiting the teachers were avoided.

Thirdly, the researcher respected and protected the participant teachers' privacy and confidentiality without doing harm to the schools and the teachers. The researcher used pseudonyms for all three teachers and other persons whom they talked about as well as their school. The researcher transcribed all the interviews and kept them only by the researcher and did not disclose to others, except in the cases of one peer debriefed and his supervisor for suggestions.

4.4　Summary

This chapter presents the rationale for choosing a qualitative case study as the methodological approach to conduct the current study after a revisit to research questions. Data collection methods including teacher and student interview, classroom observation, teacher activity observation and document analysis are introduced based on lessons learned from pilot study, followed by the introduction of a grounded approach in data analysis. This chapter closes with an introduction of the ethical considerations of conducting the present study.

Chapter 5 | The Case of Jenifer

This chapter presents data pertaining the professional identity construction of Jenifer, the first participant in the present study. It consists of 5 main sections and more subsections. Section 5.1 traces Jenifer's personal biography, language learning history and practicum in her early teaching career. Section 5.2 describes the school climate, the school-based professional activities and local sociocultural context in which Jenifer works. In order to present her trajectory of professional identity development, section 5.3, section 5.4 and section 5.5 describe Jenifer's prior teaching experiences, her experiences in taking the NTTP courses, and her changed teaching practices which have been influenced by the NTTP and local curriculum reform. The first case closes with a presentation of Jenifer's attempts and reflections in doing classroom-based research.

5.1　Jenifer's biography

Jenifer was born into a military officer's family and grew up in the city of Jinghong. She was in her late 40s when she was selected as one of the participants in this study. Jenifer received education from primary school to high school, and she began to learn English when entering the secondary school. Her high school English teacher impressed her a lot as she recalled:

> *My English teacher in high school was responsible and humorous. Although his class was enjoyable, he was very strict with us. We always had countless assignments.* (Interview, P1-1, 2016)

Jennifer's dream of higher education as a road to a better life was denied due to her failure in the College Entrance Examination, as she called to mind:

> *Perhaps because I didn't work hard enough and finally failed in the College Entrance Examination (gao kao)* ［高考］, *so I lost the opportunity to go to college or university. However, as a Chinese saying goes, when one door shuts, another opens.*
> (Interview, P1-2, 2016)

Although Jenifer couldn't go to college or university to further her education, yet she caught another chance which altered her life. Right at the time when she failed the entrance examination and had nowhere to go, the affiliated school to the local state-owned farm was recruiting some prospective high school graduates who would be able to work as primary or secondary school teachers with a two-year normal education training. The training program was the result of a joint cooperation between the local state-owned farm and Jiangsu Institute of Education in Nanjing. It was also a provincial level collaborating initiative between Jiangsu and Yunnan provinces aiming to train and dispatch qualified teachers to teach in schools scattering along the border regions in Xishuangbanna. Together with other 30 high school graduates, Jenifer was selected as one of the trainees to this program. Jenifer was neither good at math nor at physics, so she chose the subject of English as her major and made decision to become an English teacher for her future profession. The training program in Jiangsu Institute of Education prepared Jenifer for becoming a professional EFL teacher. The old fashioned but effective pedagogy affected her later teaching, as Jenifer recalled in the interview:

> *The teaching methods they used in Jiangsu Institute of Education (su jiao yuan)* ［苏教院］ *were typical grammar translation; however, they were very effective. I still remember those teachers and teaching methods they used, and I have been replicating their methods for many years in my own class before the curriculum reforms in recent years* ［…］
> (Interview, P1-3, 2016)

When she graduated from Jiangsu Institute of Education, Jenifer went back to the city of Jinghong, and became an English teacher in the same middle school where she had studied. After three years of practicum in the junior department, she was transferred to the senior department where she strengthened her subject knowledge about the language and her pedagogical competence:

> *The practicum years were difficult. For me, teaching subject knowledge to senior high students was an enormous challenge. Out of my sense of responsibility, I prepared every class carefully. Nevertheless, I still encountered numerous grammar points, especially those about the detailed usage of grammar rules were much beyond my expertise and I had difficulty in explaining them to my students. In order to be able to answer those challenging questions raised by students and improve my proficiency in English language as well, I consulted other teachers and bought grammar books that I could find in the Xinhua Book Store which was the only place where English books were available. Three years of hard practicum work in senior high department yielded many fruits and when I was assigned back to teach English courses to junior students again, I was much more confident.*   (Interview, P1-4, 2016)

Jenifer continued to teach in the junior department to date when she finished teaching in the senior high students. In her teaching for two decades, she had not attended any formal professional training until the NTTP. From 2012, the Ministry of Education launched a series of nationwide training programs specially focusing on improving teaching quality of teachers in the rural or remote border regions. Jenifer began to participate in different levels of training programs supported by the NTTP, as she stated:

> *From many perspectives, the NTTP training changed my understanding about language, cultural diversity, teaching methods, teachers' diverse roles in the classroom, and especially my beliefs about students... What a pity it is! Now I'm going to retire, how I wish I had learned those knowledge earlier!*
>
> (Interview, P1-5, 2016)

The description of Jenifer's personal biography, trajectory of becoming a practitioner of English language and her brief reflections on attending the NTTP training are well presented. Jenifer's biography helps to sketch a general picture of Jenifer's professional identity. In the next section, a picture about her school enviroment will be painted.

5.2　The teaching context

The teaching context like school culture, students and teachers' relationship with their colleagues includes important factors that influence the construction of teachers' identity. In this section, the situation about Jenifer's school, students and colleagues will be presented.

5.2.1　The school

Photo 5.1　Green Hope Middle School

Green Hope Middle School (pseudonym) where Jenifer teaches was established in 1974. The school was affiliated to the local state-owned farm, and functioned mainly as an education adjunct in the farm system, providing compulsory education service from elementary school to high school only for the children of the farm employees. Before the 1990s, the local state-owned farm had managed an independent schooling system which was parallel to the local education system. The farm could recruit teachers in line with its own need and requirements. Although the school is located in multiethnic regions, most of the teachers and heads are Han people (*Han Zu*)［汉族］who migrated from hinterland provinces as Sichuan or Hunan. The school has a tradition of recruiting Han teachers but not those who grew up in multiethnic communities. For one thing, it is believed that Han teachers usually receive more normal education and are more competent in teaching; for another, there are virtually not many qualified teachers available who are from local ethnic groups.

Before 2010, Green Hope Middle School had enjoyed a good reputation for better teaching quality and higher college enrollment rate. However, things began to change in 2011. All schools established or affiliated to the stated-owned enterprises must be detached as independent schools, or merge into local schools. Because of this change, the school was no longer an adjunct to the local farm but a secondary school under management of the city education bureau. In 2012, two more local township-level middle schools merged into Green Hope Middle School. Combination of two other schools brought not only more students but also caused problems such as inadequate faculties, overcrowded classrooms and lack of infrastructure.

Among the problems that arose from the merging, the students were the thorniest one. Quite a number of the students from two other township-level secondary schools demonstrated, as Jenifer commented, "low motivation in learning and extremely mischievous in their behaviors" (Interview, P1-6, 2016). The academic performance of this group of students was "disappointing" (Interview, P1-6, 2016) and they had negative influence on the general performance of the school. Taking students' performance in the final graduation test (happened on July 3rd, 2017) as an example, 598 students from Grade 9 averaged 52.75 out of 100 as the full mark in the English subject, which only ranked No.10 among 12 schools in Jinghong city (Document, P1-1, 2017).

5.2.2　The students

One of the most critical reality in the classroom is the considerable ethnic, cultural and linguistic diversity. Jenifer is teaching two classes in Grade 8 with 50 students in each class. Taking the demographic constitution in Class No.151 as an example, the majority of students are Han people, taking up about 40% of the total student population and the number of Dai people (*Dai Zu*) ［傣族］ students is second to Han, accounting for about 30% of the total. Other students are from ethnic groups of Yi, Miao, Jinuo and Blang (*Yi Zu, Miao Zu, Jinuo Zu*, and *Blang Zu*) ［彝族，苗族，基诺族，布朗族］.

The students in Jenifer's class speak at least three different languages and four local dialects. Standard Chinese is not their mother tongue and English is virtually the third language for them to learn. Although most of the students are able to speak Standard Chinese to communicate in discourse like answering teachers' questions or participating in classroom activities, in daily conversations, they prefer to switch to their own ethnic languages or local dialects.

Both students and teachers are from an extraordinary array of cultural background. Most teachers in Green Hope Middle School are Han people and have been brought up and educated in the context of traditional Confucian culture. However, students from multiethnic regions are less influenced by Confucian thinking, and they believe in Buddhism or other ethnic religions. The remarkable differences in belief systems between teachers and students from different ethnic backgrounds sometimes give rise to obstacles in achieving agreement in educational values.

In addition to ethnic, cultural and linguistic diversity, students from the multiethnic regions are also poorly motivated to learn. Thanks to the tropical climate, fertile land, as well as favorite agricultural policies, farmers in Xishuangbanna have been growing rubber trees, banana trees and various tropical plants on an unprecedented scale. The tropical economic plants yield not only abundant produce but large seasonal cash income. However, cash income usually would not be advisably deposited in banks or to enlarge the production, instead, most of the income may go for excessive or conspicuous consumption, with only a meager part spent on education.

Moreover, most parents in multiethnic regions in Xishuangbanna maintain a naturalistic belief in educating their children and consider that the children should grow up in a natural environment. The researcher's visits to local ethnic families in fieldwork show that most parents there hold the life philosophy that children should not be forced to learn anything which they would not like. If the child hates going to school, for example, the parents would choose not to interfere or impose their own will or values on the child. Nevertheless, if the child demonstrates capability and interest in learning at school, they would be willing to provide their children with available financial and mental support.

5.2.3 The school-based professional development

For most secondary school language teachers in China, the accessible way of professional development is various school-based and self-directed peer mentoring activities. In Green Hope Middle School, teachers instructing the same subject are working in the TRG (*jiao yan zu*)［教研组］according to different grades. In the TRG, a senior or experienced teacher is in charge of all teaching relevant affairs. Jenifer is the head of TRG of the English subject. 18 teachers who belong to this TRG meet weekly, and their routine practices include exchange of reflections on classroom teaching, such as discussion on teaching plans, preparation of tests, helping each other with problems in using computers or helping students prepare for various competitions or contests.

Another important aspect of the TRG meetings is the preparation of novice teachers (teachers who have been teaching for no more than 5 years) for demonstration classes (*gong kai ke*)［公开课］or teaching competitions. In the meetings, young teachers first present their teaching plans or give a complete demonstration, other veteran teachers would observe and evaluate young teachers' performance. When young teachers finish their presentation, senior teachers would give feedback and suggestions for young teachers for further improvement or revision. Being interviewed about the differences between the school-based professional development and the training in the NTTP, Jenifer commented:

> *Only a very small number of teachers can be selected as trainees to participate in the NTTP training. Compared with the NTTP, the school-based peer mentoring is a more pragmatic and convenient way for all teachers to grow professionally, because they can get immediate suggestions or creative ideas, hence they can change their plans, design new activities and try their improved plans through classroom teaching. Regardless of age or experience, the* TRG *meeting is valuable for those who are willing to improve their expertise.*

> (Interview, P1-7, 2016)

In the school-based professional development, novice and experienced teachers work together creating a face-to-face learning community through intensive peer coaching or mentoring, creating opportunities for both novice and experienced teachers to construct or reconstruct professional identities.

This section denotes the situations about the school, the student and school-based professional development activities, as these contextual factors are essential in shaping

Jenifer's professional identity. In the next section, Jenifer's past instructional practices will be presented in detail.

5.3   Jenifer's classroom practices before attending the NTTP

"Student activities are most vital in a successful class."

(Interview, P1-9, 2016)

In this study, three case teachers' classroom practices are examined in two time periods: classroom instruction before their attending the NTTP courses, and after the NTTP. In this section, Jenifer's past classroom practices are presented through stimulated recall interview and video recordings of her language instruction class before she went to attend the NTTP. The stimulated recall interviews were conducted in the second phase of fieldwork, and the classroom video were also collected at that time. In addition to the interview data and video footages, Jenifer's teaching documents, such as lesson plans, PPT slides (electronic version), and the field notes are all used to represent her classroom practices in the past before the NTTP.

As explained in the chapter of research design, the data collection procedure of present study constitutes three phases. The first phase of pilot fieldwork lasted for two weeks from June 6th to 17th 2016. The second phase of fieldwork was carried out from October 1st to December 10th, and the third phase of data collection changed to sustaining online collection to the end of 2017. Eight rounds of semi-structured interviews were conducted and four classroom videos were collected. In the four video-recorded lessons, there are two footages of listening and speaking class, one reading class and a reviewing class. Table 5.1 summarizes the four classroom videos:

Table 5.1   Summary of four video recorded classroom observation

Time	June 13th	June 14th	June 15th	June 16th
Class	Class 151	Class 152	Class 152	Class 151
Grade	Grade 7	Grade 7	Grade 7	Grade 7

continued

Time	June 13th	June 14th	June 15th	June 16th
Venue	Green Hope Middle School	Green Hope Middle School	Green Hope Middle School	Green Hope Middle School
Contents	Listening & Speaking Material: *Project English* Unit 4 Having Fun Topic 1 Section A, B	Listening & Speaking Material: *Project English* Unit 4 Having Fun Topic 1 Section C, D	Reading & Writing Material: *Project English* Unit 4 Having Fun Topic 2 Section A, B	Review Material: *Project English* Unit 4 Having Fun

Four classroom videos were carefully watched and examined. At last, the listening and speaking class was the most appropriate for further analysis. Compared with other samples, the listening and speaking class was guided by explicit teaching objectives and featured in Jenifer's inverted arrangement of activities and assessment. In spite of the unique lesson plan, she explained the reason and reflection for such lesson plan and activities in the stimulated recall interview. Therefore, the listening and speaking class is a good sample to reflect Jenifer's "Identity-in-Practice". The data presented is the lesson plan, episodes of classroom activities and analysis of the roles played by the teacher and students in the activities.

5.3.1   The lesson plan

A lesson plan is a teacher's understanding of material, pedagogical strategies and implementation of beliefs. The lesson plan generally includes teaching objectives (what the students are supposed to learn), how the objectives will be reached (the method, tasks or activities) and the way of measuring how well the objectives are reached (homework or test, etc.). Jenifer's lesson plan consists of four phases and features with various student activities. Being guided by specific learning objectives, different activities are arranged to improve and strengthen listening and speaking skills. Table 5.2 demonstrates Jenifer's planned pedagogy to teach a listening class.

Table 5.2　Jenifer's lesson plan

Project English, Grade 7, Unit 4, Section B, Topic 1				
	Objective	Activities	Assessment	Focus
Phase 1 (Pre-listening) 5 minutes	Review and warm up	Read out the learning objectives; Learn new words on page 83-84 by Ss themselves; Check pronunciation by reading out new words to the desk mates.	English—Chinese Translation Exercise; Chinese—English Translation Exercise	Spelling and pronunciation of new words; Translation of new words
Phase 2 (While-listening) 15 minutes	Learn expressions for inquiry and shopping.	Student presentation (Group1) Listen to dialogue 1a and answer question1; Listen to the dialogue for the second time and answer question 2.	Ask Ss to repeat the answer to the questions.	Listening and Speaking Skills
Phase 3 (Post-listening) 15 minutes	Evaluate Ss if they grasp the expressions	Listen to the dialogue for the third time. Complete the *Blank Filling* exercise.	*Gap Filling* exercise in the textbook.	Listening Skills
Phase 4 In-Class Test 10 minutes	Check Ss if they can properly use the expressions	*Multiple Choice*		Pragmatic competence

Jenifer's lesson plan is roughly divided into four phases and each phase has its specific objectives, student activities and assessment. Jenifer commented on the design of the lesson plan in the interview:

> As a teacher I don't have much right and room to make a flexible lesson plan, and the lesson plan is rather fixed. For example, the "three-phase" format is not my original invention but all teachers are required by the education bureau to follow the same format in planning the lessons.　　（Interview, P1-8, 2016）

Although teachers are required to follow the same format for lesson plans, they are encouraged to design various student activities. Jenifer enjoyed the flexibility and adopted a creative way to design and arrange student activities, as she gave her opinion in the interview:

> *Student activities are vital in a successful class. Based on the textbook, I designed many peer work and group work for students to practice the dialogue, which I believe is very helpful to improve their ability in listening. Moreover, most of my students are from ethnic families with their ethnic tradition of singing and dancing a lot in daily life. Thus, it would be very boring if you keep them sitting in silence and just listen to the teachers. If you offer chances for the students to play a part, they would be excited and active and do their best. I have noticed their talent and try to guide them to use their talent in learning English.* (Interview, P1-9, 2016)

In spite of using peer work or group work as activities to activate students' agency, Jenifer inverted the sequence to carry out the activities. Jenifer explained her design for the "flipped classroom" in the interview:

> *I heard the term "flipped classroom" from a teacher training lecture about two years ago, and the new term attracted me much. I used to design many student activities in listening and spoken English class and asked students to join the activities. However, the fact is that I have more than 50 students in one class and there are roughly 10 to 12 groups, and it is very hard for every group to present their activities in 45 minutes. For example, they are very interested in playing a mini-play and want to participate in this activity, but fail to get the chance to present their work, and the students then become very disappointed. The term "flipped classroom" caught my attention and later I learned the theory and practiced carefully about the flipped classroom and then tried to apply this method in arranging in-class activities. Based on the syllabus, textbook and students' ability, I usually use the last 5-10 minutes of each class to discuss activities with my students, then design proper activities and finally assign them to different student groups. Following my instruction, the students practice the activities with their peers before the next class. When they come to the class, they just present their prepared peer work or group work activities. By "flipping"*

the instruction and student activities, I save a lot of time for instruction and make the learning process more effective.　　　　　　(Interview, P1-10, 2016)

The document data of Jenifer's lesson plan and interview data suggest that though the teaching is fragmented into three fixed phases and only lasts for 45 minutes, Jenifer has tried to design many classroom activities based on the character of her students. Jenifer believed that the tailored activities would motivate the autonomy of her students. Jenifer's lesson plan also features in the "flipped" arrangement of the activities. Because of the time pressure, she assigned the peer and group work as tasks before class, and when students came to class, what they would do was to make the presentation. In addition to rich design of student activities, Jenifer also paid attention to the assessment. She incorporated different exercises and quiz to help her students learn the new vocabulary, expressions or grammar points. Jenifer's flipped classroom and teaching practice are evidenced by the classroom observational data. In the next section, the researcher will present how Jenifer designs and carries out the student activities.

5.3.2　The classroom activities

This subsection aims to illustrate and analyze Jenifer's classroom practice, showing how she conducts student activities. As stated in the introduction part of this chapter, the researcher chose to describe the episodes of Jenifer's listening and speaking class, which was videotaped. The sequence, contents and focuses of student activities are summarized in Table 5.3:

Table 5.3　Summary of student activities in Jenifer's
listening and speaking class (Jenifer, Video Recorded Data, 2016)

Source of data	Types of activities	Contents of activities	Focus of activities
Video recording (12 minutes)	Mini Play	Role play acted by 3 boy students	Speaking skill
Video recording (5 minutes)	Pronunciation Exercise	5 students pronounce the new words in the word-match quiz	Pronunciation

continued

Source of data	Types of activities	Contents of activities	Focus of activities
Video recording (8 minutes)	Word Match Quiz	Students do the vocabulary quiz	Vocabulary
Video recording (10 minutes)	Sentence Translation	Students work in group to complete the sentence translation	Sentence translation
Video recording (15 minutes)	Listen to the tapes	Audio recording is played and questions about the contents are asked	Listening skills

Episode 1

The first student activity that was performed in Jenifer's listening and speaking class was a mini play, a teaching task aiming to imitate a situation for students to practice sentence patterns that would be frequently used in shopping context. With brief greetings to the class, Jenifer started her teaching by inviting three boy students to the podium, presenting their prepared mini play—*Buying Clothes*. Students acted as the shop assistant and customers in order to practice drills and expressions. Conversations between "shop assistant" and "customers" were observed and recorded:

> Shop assistant (S1): Welcome! What can I do for you?
>
> Customer A (S2): I want to buy something for my son. Where can I find clothes?
>
> Shop assistant: Follow me please. (*Showing a piece of clothing for customer B*)
>
> Customer B (S3): Can I try it on?
>
> Shop assistant: Sure.
>
> Customer B: Trying the jacket …
>
> Customer A: It looks good on you! (*To the shop assistant*) How much is it?
>
> Shop assistant: 70 *Yuan*.
>
> Customer A: OK, I'll take it.

When the three boy students finished their mini play, Jenifer asked the whole class to make comments. A student volunteered to stand up and gave his comment:

"I think their performance is good but, not as what our teacher required, the shop assistant forgot to introduce the color and size of the clothes."

Jenifer agreed and graded the mini play performed by the three boy students by saying:

"Yes, you did a very good job, but just as what Wang Dong said, you didn't describe the color and size of the clothes. Therefore, I give you 8 points for your performance."

Episode 2

The second activity performed in the class was pronunciation. Jenifer requested all students to read out the teaching objectives which were projected on the screen. There were two teaching objectives in the class: Objective A: Ss were able to pronounce, spell and translate all the new words in the text; Objective B: After learning Passage 1a, Ss should be able to use drills and expressions properly to solve practical problems in real life. Jenifer explained in the interview why she required the students to read out the teaching objectives:

It is very important for the students to know what they are going to learn in my class. The teaching objectives for every class and goals for every unit function like the compass for a sailing ship. If the students were aware of the objectives in the process of learning, they would be clear about their destination and what efforts they should put in. (Interview, P1-11, 2016)

When the whole class finished reading the teaching objectives, Jenifer asked her students to open their books and read the new words and expressions together. Next, a boy student from Group 2 was invited to come to the podium, taking lead to pronounce the new words again, but he made some pronunciation mistakes, and then another girl student from Group 4 was asked by Jenifer to identify and correct his wrong pronunciation. At last, Jenifer pronounced the words herself and led the whole class to read them three times. Jenifer commented this peer coaching activity in the interview:

It's an effective way for them to learn pronunciation of new words. I make the pronunciation practice as one of their assignment and I check and help them to read. If there are mistakes or wrong way of articulation, I will notice and help them to correct. If I teach them how to read, they are free from pressure, but if I ask them to do the pronunciation before the whole class, they would feel the stress and accordingly want to do a better job. In this way, their agency will

be activated.　　　　　　　　　　　　　　　　　　(Interview, P1-12, 2016)

Episode 3

After the practice of pronunciation, the third activity was carried out, which was a match quiz about English vocabulary and their Chinese meanings, with focus on strengthening memories of words. Instead of requiring students to remember new words by rote, Jenifer used amusing and animated cartoon figures to facilitate the memorization. The students were grouped before class and Jenifer asked the student groups to race for opportunities to do the match. Because the Chinese-English word match quiz was made in animated forms with sound effect, soon the class became lively and relaxed, and all students were attracted and enjoined the competition to give their answers.

Episode 4

The fourth activity conducted in this listening and speaking class began with four group presentations. Each group carried a small white board on which the students had prepared writing contents of their presentation. Jenifer organized the sequence of student presentations. The first group rose to explain how each member completed a Chinese-English word match exercise. The English words and equivalent Chinese meaning were written on the white board in two columns and in random order. Each group member first picked the English word to match its Chinese version, and then explained the reason for his or her choice. After Group 1 finished their work, Jenifer asked the class to spot possible mistakes they made in the presentation. The class were very active to detect grammar or pronunciation errors and also offer some additional answers.

Next, members from the second group came to the front in turns presenting their result of sentence translation work:

---

1. 你认为这条裤子怎么样？ How do you like the trousers?
2. 为什么不试试那条？ Why not try on that pair?
3. 我只是看看，谢谢。I'm just looking, thanks.
4. 您是在开玩笑么？ Are you kidding?
5. 仍然感谢您。Thank you all the same.

Each student chose a Chinese sentence and then offered the whole class his or her explanation for the English translation.

Argument arose when each member finished the translation, because a boy student gave a wrong explanation on the usage of "pair". Several students raised their hands trying to correct his error as soon as they identified his inappropriate explanation. Jenifer smiled and asked two girls to give the right answer. Jenifer realized that the usage of "pair" was an important grammar point and her students might have a problem in using it, so she walked to the front asking: "一条裤子，用英语怎么表达？（*How to express a pair of trousers in English?*）" The students volunteered actively to answer the question, and Jenifer followed their response and raised another question: "那么两条裤子呢？（*Then how to express 'two pairs of trousers' in English?*）" More students wanted to grasp at the opportunity, and finally Jenifer wrote the idiomatic expression of English quantifiers on the blackboard.

Episode 5

The videotaped classroom observation shows that Jenifer has changed to a traditional way to teach listening skills by playing the audio recordings sentence by sentence. Jenifer began her listening instruction by trying to contextualize the dialogue in the recording:

Jenifer: Any one of you know Christmas?

Students: (*in loud voice*) It is 圣诞节 (*Christmas*).

Jenifer: Good, Christmas is a Western festival, 圣诞节. When Christmas is coming, Jean, Maria and Michael decide to go shopping, and they want to buy some clothes for Christmas. Let's open your book… what do you see in the book?

Student a: I see two girls. They are Maria and Jean.

Student b: I see Michael.

Student c: I can see four pairs of trousers.

Jenifer: Very good, from the picture in the book we can see that the three children are now in a clothes shop, and they are talking about trousers… Now let's listen to the recordings and please look at the first question in your book. When the dialogue stops, I'll ask someone to tell us his or her choice. (*Playing the first dialogue…*)

Jenifer played the tape recorder and all the students listened attentively. Jenifer stopped the recorder after every two or three sentences and asked her students several related questions. If the students could give right answers, Jenifer preceded to play more dialogues. Similarly, she asked students to answer questions based on the contents of conversation in the next round. The listen—explain—answer pattern of instruction was applied to the end of class.

In the previous five subsections, the researcher described the activities carried out in Jenifer's listening and speaking class. The detailed description suggests that in her "flipped" classroom, Jenifer has implemented different activities in order to achieve the teaching objectives and foster listening and speaking skills. Jenifer's design and arrangement of teaching activities show her practiced identity. In the following section, the researcher will analyze diversified roles played by Jenifer and her students in the listening and speaking class.

5.3.3   The teacher's and students' roles

Teachers and students are the major actors in the classroom and they take many roles in the process of teaching and learning. In this section, the researcher presents and analyzes the roles played by Jenifer and her students in the listening and speaking class.

Roles in the mini play

The first student activity carried out in Jenifer's listening and speaking class was a mini play, in which three boy students acted as shop assistant and customers practicing drills frequently used in shopping conversations. The task of mini play had been assigned to the students before they came to the class. When the three boy students were performing the task, Jenifer and other students were involved in the observation and assessment of their performance. Jenifer took the teacher's role as an organizer and evaluator and her students took the roles of participants and also evaluators. The teacher's and students' roles and the method applied in the class can be summarized in Table 5.4:

Table 5.4　Summary of the teacher's and students' roles
in the activity of mini play

Classroom activity	Pedagogy	Teacher's roles	Students' roles
Mini play （3 Ss）	Task-based	· Organizer · Observer · Grader	· Participants · Team players · Evaluators

Roles in Pronunciation Exercise

Before the pronunciation exercise, Jenifer asked her students to read out the teaching objectives because she held that her students should be clear about the contents that they would learn in the class. Jenifer demonstrated a strong belief in how to direct her students in the process of learning thus she played the role of a director. In the next activity in which pronunciation skills were focused, Jenifer shifted her role from the director to an observer and grader. She observed the students' performance in doing the pronunciation practice and graded their work as a way of incentives. In this section of learning, the students prepared their work before the class and when they came to the class, they demonstrated enthusiasm in doing this type of task and took roles as team players and collaborators. See Table 5.5:

Table 5.5　Summary of the teacher's and students' roles
in the activity of pronunciation exercise

Classroom activity	Pedagogy	Teacher's roles	Students' roles
Pronunciation exercise （T）	Task-based	· Resource provider · Organizer · Controller · Activator	· Team players · Collaborators

Roles in the Activity of Word Quiz

The activity of word quiz lasted for about eight minutes and Jenifer took on roles of a resource-provider and organizer. Jenifer prepared an enjoyable way for the students to remember the new vocabulary as she believed that young students would be attracted by animated cartoon figures. She organized the whole class to join a competition, by doing so, students were motivated. Students played the roles of participants and knowledge receptors. Following Jenifer's direction, students remembered meanings of the words and joined the competition to give answers. See Table 5.6:

Table 5.6   Summary of the teacher's and students' roles
in the activity of word quiz

Classroom activity	Pedagogy	Teacher's roles	Students' roles
Match quiz （T）	Task-based	· Resource provider · Organizer	· Participants · Knowledge receptors

Roles in the Activity of Sentence Translation

As the class proceeded, a new student activity was applied. Jenifer and her students changed their roles accordingly. It can be indicated that in the third activity, the teacher and students took on diverse roles to complete different tasks, and they even exchanged their roles during classroom interactions. In the preparation of group work, student members in the group not only previewed the language points by themselves, but had to collaborate them to produce a successful presentation; therefore, students played their roles chiefly as cooperative team players and presenters. When some students demonstrated their presentations, other students learned language knowledge from them; at this time, the students' roles could be regarded as instructors.

As the organizer of the class, Jenifer managed the time and pace of the class. In addition, she tried to enhance the lively atmosphere in the class by encouraging students to rectify errors and present their own ideas. When students encountered grammatical puzzles, Jenifer helped the students to solve the possible problem and offered further explanation. Jenifer's role in the activity of sentence translation can be summarized in Table 5.7:

Table 5.7   Summary of the teacher's and students' roles
in the activity of sentence translation

Classroom activity	Pedagogy	Teacher's roles	Students' roles
Presentation (12 Ss in 2 groups)	Task-based	· Organizer · Observer · Judge · Error corrector · Knowledge transmitter · Environment creator	· Team players · Presenters · Instructors · Observers

Roles in Teaching and Learning Listening Skills

Data from video recorded classroom practice show that Jenifer's teaching of listening contents has shifted to traditional way of instruction. Jenifer used a tape recorder to play the listening contents. She stopped and asked questions to test if students captured the meaning of the conversation. There were not many student activities and interactions between the teacher and students or among student groups. The teaching procedure observed in the fourth episode suggests that Jenifer has pragmatically adopted the grammar-translation method to impart the language knowledge. Students were actually passive in the process of knowledge transmission and their listening competence were not well developed. The roles that the teacher and students played in the process of teaching and learning listening skills are summarized in Table 5.8:

Table 5.8　Summary of the teacher's and students' roles in

teaching and learning listening skills

Classroom activity	Pedagogy	Teacher's roles	Students' roles
Listening instruction （T）	Grammar-translation	· Resource provider · Organizer · Controller	· Knowledge receptors · Listeners

In this section, Jenifer's classroom instruction has been described in great detail. From the lesson plan and class video, it is evident that Jenifer holds a teaching belief that the classroom activities play vital roles in her teaching. In the coming section, her experience in participating in the NTTP will be presented.

5.4　Jenifer's experiences in attending the NTTP

"The training deepened my understanding about my roles in class."

(Jenifer, Interview, P1-13)

As explained in section 2.4, the NTTP has been designed to assist teachers in rural areas especially those in remote and border regions, strengthening their pedagogical competence. There are three major modules that constitute the NTTP namely, Trainer-Training Module

(*pei xun zhe pei xun*)〔培训者培训〕, Demonstration Module (*song jiao xia xiang*, sending demonstration classes to countryside schools)〔送教下乡〕, and Distance Education Module (*wang luo yan xiu*)〔网络研修〕. Functioning as opportunities for situated learning, the three modules prepare both novice and veteran teachers for strengthened expertise, as well as being a good chance to form new professional identities.

As a senior teacher in school who was selected as the backbone teacher (*gu gan jiao shi*)〔骨干教师〕in the NTTP, Jenifer experienced all the three training modules. She considered her learning experience in the NTTP as a "turning point" on the road of professional development, for these training programs significantly influenced her perception about language teaching and dramatically changed her practices in classroom.

5.4.1   The Trainer-Training Module

The Trainer-Training Module can be succinctly explained as sending selected "backbone teachers" from rural secondary schools to learn in university. When the trainees complete their training session (usually no more than 20 days) in university, they return to their school and give demonstration classes to more schools in rural areas. The training is beneficial to those who have plenty of teaching experience but few pedagogy theories. This subsection presents Jenifer's reflections after taking the courses in a normal university. In this section, interview data is used to report Jenifer's reflections, mainly on subject knowledge, pedagogical beliefs and her new understanding about teachers' roles in the classroom.

In 2015, Jenifer was assigned to Yunnan Normal University for three weeks of professional training. A wide range of courses were included in the short but intensive training program with focus on pedagogical knowledge.

When asked about her training experiences, Jenifer commented that: "The training courses that I took in 2015 did widen my eyes, especially those lectures really strengthened my subject knowledge, changed my perceptions on teaching and I began to realize I should take more roles in classroom teaching" (Interview, P1-13, 2016). Regarding subject knowledge, Jenifer stated that:

> […] *contents of the training courses offered by the university were quite*

diversified. I took courses like Phonetics, Designing Classroom Activity and Second Language Writing. Those courses helped me a lot to enhance my subject matter knowledge. Moreover, I also took Action Research—a course focused on how to conduct classroom-based research. In addition to courses about the language and research methods, I attended lectures on Traditional Chinese Culture and Ethnic Culture in Yunnan… These courses provided by the NTTP not only broadened and strengthened my content knowledge about the language from both theory and practice perspectives but also changed my understandings about my roles and positions in my classroom. What I learned from the training courses altered my beliefs as an English teacher. (Interview, P1-14, 2016)

Jenifer's reflections suggest that the cross-discipline training courses offered by the normal university about content and pedagogical knowledge have generally broadened and enhanced her teaching expertise. Jenifer also mentioned that attending these courses deepened her beliefs about her roles and positions in the classroom. She continued that:

I used to complain a lot about my students for their clumsiness in learning language but failed to find any appropriate ways to improve their performance. My beliefs in teaching and students changed after attending training courses in the NTTP. It is not students' fault to have problems in learning, but the teachers' ignorance of suitable or creative methods in teaching. Teachers should play diverse roles in the classroom instead of only being a classroom controller, organizer or knowledge resource provider, just like a monodrama player or standing in the classroom like a tape recorder, repeating instructions over and over. Teachers should design some enjoyable tasks and even work with students to practice the tasks... If teachers know how to scaffold the students and to work with them, I'm sure that they will love this subject and make rapid progress. (Interview, P1-15, 2016)

The interview data shows that Jenifer's disciplinary and pedagogical knowledge have been broadened, and her teaching beliefs have been renewed. In addition, her understanding about roles in the classroom has been deepened through participating in training courses in the NTTP. These changes contribute to enhancing her professional identity. In the next subsection, Jenifer's experience in practicing the Demonstration Module will be elaborated.

5.4.2   The Demonstration Module

The Demonstration Module is another creative approach to enhance the effect of teacher training. When trainees graduate from the teacher trainer program and return to their schools, some of the trainees who are experienced and have better performance during the training are selected as trainers and assigned to give lectures or demonstration classes in rural schools. That's why this program is literally translated into "sending demonstration classes to countryside schools". Giving demonstration classes in other schools provides the trainees with the opportunity to exercise the theoretical knowledge, putting pedagogical theory learned in university into classroom practice. Jenifer recalled one of her experiences of delivering a demonstration class to a countryside school:

> *When I completed training courses from the Trainer-Training Module in the university, I was assigned as a trainer to train other teachers. The school which I was assigned to present the demonstration had a good reputation for better teaching quality. However, compared with other subjects, their students had been achieving poorly in English. To make things worse, the students I was about to teach were mostly "underachievers" in the grade. Low performance of the students made me feel anxious and unconfident to give the demonstration class. Fortunately, my training experiences in the "Training of Teacher Trainers" helped me a lot in preparing for the demonstration class. I considered the demonstration as a good opportunity to practice my learnt skills in designing the classroom activity. Since the lesson was about the body language, I designed 2 group tasks and a classroom game in the demonstration, and I also invited students to sing songs and play games with me. The demonstration class was rather successful; much to my surprise, the class was not that horrible as what I was told and imagined, and the students were very active and showed great interest in learning English!*   (Interview, P1-16, 2016)

Comparing the two different approaches, Jenifer had that:

> *Comparing the programs of "Trainer-Training Module" and "Demonstration Module", I regard the latter challenging but rewarding, for that will be a very good opportunity to examine teachers' pedagogical competence and to practice newly learnt skills. To give demonstration classes in a new school and to strange students would be a very difficult and trying experience, but you will definitely learn more than teaching your own class.* (Interview, P1-16, 2016)

The learning experience of "Training of Teacher Trainers" in university considerably reshapes pedagogical knowledge of the trainees. They would accordingly gain lots of reflections on their previous teaching practices. Then the program of "Sending Demonstration Classes to Countryside Schools" comes at a critical juncture linking teachers' pedagogical beliefs and practice in the past with new understandings about teaching at present.

5.4.3   The Distance Education Module

In the NTTP, training programs and sessions offer both face-to-face and in Internet facilitated learning context for teachers to join collaborations to grow professionally. The present study observes three types of communities of practice established by teachers in the NTTP, namely the School-based Peer Mentoring, Outside-school Training and Online Group Discussion. School-based Peer Mentoring refers to the practice community within subject department and it is the most common approach for teachers to their professional growth and professional identity formation. The second type of communities of practice is the Outside-school Training, which means that teachers are assigned to attend various outside-school trainings organized by different level of authorities. Online Group Discussion, the third type of communities of practice, established along with the fast development of information technology and rapid emergence of social networking applications (software), has become a novel discourse in which teachers construct professional identity.

Cellphone based social networking applications like WhatsApp in America, LINE in Japan and WeChat in China have become obligatory instruments for people to stay connected in the information age. Thanks to many handy functions like voice messages and grouping, social networking applications have made it possible to establish a new type of learning environment where teachers can share ideas, discuss teaching plans or watch classroom video recordings, and finally, construct a shared online community of practice. In this Internet-based and social networking application-assisted community— the online community, new culture of learning, collaboration, peer mentor activities and role of participation are fostered and accordingly develop language teachers' professional identity.

Jenifer reported her reflections when she immersed herself in the WeChat Group Discussion which was established by English teachers from secondary schools in Jinghong. Jenifer commented that:

> *The information technology is developing so fast that you won't find anyone who doesn't have a cellphone or doesn't know how to use it to obtain information. It is very common for teachers to join different online discussion groups or subscribe to public accounts via social networking apps like WeChat. It's very convenient for teachers working in the same subject department to establish an online network or a community among themselves, contacting each other or exchanging ideas…, for example, I subscribe to two WeChat discussion groups relevant to the NTTP. The first one is huge and general, and members in the group are almost all secondary English teachers in Jinghong, but I don't talk in that group, because the function of that group is to receive notices issued by the city education bureau.*

> *The second one is called "Learning and Research Forum". It is an important web platform for me to learn from others. Teachers in the group are active and discussions are vibrant. In the group we can ask very detailed questions like detailed usage of vocabulary or grammar, share reflections after attending training courses. What's more, every semester, two or three experts in the field of pedagogy or language teaching are invited to give online lectures. They send voice message in the group, we listen and put up questions afterword.*

It makes me feel so good that every time I am greatly encouraged and inspired by their new educational concepts and creative teaching skills.

In addition to the convenience and mobility of the online discussion group, another reason that makes this online group discussion attractive is the democratic and vibrant atmosphere in the group. When questions pop up in the group, you would get many active responses; therefore, I'm quite willing to answer questions or to offer my suggestions and comments, not afraid of authorities or making mistakes, or losing face... The online peer coaching is not limited to asking and answering questions. We demonstrate our classroom practice by sharing audio or video recordings, and those recordings would trigger more heated discussions. (Interview, P1-17, 2016)

Compared with the face-to-face training, the Internet-based and social networking app creates a more relaxing environment that attracts teachers to learn in collaboration. Moreover, the online community greatly encourages teachers' agency, as Jenifer mentioned, "I'm quite willing to answer questions or to offer my suggestions and comments", which she would not do in the face-to-face communication. As a new form of situated learning in the NTTP, the WeChat online group discussion has become a novel way for teachers to construct professional identity.

In section 5.4, the researcher reports Jenifer's learning experience and her reflections on trainings through different programs in the NTTP. The three major training modules have greatly enhanced Jenifer's knowledge and belief about language teaching. In the next section, based on the classroom video, the researcher will continue to describe her changed instructional practices after her attending the NTTP.

5.5 Jenifer's classroom teaching in the post-NTTP period

"Whatever the methods or teaching model in use, they should be effective."

(Jenifer, Interview, P1-19)

Teachers' identity is never a stable entity, but a dynamic, active and on-going process, changing and developing over time and continually being influenced by teachers' own character, learning history, teaching experience, institutional context, training experiences and reflections. In the previous section, Jenifer's professional identity as a classroom practitioner was demonstrated through detailed illustration of her classroom practices and analysis of the roles played by the teacher and students in a listening and speaking class. Apart from describing her past teaching practices, the researcher also reported Jenifer's immersion in the NTTP training programs and her reflections on those trainings. When taking training courses in the NTTP, Jenifer was a trainee, and her professional identity accordingly changed to a learner whose knowledge about the particular subject, pedagogy and students was enriched and strengthened. The three-year-long NTTP training has sustainably influenced teachers' pedagogical practices and created opportunities for teachers to form new professional identities.

In this section, following the same format of data display, the researcher will elaborate on Jenifer's changed teaching practices by enlisting documents and observation data of lesson plans, classroom activities and roles.

5.5.1　The lesson plan

As introduced in Chapter 2, the National Teacher Training Plan launched by the MOE is a general framework with the goal to facilitate teachers' professional development in the broader rural regions in China. Based on the guiding principles of MOE, the Education Bureau of Jinghong city collaborated with curriculum experts from Yunnan Normal University and worked out a new model to teach English lessons for secondary schools in Jinghong city. All English teachers in the 13 secondary schools began to implement the so called "Three Stages and Seven Steps Teaching Model" (*san jie duan, qi bu zhou*)［三阶段，七步骤］as a new approach to direct their teaching. The Municipal Educational Bureau issued a detailed instruction clarifying what teachers should do in each step. Taking the direction of reading and writing model as an example, Table 5.9 presents the new model:

Table 5.9　The Three Stages and Seven Steps Model for teaching

reading skills (Document, P1-1, 2016)

	Stage I Pre-Reading	
Step 1	Activate background knowledge. Teacher may start the lesson by reviewing language points or other contents learned at the previous class. Teacher is also advised to activate background knowledge, creating a situation/context to help Ss to recall prior knowledge on the topic.	
Step 2	Learn new words, present and practice. Teacher presents the sentence structure and teaches 5-8 new words. Teacher may use games or other activities to teach the vocabulary or grammar points.	
Step 3	Predict the passage in different ways. Teacher helps Ss to make predictions about the passage in different ways. Before learning the contents, teacher may use conversations, tell stories or create a real context that contains language points in the contents, thus get Ss familiar with what they are going to learn next.	
	Stage II While-Reading	
Step 4	Skim questions for the first-time reading. Before teaching the passage, teacher may raise 2-3 questions. Then Ss skim the passage for the first-time reading and try to answer the questions. The goal for the first-time of reading is to help Ss establish a global understanding of the passage. It is reasonable for Ss if they fail to provide any answers to the questions.	
Step 5	Scan for detailed information for the second-time reading. Teacher asks Ss to scan the passage for the second time. Before Ss begin scanning, teacher may repeat 2-3 questions raised in Step 4, 1 or 2. More questions can be added to ask the detailed information.	
	Stage III Post-Reading	
Step 6	Read out the passage. Teacher asks Ss to underline the key language points, then may ask Ss to read out loud in different ways (in pairs or groups).	
Step 7	Do exercises or practice language points. Teacher presents exercises according to the texts, strengthening Ss' knowledge about the comprehension ability or language points. Teacher can also raise questions to improve Ss' critical thinking ability or ability to express their opinions.	

The new teaching model is a fruit of the collaboration between the local educational bureau and curriculum experts from universities. This top-down direction divides classroom teaching into three stages/phases and requires teachers to carry out a lesson in seven to eight steps. The administrative staff from the educational bureau stated in an interview that:

This model is tailored to help teachers in our region to enhance their teaching. It looks rather fixed than flexible, but it works well. Our teachers are responsible, hard-working, but they are short of subject knowledge and pedagogical knowledge. This has been a serious problem and prevented us from improving teaching quality and students' performance. It is important and urgent for them to teach in a scientific and effective way. Therefore, we take the NTTP as an opportunity and invite experts from the Normal University to develop this new model, hoping to help teachers to improve their teaching quality. (Interview, P1-18, 2017)

From the fall semester of 2016, teachers from 13 secondary schools in Jinghong city were trained with the new teaching model. Based on the new model, Jenifer gradually changed from her past "flipped" teaching method to the "Three Stages and Seven Steps" pedagogy. In May 2017, the educational bureau launched a teaching competition among English teachers to test their teaching competencies using the new model. Jenifer participated in the competition and tried to apply the new model to teach a writing class. She recorded the class and sent me the footage; therefore, the researcher chose to analyze these documents and video recorded data. The first data the researcher will present and discuss is Jenifer's lesson plan. Jenifer's lesson plan for writing class is shown in Table 5.10:

Table 5.10   Jenifer's lesson plan to teach a writing class (Document, P1-2, 2017)

Unit 7—Topic 3—Section D		
Teach Reading and Writing Skills	Date: May 20th, 2017	Grade 7
Teaching Objective: Write a short passage about Mother's Day		
Topic	Mother's Day	
Key Sentences	She was born on … I bought some flowers for her.	
Vocabulary	carnations, buy/make/cook sth. for sb.	
Ability Objective	Write a short passage about Mother's Day	
Strategy Objective	Integrating reading and writing	
Culture and Emotion Objective	Offering Ss an opportunity to express affection for their mothers	

continued

Unit 7—Topic 3—Section D		
Teaching Aids: Multimedia Courseware		
Teaching Methods: The Communicative Approach		
Expressions and language points: I bought some flowers for my mom. I made a card for my mother on Mother's Day.		
Teaching Procedures		
Stage 1 Pre-Writing	Step 1 Warming-up and revision	Listen to the song: Mom, I Love You. Watch a video clip made by Ss.
	Step 2 Activation	Activity 1: Free talk Talk about the activities that Ss will do for their mothers on Mother's Day. Activity 2: Learn a passage about Mother's Day. After reading the passage, answer three questions. Activity 3: Filling the blank "Do you know ___ your mother?" Activity 4: Write a short passage about your mother.
	Step 3 Mind map	Develop ideas in a logical way by drawing a mind map.
Stage 2 While-Writing	Step 4 Writing or drafting	Individual writing: Ss start to write.
	Step 5 Peer proof reading	Ss check each other's writing.
Stage 3 Post-Writing	Step 6 Evaluation/ feedback/editing	Teacher checks Ss' work and give feedback.
	Step 7 Summary and Assignment	Ss write the passage again and peer review.
Blackboard Design Mother's Day (a student's name) bought some flowers for her mother on Mother's Day. (a student's name) made a card for her mother on Mother's Day. (a student's name) cooked a big dinner for her mother on Mother's Day.		

In the model of classroom teaching made by the educational bureau, there is no specified guidance for the teaching of writing skills, instead integrated instruction for reading and writing class is provided. Following the reading model, Jenifer made her plan basically in line with the requirement and format demanded by the educational bureau. With a clear teaching objective, she divided the lesson into three major stages/phases and in seven steps. In the Pre-Writing phase, Jenifer designed six activities which would be carried out in three steps, aiming to create a context/situation for the students to get familiar with the task. There were two steps in the phase of While-Writing in which students began their composition. This phase was designed to last for about 15 minutes and, in the end, when students completed their writing, they were asked to begin peer proof-reading. In the last phase, the teacher would comment on some of the compositions and give feedback. Jenifer stated her understanding of the teaching of writing skills and her perceptions about the new teaching model:

> *Honestly, the teaching of writing skill has been ignored for a long time. There are two reasons: the first reason is that teaching writing skill takes a long time and the second reason is (that) we as teachers seldom write. We usually spend much time in teaching vocabulary, explaining texts or doing grammar exercises, leaving very little time to develop students' writing skills. The less devotion from teachers results in students' poor performance in writing composition. I began to realize this problem when I was participating in the NTTP. I learned some pedagogy from the NTTP for teaching different skills including writing. From this year, our Municipal Educational Bureau has began to improve teaching quality with the focus on pedagogy. With the help of my colleagues and the Teaching and Research Coordinator (jiao yan yuan)［教研员］ from the educational bureau, I tried to integrate reading and writing instruction into one class.*

> *When I was taking courses in the NTTP, the professor mentioned the concept of need analysis in his lecture. After the training, I carefully learned relevant knowledge about the student need analysis by myself, and when it came to the lesson plan, the principle my design underlined was the real need and practical situation of the students. Now I'm teaching Grade 7 and the*

students in my class are quite young and active; therefore, I begin the class with a lovely song. Many students in the class are from ethnic families, and English is actually the third language for them, so learning a foreign language is not an easy job for them. I pay attention to linguistic cognition of the students, and try my best to make the contents easy, and I speak slowly and try to be nice and very patient during the class. (Interview, P1-19, 2017)

As a language teacher working in secondary school in the local educational context, Jenifer didn't have much flexibility to design and teach the class in her own ways but to follow the pedagogical directions and meet requirements made by the local educational authorities. Although teachers need to teach in a fixed framework, they still enjoy great flexibility in practicing pedagogy as they can be very creative in contextualizing linguistic input and designing diverse activities. As a senior teacher, Jenifer was experienced in designing activities which were demonstrated in her previous teaching.

When it came to the lesson plan based on the new teaching model, Jenifer's focus was no longer the activities or contextualization but the students' practical need. She came to realize that teaching should match students' true learning ability and their practical level of learning.

It is evident in the interview that when Jenifer is making the lesson plan, the principle directing her instruction is to meet the practical need of the students in her class and her lesson plan is made according to her knowledge and understandings about her students in the class. In the next section, the researcher will examine Jenifer's design of student activities and how she implements the lesson plan, expecting to show her practiced professional identity.

5.5.2　The classroom activities

Jenifer mentioned her changed perceptions on the design of classroom activities in the interview, which can be observed that Jenifer has become more decisive and clearer in planning the class and preparing classroom activities than she did in the past. In this section, the researcher will illustrate how Jenifer carries out classroom activities in a writing class as well as presenting a window to observe how Jenifer constructs new professional identity through classroom practice.

Episode 1

The topic for the class was "Mother's Day". In preparation, Jenifer searched the Internet and downloaded a short but lively children's song to start the class. The classroom was equipped with a computer and a LCD projector; thus, materials and contents could be displayed on the whiteboard. When Jenifer played the song, all students stood up watching the video on the screen, singing along the English lyrics and clapping their hands with the cartoon figures in the video. Because of the simple lyrics, rhythmic tune and the animated cartoon figures, the young children in the classroom were quite absorbed in singing while enjoying watching the video. The song was repeated twice and when students finished singing, Jenifer asked three students to explain the general meaning of the song. Jenifer explained why she started the class by teaching students a children's song:

> There are many reasons for me to begin the class with an English song. The students I'm teaching are in Grade Seven. Most of them are from ethnic families in rural regions and just finished their primary education. The students are quite young and active. Though having little knowledge in English language, they are quick in learning and singing songs, which is the nature of children. It would be better for the teacher to start a lesson by singing songs than learning by rote.

> I remember that in one of the lectures of the NTTP, the teacher mentioned the importance of recreational activities like singing songs in teaching second or foreign language to young children. A lot of studies have proved that language learning can be enhanced by music and songs; therefore, I think my teaching of English songs has sufficient theoretical foundations.

> (Interview, P1-20, 2017)

Jenifer's first classroom activity for this writing class was to teach her students to sing an English song. As manifested in the interview, she decided to do so because of her understandings about the disposition of the students; meanwhile, her early learning experiences under the NTTP also helped to construct this new belief. Evidences can be found in literature that using music and songs in language acquisition can benefit learners for both the linguistic and motivational interests generate. The interview and her practices in the classroom signal that Jenifer has began to construct her new professional identity, instead of relying on intuition or experience, as she has began to teach under the guidance of language teaching theories and this change mainly results from the NTTP.

Episode 2

Unpon completion of teaching the English song on the theme of maternal love, Jenifer began to carry out her second classroom activity that she had prepared before the class. It's not uncommon for teachers to use video materials in their class because compared with teachers' instructions, students would be easily attracted by the story or figures in the video. What made Jenifer's video special was that the character in the clip was a boy student in her class, and it was the boy student himself who produced the video. When he appeared on the screen, his image surprised his classmates and they began to talk. Some even stood up and shouted out the boy's name. The short video lasted for about three minutes and was recorded by cellphone describing that the boy bought a carnation flower and sent it to his mother as a Mother's Day gift. The boy spoke in English when introducing himself and then told why he chose to buy a carnation flower. At the end of the short video, he sent the flower to his mom saying that "Mom, I love you and I wish you healthy and beautiful forever!" The boy forgot how to pronounce "healthy" in English, he thought it for a second and switched to a Chinese word " 健康 (*jian kang*)" for the English word "healthy". The unexpected mistake embarrassed the little boy and he made a face, which amused the whole class and Jenifer laughed a lot.

Before Jenifer played the video for the second time, she asked her students to notice the words used by the boy in the video. She also emphasized the past tense of the word "buy" and asked students to identify more verbs in the past tense in the dialogue.

Together with the English song, the student video was used as creative techniques by Jenifer to motivate her students to learn the English subject. She perceived that her students were from multiethnic regions, and they were young and liked singing and dancing. The students would be quickly bored if the teacher constantly taught the contents by memorizing vocabulary and stressed too much on grammar. As mentioned in previous section, the teaching of English songs was inspired by the lectures she attended under the NTTP, and the new idea of self-made student video was from a discussion with a young teacher in the online WeChat group. She confessed in the interview:

> *I learned this teaching technique from one of my young colleagues when we had some online discussion in the Wechat. Thanks to the information technology, the cellphone today becomes multifunctional. It is not just a phone, but also a camera and a video recorder. My knowledge about smart phones is limited to making phone calls or taking pictures until one of my young colleagues shared her experience of using a smart phone to make short videos. She asked her students to make short videos using dialogues in the textbook. She suggested that I could have a try. I took her suggestion and tried to assign a video project to my students. As what you can see in my class, students like the video very much. I think students like this way of teaching because not only they can see themselves acting in the video but also they are able to speak in a foreign language. Such novel learning experience make them feel excited and thus motivation in learning the language is activated.*

> *I also find it necessary to learn from other teachers in the online learning community. Taking this student video technique as an example, I learned this method from a colleague in our Wechat discussion group. A young teacher from other schools shared a video footage which was recorded by her student, and this video aroused many teachers' interest and we discussed it a lot from recording techniques to feasible topics.*

> *The new generation of teachers was born in the information age in which Internet, cellphones and computers are common in their life, and they are quite able to apply new technologies into their classroom teaching. As an "old" teacher, our information literacy is limited, and it may take me a very long time to make the video. However, I'm quite willing to learn new things and fortunately we have an online learning community. If I have any problem, I can*

consult those young teachers via Wechat, and they are quite willing to help.

(Interview, P1-21, 2017)

The interview data reveals Jenifer's two-folds concept of professional identity construction. Teachers' agency and professional learning community are two pivotal factors that influence the construction of professional identity. As a senior secondary school teacher who was approaching retirement soon, Jenifer was still active in acquiring new knowledge and her willingness to learn has been realized in the online Wechat discussion group—an online learning community beyond time and place which offered her the opportunity for professional growth.

The classroom observation data shows that Jenifer's classroom practice evidences her perceptions. The students' feedback to the short video made by a student himself is positive and the video has effectively activated students' learning motivation.

Episode 3

Based on the short video made by a boy student himself, Jenifer asked the class more questions:

"Just now we watched what Luo Yusen (name of the boy student) did for his mother on Mother's Day, and I know every one of you in this class loves your mother, now can you tell me what you did on Mother's Day?"

Students in the class made a quick response and seven students described what they had done on Mother's Day. Students expressed their love for mothers in various ways:

"Luo Yu made a cake.

Zhang Fan helped her mother clean the room.

Lou Wei sang a song for her mother…"

Jenifer summarized replies and wrote them on the blackboard, instructing her students that these sentences could be used as building blocks to compose their writings later. Then, Jenifer asked the students to open their textbooks reading a passage. The passage which was entitled "Say Thanks to Your Mother" told a story about the origin of Mother's Day. In order to help her students to gain a better understanding about the passage, Jenifer wrote four questions as a mind map on the blackboard. Starting with the core question "When is Mother's Day?", other questions were asked about "What is the true love in the world?", "What does John's mother often do for him?" and "What did John do for his mother on Mother's Day?"

Following the questions, students began to read the short passage. About five minutes later, Jenifer asked her students to stop reading and some of them were invited to give answers to the questions in the mind map. In addition, Jenifer projected a gap-filling exercise on the whiteboard and more students were called to fill the gap.

Jenifer regarded the classroom activities like teaching of English songs, self-produced student videos and mind maps as preparations for the teaching of writing skills. Jenifer elaborated her perception of this way of teaching in the interview:

> *In my past teaching, though many student activities were applied, I used to instruct skills separately and put emphasis on rote learning. Now, as what you observe in my class, I change to integrate different skills into an interwoven process, that is to say, every design and practice pave the way for, or scaffold the next step* [...]

> [...] *I use the song and video to catch their attention and interest. Then prepare my students with the dialogue in the video and the sentences in the passage as the material for essay writing, then students would have enough input to write with. They are becoming more confident, and I'm becoming more confident, too.*

> *However, after practicing the new teaching model for some time, I've realized that whatever the methods or model teachers apply in their class, they (the methods or model) should be effective in improving students' language competences.*   (Interview, P1-22, 2017)

Jenifer concluded her practice as "integrated instruction of different skills". She changed from teaching language skills independently to combine different teaching objectives into an interlinked process. As reflected in the interview, this way of teaching made both her and her students "more confident".

In line with the lesson plan, the writing class entered into its last step. Jenifer projected a mind map on the whiteboard. The mind map was made up by four rectangular shapes, and in each rectangular shape, there was a question for students, namely "What does your mother do? What does your mother like to do after work? What does your mother often do/say to you? What did you do for your mother on Mother's day?" Jenifer first asked her students to read out the questions and then explained the task of essay writing, which required students to compose a short essay with a given title "I Love My Mother".

Being guided by the questions, students started to write while Jenifer moved around the classroom offering help and monitoring the writing process. Ten minutes past; when most of the students finished their writing, Jenifer asked the whole class to exchange their works for peer proof-reading. She outlined three standards for the proof reading, namely tense, spelling, and word count. In the end, Jenifer selected three compositions as samples and projected them on the whiteboard through the LCD projector. Together with her students, Jenifer checked and analyzed each of the compositions for mistakes in spelling, third person singular, past form of verb or other grammar misuse.

Examining classroom practices can shed light on exploration of teachers' professional identity construction process. In the previous three subsections, the researcher demonstrated how Jenifer formed new professional identity through description of Jenifer's classroom activities aiming to improve students' writing skills. Comparing with her past teaching practices before attending the NTTP courses, it is noticeable that Jenifer has intended to embed different teaching tasks into an interlinked process, and considered to change the response to the pedagogy reform required by the Municipal Educational Bureau. Jenifer regarded this change as a positive shift because the new teaching model made her more confident.

5.5.3 The teacher's and students' roles

In addition to the illustration of Jenifer's classroom practices, analysis of the teacher's and students' roles in class has equal importance to reveal the process of teachers' professional identity construction. In this section, the researcher will identify a number of roles that Jenifer and her students played during the classroom interaction in the past time before the NTTP. Jenifer's learning experiences under the NTTP have changed her a lot both in pedagogical perceptions and in classroom practices. In her later teaching, she made considerable changes in her practices, and her roles in classroom interaction with students changed accordingly. In this section, the researcher will use the data of classroom videos to distinguish and analyze multiple roles that Jenifer and her students played in a writing class.

The first role Jenifer played in the classroom is an organizer. Based on the teaching plan, Jenifer first divided the writing class into three stages/phases, and she arranged various activities in each stage, step by step, preparing the students for the instruction of writing skills. The second role Jenifer undertook is a resource provider. For instance, in preparation of teaching students an English song on the theme of mother's love, she first searched the Internet for suitable songs, and later displayed lyrics and tunes via PowerPoint. In this process, Jenifer acted as a provider of content. When the class progressed into the activity of student video, Jenifer changed her role to a controller and manager. Immediately she designed and gave assignments to students to record a short video reporting how they celebrated Mother's Day with their families. In the classroom, Jenifer selected video footages in good quality and helped students to do the editing. In this student video activity, Jenifer worked as a project/task manager, —she designed, carried out and guaranteed the implementation of the project. Moreover, Jenifer's role in the instruction of writing skill is first an organizer, activator, knowledge-transmitter and then an evaluator and feedback-provider. Being an activator, she used dialogues and sentence patterns in the student video as building blocks, scaffolding students to compose their own paragraphs. When students completed their writing of the short essay, Jenifer collected three writing samples from the student works, showing her students wrong sentences and together with students correcting the mistakes. At last, she graded the writing samples and asked each student to identify their own mistakes in the writing. In order to enhance students' awareness of their misuse of past tense, especially the irregular form of past tense of verbs, she recognized all verbs that were used by students in the three samples, and summarized principles that guided the change of verb in forms of past tense. In doing so, Jenifer worked in her class as an activator, assessor, grader and feed-back provider during the writing class.

According to classroom video of the writing class, students played diverse roles. When learning to sing the English song, students were active participants and knowledge receptors. But in the activity of student video, students were working with their teacher. Thus, they were not only the learners in the classroom but also content creators and resource provider. In addition, in other classroom interactions, for example, when students began to compose their own essay, they followed the mind map and adopted sentences that Jenifer had suggested. In this apprentice—master relationship, as students were learning skills and craftsmanship from their master, they were active knowledge receptors.

In brief, the teacher's and students' roles in a writing class could be summarized as follows (see Table 5.11):

Table 5.11   Summary of the teacher's and students' role in a writing class

Classroom activity	Pedagogy	Teacher's roles	Students' roles
English song	Task-based	· Resource provider · Organizer · Controller · Activator · Grader/assessor	· Participants · Content providers · Active knowledge receptors

5.6   Jenifer's reflections on doing teacher research

"I know it is difficult, but I'm willing to try."　　(Jenifer, Interview, P1-24)

A teacher as the researcher refers to is the education practitioner who volunteers to conduct action research to solve problems in the classroom. This type of inquiry involves initiating some action in one's teaching and then systematically analyzing the teaching processes and outcomes. Based on the interview and document data, this section will report how Jenifer constructs her professional identity as a teacher researcher when she is engaged in two different action research projects.

5.6.1   The motivations for doing action research

Teachers vary in their motives and desires to participate or initiate classroom research. Jenifer, as a senior secondary school language teacher, explained her reasons for doing action research in the interview:

> [...] *to be honest, I didn't know what the term "action research" meant until you mentioned it just now. I was engaged in two action research projects so far: one was in collaboration with the TRG and the other one was an ongoing project of my own. The year before the last, I had been invited to join a research project which was conducted by the jiao yan yuan from the educational bureau and the study was about teachers' classroom language use. Initially, I had been required to videotape one of my classes teaching speaking skills. Then, I was asked to transcribe every sentence I used during the class. Finally, the task went on watching the video and reflecting on the language I used in that class.*

> *At the beginning of this project, I didn't know how and why they asked me to do so, and I just followed their instructions. The project was complicated and "troublesome" but I was very patient, because firstly I wanted to learn from them, and secondly I wanted to be promoted as senior teacher (zheng gao ji jiao shi)〔正高级教师〕. To apply for the higher title, I need to win national or provincial-level awards, and I must have published papers. The title, I think, would not only be evidence of my teaching competence but also a recognition for my 30 years of hard work.*   (Interview, P1-23, 2017)

The interview data suggests that teachers' agency and institutional incentives are the major impetus for Jenifer to make the decision to be engaged in research activities. Jenifer's active agency was evidenced by the interview data in section 5.4.3 when she mentioned about her perceptions about online communities. Jenifer had strong curiosity about and interest in learning new things though she had only four years to teach before retirement. The teacher' assessment and incentive system in the education sector encourages teachers to promote themselves from the primary level to the senior level. When being interviewed, Jenifer was "associate senior teacher" (*fu gao ji jiao shi*)〔副

高级教师〕and she was ambitious to be promoted as "senior teacher" during the last four years before retirement. Besides increased salary, higher professional title not only benefits teachers in terms of public reputations, it is also a testimony of their long and hard teaching career, as Jenifer said in the interview that the title was "a recognition for my 30 years of hard work".

5.6.2 The personal and contextual constraints

Various personal and contextual factors are influencing teachers in constructing their identity as researchers. According to the interview data, the present study finds that limited research repertoire and insufficient institutional support are two major contextual obstacles that hinder teachers in developing the identity of researcher. As found in the interview data (P1-24, 2017), Jenifer had limited research knowledge and experience, and she confessed that she had no idea about the meaning of the term "action research". She further elaborated on that in the interview:

> *I attribute not having enough knowledge for doing research to two reasons: for one thing, during the time I was learning the English language, no subjects were taught on research and research methods (to do the research). No matter in middle school or in university, I mean in Jiangsu Institute of Education, we were immersed in learning subject knowledge with focus on developing reading competence and building solid grammar knowledge. As for research, it was far away from my study.*

> *For another, not like university teachers, we middle school teachers are not encouraged to do research. Schools are pragmatic, even utilitarian in teachers' professional development. Because all schools are assessed by a set of indicators showing students' performance in tests, teachers have to follow and reach stringent requirements in helping students to make higher scores. Therefore, teachers are busy in learning all kinds of practical or effective skills that can help them to manage the classroom, improve student motivation or just simply oblige students to learn by rote.*

In addition, in such "score-driven" context, there is no academic environment for teachers to do research. Things are alike in both the in-school and out-of-school professional training programs. Time was usually spent on learning new educational policies or practicing new pedagogical theories, while no specific contents were taught on research skills.

(Interview, P1-24, 2017)

Jenifer's words might explain part of reasons why secondary school language teachers are less involved in the research activity. As Jenifer pointed out, in teachers' early learning experiences, most school curriculums were designed to improve students' first subject matters then pedagogical knowledge. There are not many courses in school syllabus instructing students how to do the classroom-based research. When teaching in the school, teachers then have to conform to the school objectives which often aim at training students to achieve higher scores in tests. Moreover, opportunities are rare for most in-service teachers to conduct research even though they are encountering myriads of problems in their classroom practices. The interview data also indicates that the workplace training in which Jenifer participated mainly intends to update teachers' content knowledge or pedagogical capacity, but is not designed to enlighten them to solve problems by doing classroom-based research.

To conclude, teachers' limited personal knowledge about research, lukewarm institutional support and pedagogy-focused workplace trainings are significant constraining factors that hinder teachers' awareness and practices from doing classroom-based research.

5.6.3   Classroom-level curriculum development

In section 5.6.2, the researcher presented findings that emerged from the interview data indicating personal and contextual factors that impeded the construction of teachers' professional identity as researcher. Although being hindered by various negative personal or contextual factors in doing research, Jenifer overcame obstacles and conducted research with the help of experienced researchers and then managed to carry out research on her own, which finally resulted in her classroom-level curriculum development.

The last section of this chapter sets out to report Jenifer's attempts in developing the classroom-level curriculum.

Taking the status quo of the research capability of Chinese secondary language teachers into account, it is not possible for teachers to initiate full-scale and systematic curriculum development. Teachers may choose to supplement additional attractive materials, rearrange the sequence of contents or carry out more appropriate activities. Among the trainees in the NTTP the researcher has contacted, Jenifer is a unique example in exercising teachers' agency to do research and curriculum development. Although being frustrated from time to time for not having sufficient knowledge to do research, she finally managed to find ways to learn and carried out research independently. The trajectory of becoming a teacher researcher and a curriculum developer might not be as dramatic as "roller coaster" and "rocky" (Burns, 2017) as described in the literature. For a secondary language teacher in less developed multiethnic regions, her experience is a good try. When Jenifer was asked to comment her experience in doing research, she firstly recalled how she learned to do research in collaboration with other researchers:

> *I've been teaching English subject for almost 30 years, but never thought about doing any classroom-based research. As mentioned in the last talk, I've never heard about terms like "action research or classroom-level curriculum development" until I participated in the training programs sponsored by the NTTP. The year before the last, the TRG invited me to join a collaboration in doing a research project about teachers' classroom language use. I followed their directions and videotaped 3 of my classes teaching listening and speaking skills. By doing this project, I not only learned some basic methods and skills in data collection and analysis, but also found the attractiveness of doing research. For example, when I watched the video footage of my teaching and I transcribed my words, I came to realize how poor my classroom language was! Then I changed deliberately to use more diverse language in my class and use the "IRF"(Initiation—Response—Feedback) model attentively in conversation with students. Later when the project was completed, I found myself unconsciously using more words for encouragement and compliment, and very careful in giving feedback.* (Interview, P1-25, 2017)

The analyzed interview data may help to reveal that for secondary school language teachers, it is impossible to initiate any research without external assistance. School teachers need help from outside resources to guide or lead them to carry out a research project. It also cannot be denied that participation of research projects benefits teachers from multiple perspectives, like gaining some practical research skills. Teachers' participation of research projects catalyzes the dissemination of the research. As Jenifer noted in the interview, she began to value her language use in classroom and when she exercised the research findings to classroom teaching, she discovered that the teacher-student classroom interaction became much more effective.

When Jenifer finished the research project in collaboration with other teachers and researchers, she began to try to do research by herself. The idea of doing classroom research was not an idea on a whim but her continuing quest for effective teaching and practical solutions to the classroom problems. Jenifer explained her motivation to conduct the action research in the interview. She first analyzed the status quo of problems in her classroom:

> I had been questioning the top-down educational policy and curriculum when I began to teach. Our country has a vast territory and a large population. Geographical remoteness and economic underdevelopment make Xishuangbanna a place backward in education. The textbooks and curriculum are designed by the national-level experts, and they are facing middle school students in general at the time of selecting materials and editing textbooks but not tailored for our students. I find it problematic in teaching some units because of the sudden change in the difficulty of vocabulary or in the contents of reading materials. Other problems like irrelevance between the contents and real life of students are also found. For example, it is hard for the students from subtropical and remote border places to understand a snow storm, a hamburger or spaghetti.   (Interview, P1-26, 2017)

As a frontline teacher teaching for almost 30 years, Jenifer identified incongruence between high demand of materials and low learning competence of students, and she found that irrelevant themes in contents as one of the key problems impeded her classroom teaching. Having been plagued by the practical problems in her classroom teaching and inspired by her rudimentary experience in recent collaborative research project, Jenifer commenced to carry out an action research. She elaborated her design of the research on classroom-level curriculum development:

> *In spite of various reasons that caused students' lower performance, I consider the curriculum as one of the key factors that influence the learning and teaching process. In my daily teaching, I find many mismatches between the official textbook and students' actual situation in terms of vocabulary, themes and activities. From the last semester, I have conducted a classroom-level project on curriculum development with expectation to change the situation. I firstly used questionnaire to explore the students' true attitude and clarified the difficulties that had been preventing them from making full efforts to learn the subject well. Then based on the result, I carefully rearranged some of the contents of the textbook. In addition to supplementing some materials that were highly pertinent to the local life of ethnic communities, I designed extra activities for every unit. I intended to use the classroom activities to enhance students' learning experiences instead of teaching the contents strictly in line with the textbook. At the end of the last semester, I used another questionnaire to collect data about students' responses to my change of the curriculum. At last, I would change the activities and try to modify the changed sequence to present language points. After many rounds of adjustment, I'm becoming more confident on my research and teaching.* (Interview, P1-27, 2017)

Based on the official textbook and in line with the curriculum, Jenifer rearranged the sequence in presenting the language points to supplement more student activities that were close to the local life of ethnic communities.

The interview data also indicates that Jenifer has gripped some basic techniques to secure a valid research. She detected the research problem from her reflections, experiences and frustrations that were gained from her many years of teaching practice. Then she applied questionnaires as an effective instrument for data collection. At last, Jenifer made new changes according to the responses from students. Also as quoted at the beginning of this section, Burns (2017) describes the trajectory of teachers' research engagement as "roller coaster" and "rocky", indicating the tough experience for teachers to accomplish action research. Jenifer reflected on her experience conducting the research in the interview:

> *Doing research is like a toddler learning to walk, you need help from other people when you are stumbling ahead. I gained the research skills partly form my previous research experience in the collaborative project of teachers' language use in the classroom. I have also been supported by veteran researchers from the Normal University. Two experienced researchers in the university guided and directed my research. They were so generous in providing me with pertinent books and journal papers that I could establish a literature about action research on classroom-level curriculum development. I'm also grateful for their kind instruction on methodology, especially for enlightening me to design the questionnaire and analyze the data.*   (Interview, P1-28, 2017)

In this section, Jenifer's professional identity as researcher is manifested through semi-structured interview data. The data suggests that in constructing the professional identity as researcher, teachers' agency and institutional incentives are two major impetus for Jenifer's research engagement. The interview data also reveals that limited research knowledge and skills and weak institutional support are overt factors among personal and contextual constrains that restrain teachers from doing classroom-based research. In the end, Jenifer's practiced professional identity as a beginner in doing research is evidenced and exemplified by her attempt in carrying out research project on classroom-level curriculum development. In this trying process, Jenifer's past experiences and assistance from veteran researchers in university were indispensible to her for accomplishing the project.

5.7   Discussion and summary

This chapter has presented the trajectory of professional identity construction of Jenifer, the first participant of the present study. The data reveals that Jenifer's professional identity is developed and shaped at different time periods and stages. According to the data, it can be concluded that Jenifer's personal biography workplace context, external professional training and engagement in the teacher action research all contribute to shape her professional identity as a language teacher.

Since the formation of teachers' professional identity is not a linear process, the professional identity is formed in teachers' personal biographies and early language learning experiences, and then influenced by various contextual factors in different professional development periods. As the data reveals, in Jenifer's personal biography, the failure in *Gao Kao* has left a significant mark in her life. Having been influenced by her English teacher, she chose to be an EFL teachers for life long career. Then early language learning experiences in *Su Jiao Yuan* helped her to lay a solid foundation in both subject matter knowledge and pedagogical contend knowledge. The learning experience in *Su Jiao Yuan* had a lasting influence on Jenifer's language teaching beliefs and practices.

The working place context has a great impact on the development of teachers' professional identity. Documents and interview data collected in the fieldwork are used to introduce the historical and current situation of the school where Jenifer works. As shown in the data, because of the change of national socioeconomic policy, when the school merged with other local secondary schools, the faculties had to face a myriad of difficulties such as inadequate faculties, overcrowded classroom and insufficient infrastructure. Teachers had to face more intricate situation that was brought by the combination of different district schools, and diverse ethnic and linguistic backgrounds of students who were the most tricky ones in the classroom. As for a language teacher, Jenifer became increasingly aware that English was the third language for her students, in addition to local ethnic languages and Standard Chinese (*pu tong hua*) ［普通话］. Diverse linguistic backgrounds and weak learning motivation were pivotal factors that affected Jenifer's classroom practice and development of her professional identity accordingly.

Stimulated recall interview and classroom video data are mainly used to represent Jenifer's classroom practice in the past time before the NTTP. As the lesson plan and classroom practices show, before her attending the NTTP, Jenifer used many student activities in her class and she perceived that the classroom activities were essential in teaching language skills. While according to the interview, Jenifer took a new teaching belief that regardless of what teaching methods or models teachers applied, they (the model or methods) should be effective in improving students' linguistic competences.

Attending the NTTP courses was regarded as a "turning point" by Jenifer on her road of professional development. It was a critical event in reshaping Jenifer's professional identity, as she summarized that "various training programs not only updated her knowledge of subject matter, but greatly improved the pedagogical competence". Stimulated recall interview was mainly applied for data collection and yielded important outcomes about her reflections on the three training modules. Jenifer saw the first module as "cross-disciplinary" that broadened her pedagogical knowledge as well as enhancing her teaching expertise. As for the second module, though being put under huge pressure, Jenifer regarded the demonstration as a precious opportunity to practice her learnt skills in designing the classroom activity. Jenifer didn't give very positive comment on the distance learning module. However, according to the interview data, she demonstrated strong interest in participating in the online WeChat group discussion. She was even inspired by one of her cyber colleagues to design and carry out some innovative classroom activities.

Diverse training modules in the NTTP greatly inspired Jenifer to make a change in her traditional pedagogical practices that she had been doing for a long time, thus her professional identity as a front-line practitioner has been reshaped. Based on her renewed knowledge about the pedagogy, student and content, Jenifer reformed her teaching plan and supplement more innovative student activities. Jenifer's dramatic change in trying new pedagogy was videotaped during the fieldwork. The most distinctive change in Jenifer's plan of instruction was the implement of the "Three Stages and Seven Steps" teaching model. Jenifer redesigned the students' activities, which were more "close to the life of students". Being guided by the new teaching model, regarding the roles during the instruction, Jenifer's roles in class were more diverse, —she was a resource provider, class organizer, controller, activity activator and student performance grader/assessor. The classroom practices of all the three participants will be compared and discussed comprehensively in the discussion part of this study.

Finally, Jenifer's engagement in teachers' action research is illustrated. The journey in which Jenifer tried to develop her identity as researcher was rather difficult. Her personal aspiration for academic promotion was the major impetus to initialize her engagement in research, then her establishment of researchers' identity was mediated by her collaborative efforts in other researchers' project. Taking advantages gained from her hands-on research experience, Jenifer stumbled to carry out action research in order to solve her teaching problems. However, Jenifer's limited research knowledge and skills constrained her attempts for the research activity. Fortunately, Jenifer's endeavor to conduct classroom-level curriculum was supported by veteran researchers from the Normal University, and their aid secured the completion of Jenifer's action research.

To conclude, this chapter diachronically depicts the trajectory of Jenifer's professional identity development through her personal biography, professional training, classroom instructions, and participant of classroom-base action research and her experiments in development new curriculum for her students. In addition, the data shows that multiple contextual factors, such as the school environment, the interaction with colleagues, and the students' motivation all affect the construction of teachers' professional identity.

Chapter 6 │ The Case of Amy

Based on interview and observation data, this chapter describes the trajectory of Amy's professional identity construction. This chapter consists of 6 major sections. Sections 6.1 and 6.2 trace Amy's biographical profile and describe the school context. Section 6.3 examines Amy's teaching practices before she took the NTTP. Section 6.4 reports her experiences when participating in different professional training modules in the NTTP. Section 6.5 depicts Amy's changed classroom practices after she participated in the NTTP. The chapter ends with reflections on her engagement in the classroom-based teacher research.

6.1　Amy's biography

Amy was introduced to the researcher by the Teaching and Research Coordinator (*jiao yan yuan*) ［教研员］ when the researcher was in the fieldwork observing a workshop on teachers' professional development. Amy was relatively young who had just celebrated her 30th birthday when interviewed. Although Amy is plain-looking and a little bit on the heavy side, people would be impressed much by her melodious voice and native-like accent. Amy had a reputation for her good teaching style among the internship members in the NTTP, and because of her strong sense of responsibility and notable achievements in her career, she was appointed as the head of the TRG of English subject in her school.

Like other junior language learners, Amy's interest in English language was aroused by English pop songs when she entered her secondary school, Amy had that:

I was fascinated about English songs when I was in middle school, and this became a hobby after my father bought me a Walkman [随身听] (portable cassette player manufactured by Sony company). When I was alone after school, I would put the tape into the cassette player and sang along with the singer. English Pop music in early 1990s was pure and melodious and the styles were not as diverse as the music today. Despite the enjoyment that brought by the songs, I found many other important functions that music could play in learning language. For secondary school students, music and songs can enhance their language acquisition directly from at least three perspectives—listening, vocabulary and pronunciation. I've been amazed by the delightful and artistic lines in the lyrics. When it comes to English songs, I would take notes of beautiful words, then look them up in the dictionary, and finally use them in my writing samples to show my students how the word could be used in their writing of sentences or passages. Singing English songs also benefits pronunciation. For example, there are many liaisons in the songs, and I would practice those sound connections even hundreds of times until the liaisons could be pronounced fluently without any stutters. I treat such practices as kind of phonetic exercises and this benefit me a lot in my classroom teaching. My students would often compliment me about my pronunciation as "native like". Now, if time permits in class, I would play and teach English songs for my students, demonstrating the rhythm, sound connection and stress in detail.

(Interview, P2-1, 2016)

It can be inferred that teachers' hobbies would have a significant impact not only on their personal lives but also on their teaching practice. Being aware of her talent in singing English songs, Amy has developed her personal hobby into a strategy in the foreign language acquisition. It is undeniable that Amy has managed to pursue her diverse interests in parallel with her fast-moving teaching career, acting as a role model for the students in learning phonetic knowledge of English language.

Life experiences in the past, especially which were gained in language learning period, would shape and influence the emerging identity as a language teacher at present. This is no exception for identity formation of Amy as a language teacher:

My interest in learning English language grew stronger because of two native speakers in high school and college respectively. The first foreign teacher in high school was an old lady. She was from the U.S. and serviced as a volunteer for a local NGO. Foreigners were rarely seen in the remote border towns like the place where I lived, and students were extremely curious about her but too shy to say hello or start a talk. Because of my better pronunciation, I was so lucky that I had been selected as the student coordinator to assist my English teacher to arrange the daily activities for the foreign teacher. Therefore, I occasionally had the chance to speak to the native speaker in person. During her short stay in my middle school, I talked a lot with the old lady who was very kind, patient and friendly to the kids around. Her class was also interesting and full of laughter, much different from that of Chinese teachers, and I still remember how she taught words of animals with vivid gestures and hand-made paper cards. You can not imagine how greatly that short encounter with a foreign teacher could ignite my passion for English. After that, I worked very hard to learn the English subject and finally chose to become an English teacher.

(Interview, P2-2, 2016)

In addition to those "significant others" who strongly influenced Amy's learning process and the choice of career, professional learning experience was indispensible to her development of professional identity as a language teacher. Life in college made significant contribution to Amy's construction of professional identity:

Life in the teachers' college was very busy. In all the four years, despite attending numerous courses, lectures and seminars, I had been immersed in all kinds of school activities. I believed that it was the way I prepared myself for future career development. For one thing, I attended General Linguistics courses like phonetics, syntax to pragmatics, which helped me to lay a solid foundation for the subject matter knowledge; and other courses like English and American Literature, Cross-Cultural Communication, which broadened my horizon about Western culture. There were other courses such as Child Psychology, Curriculum Theory and Pedagogy. These courses were vitally important for me as a student teacher and had lasting effects on my classroom teaching at present. As the years went by, I was increasingly aware that such sound and broad-ranging knowledge base contributed significantly to developing my confidence as a teacher. For another, I caught every possible chance to put myself into various student activities like English speaking contest or teaching skill contest, different levels of contest activities held by both the college or student union. I gained both confidence and experience through participating in these student activities. I have actively prepared myself for future teaching work.

(Interview, P2-3, 2016)

Amy was an earnest learner in accumulating the subject matter knowledge which would be essential for becoming a language teacher. Upon engaging in the public activities, she built confidence and gained extensive work experience. In spite of the fact that smart learning strategies assisted her in achieving academic performance, Amy also shared her mature teaching advice for the teacher preparation program in the college:

I extend my thanks to the college where I had been forged as a language teacher. However, based on the teaching experience I have gained in these years, I would like to make some suggestions for the language teacher preparation programs in the teachers' college, that more classroom-based "hands-on training" should be integrated into their preparation program or practicum. Whatever courses we took in college, they would finally turn out to be too weak to support us as student teachers in managing the complex classroom realities which were remarkably different from their short practicum.

(Interview, P2-4, 2016)

Amy's advice for the teacher preparation programs in normal education echoes research results in literature that efforts should not only be put to train students to consolidate their basic knowledge, strength is also valued to integrate the pedagogical theories and principles codified in textbooks into real-time and hands-on classroom practice during the practicum period.

The sheer emphasis in this section is on Amy's personal life experience as well as her early language learning experience. Semi-structured interview was applied as a major instrument for data mining, from which the features of Amy's teacher identity construction emerged. As a language learner, Amy was active in integrating her past learning experience (singing English songs) and language learning skills (vocabulary and pronunciation) into her classroom teaching; Amy was also active in building her knowledge base. What's more, during her school life, she learned the subject matter knowledge attentively. These agentive qualities and reflective practices were vital parameters to form her burgeoning identity as a language teacher.

6.2   The teaching context

Language teachers have developed their professional identity through both early language learning experiences and teacher preparation programs. In addition, teachers' identity has also been shaped and reshaped by a variety of contextual factors, as Beauchamp and Thomas (2009) identify the contextual influences on identity as the school environment, characteristics of the learners, school authorities, and other teachers (p.184). In this vein, section 6.2 explores some key contextual factors that have been influencing Amy's construction of her professional identity from three perspectives, namely the school, the students and the school-based professional development before the start of the NTTP.

6.2.1   The school

Unlike the secondary school where Jenifer teaches, which used to be supervised by the educational department affiliated to the local state-owned farm, Green Leaf Middle School (pseudonym) where Amy teaches, founded as a public school, has provided secondary school education for the local town since 1976. Through the joint efforts of teachers from generation to generation, it has developed into the fifth largest among the 12 secondary schools in Jinghong city. Being located in the north, 78 km away from the Municipality of Xishuangbanna Autonomous Prefecture, it boggles your mind to imagine the school infrastructure and local teachers' work ethics compared with that of the urban schools in the core multiethnic community regions. Roaming the small rural community where the school is located, one may not expect to see too many Buddhist

Photo 6.1　Green Leaf Middle School

temples or architectures in ethnic style. A huge statue of Confucius standing at the entrance of the campus strongly indicates the influence of Confucian educational philosophy, which makes the school more like any ordinary schools in hinterland except the greener and fresher coffee bushes on hills near and far, signaling the typical geographical features.

Most of the teachers are not local, who graduated from a teachers' college in Pu Er, another large city about 40 km far from the town. In Green Leaf Middle School, 80% of the teachers hold the BA degree and have received comparatively complete and systematic normal education. It is known to all that the higher quality of teachers, the better academic performance of students. Document data collected from fieldwork shows a good example of the student performance in the final graduation test (dated on July 3rd, 2017). 461 students from Grade 9 averaged 55.53 out of 100 as the full mark in English subject, ranking No.5 among 12 schools in Jinghong city (Document, P2-1, 2017).

6.2.2　The students

From the sociocultural perspective, Reeves (2009) contends that teachers' identity is constructed in relation to others, including other teachers and students. The students in Green Leaf Middle School have two prominent features. Initially, the students in this school are less demographically and linguistically diversified than those from schools in the central multiethnic area. The majority of the students are Han people whose communicative language is Standard Chinese and they are less influenced by multiethnic culture. Secondly, with sufficient family educational investment, the students possess comparatively higher motivation in learning school subjects.

The demographical features of the students of Green Leaf Middle School differ from those in other boarder regions. Located in the north part of Xishuangbanna, the school is far away from the core area where multiethnic groups dwell in. In the classroom, most students are Han people and the rest are from ethnic communities such as Dai, Yao, Yi or Blang. Because of the rapid development of construction industry and coffee plantations, a large number of rural farmers left their native place and migrated to cities where jobs were available. Having worked for several years, many of them decide to stay and begin to start life in the towns and cities. Hence the children from migrant worker families and from local rural farming families constitute the major student body.

Since the early 1980s, advent of migrant population not only has enforced the local socioeconomic development but also greatly influenced the culture, which, in turn, strengthened and transformed local people's belief about parental investment (Norton, 2013) and involvement in educating their younger generation. The migrant workers whose education opportunity was once deprived by poverty and ignorance at an early age, now firmly believe that decent school education is vital to the development of their children in their future career. Therefore, they have great expectation for their children to receive complete and good quality schooling. Positive and corporative parental involvement and investment were evidenced during the fieldwork. Despite the differences in family backgrounds, in the researcher's visit to five students and their families, all the parents demonstrated their enthusiastic support for education. Here is the quotation from a mother of twin sons, who was working on a coffee farm:

> *I suffered and was frustrated a lot for not having enough schooling in my childhood. Now, as a mother of my twin sons, I worked very hard in this coffee farm to support them to study in school. I would offer any possible help for my sons to learn well, and I do expect them to go to university [...]*

(Field notes, P2-1, 2016)

Being motivated by parental encouragement and expectation, students in Green Leaf Middle School generally display positive attitudes and strive for inclusive excellence in classroom activities. Students' desire and curiosity for knowledge are evidenced in my classroom observation and group interview conducted in Green Leaf Middle School. It is extremely impressive to notice the students' strong motivation in learning different subjects, especially in learning English language by actively engaging in various creative classroom activities. Compared with Jenifer's case study, in which Jenifer has long been frustrated by the low student motivation, Reeves's (2009) argument is particularly true in Amy's case, which means Amy is aware of the importance of forming her professional identity through the teacher-student interaction pattern. This model will be discussed in later sections with its focus on analyzing Amy's classroom activities.

6.2.3 The school-based professional development

As stated in Chapter 5, for language teachers working in rural schools with scarcity of educational resources, the most practical channel available for teachers' professional development is the school-based peer mentoring activities. The TRG provides such a milieu where teachers can develop their professionalism as well as constructing new teachers' identity through peer coaching or collaboration. Although there were many other experienced teachers in her TRG, Amy was elected as the head of the teaching and research group for English teachers because of her devotion to job. Amy commented her colleagues as below:

> *I consider my TRG as a family, —young teachers learn from the experienced teachers, and old teachers are quite willing to share reflections on teaching with novices. When it comes to the prepatation for the tests or young teachers' preparation for the teaching skill contest, all teachers are cooperative and would contribute their efforts. Working in such a harmonious environment, everyone here in our group can learn and grow.* (Interview, P2-5, 2016)

Although working in a supportive community of English teachers, Amy had her own concerns for professional development:

> *Honestly speaking, before the NTTP, there was not any systematic professional development for our language teachers in the rural secondary school, despite learning from other experienced teachers in the TRG, and the resources for teachers' professional development were scarce. I remembered that when I started teaching, all new teachers were required to attend the online courses, a series of distant education programs organized by the city education*

bureau. We had higher expectation for that online training because it was a novel way that we never tried before. However, the online training turned out to be a general instruction for teachers from all subjects, and just about some basic teaching skills and work ethics. I felt disappointed about the online courses that the content was rather dull, and without any off-line practices or activities. The so called distant professional training was not very effective, and teachers finally changed to learn from experienced teachers and tried their own pedagogies through classroom practices.   (Interview, P2-6, 2016)

As Amy stated, before the NTTP, due to the lack of educational resources in rural schools, the opportunity for professional development was very limited. However, problems and challenges continuously arose from the classroom, calling for teachers' professional methods to tackle the dilemma. It is virtually inevitable that professional development may take arrays of forms, but the best available evidence indicates that effective practice in professional development for teachers depends on both their self-driven innovation and their independent thinking.

Based on her own classroom observation and reflection, Amy summarized three assessments that teachers should refer to:

For the teachers who are approaching retirement, they are satisfied with the current state and reluctant for any change or reform; for those who are experienced in teaching, they are so content that they think any additional training would be unnecessary. And, for those novice teachers, whose active practice is essential, they should learn to be aware of and prepare themselves for a long term career development.   (Interview, P2-7, 2016)

Amy's personal and professional experiences suggest that language teachers' identity is multifaceted and constructed with complicity which is affected by myriads of factors related to language learning history, experiences in teacher education program, school environment and performance of the students. In Amy's case, teachers' agency should be noted as a distinctive feature in the development of professional identity. As mentioned in the previous sections, Amy was capable of integrating her language learning habits into her classroom teaching practices, whose agentive quality was also manifested in her reflections on her early teaching experience. As she stressed, in the less resourced school environment, novice teachers should use their agency to seek opportunities for self-development.

It is not enough to observe the development of teachers' professional identity only from personal biography or school environment. In the next section and following the format of data displayed in the previous chapter, Amy's professional identity construction will be probed into through the presentation of classroom practices. Hence, a full picture of language teachers' professional identity-in-practice is profiled.

6.3 Amy's classroom practices before attending the NTTP

"Language should be learned in a real context." (Amy, Interview, P2-9)

Because of the geographical remoteness, schools in the underdeveloped regions in hinterland or boarder areas in the southwest of China have long been short of financial and intellectual support. For the teachers who just started their teaching career, pedagogical expertise acquired from practicum or experience shared by veteran teachers are two common resources that shape their classroom practice. Since teachers' professional identity is constructed through an ongoing and longitudinal process, it is necessary for researchers to observe what teachers' original teaching perceptions and actual practice are like. In this section, stimulated recall interview data and classroom video collected during the fieldwork from September to December, 2016 are used to represent Amy's classroom practice and her pedagogical perceptions before she attended the NTTP. Through detailed description and analysis of Amy's teaching plan, classroom activities, the teacher's and students' roles in the classroom, Amy's professional identity as novice language teacher can be well illustrated.

6.3.1 The lesson plan

Lesson plans are teachers' understanding of materials, pedagogical strategies and implementation of beliefs and enactment of teaching philosophy. Brown (2007) argues that the lesson plan should generally consist of six components, namely goal (an overall guideline that provides a pedagogical context); objective (an explicit roadmap that directs students at what is about to gain from the lesson); materials and equipment (handouts, posters, textbooks, student workbooks or devices like tape recorders, overhead projectors); procedures (a set of activities and techniques); assessment (use quiz or formal test to determine whether the objectives have been achieved); extra-class work (application or extension of classroom activities for students to do beyond the class hour) (p.167).

It is hard for the novice teacher to design the lesson plan or to implement the curriculum. Many new teachers in Chinese schools usually follow the traditional teaching style in which they would first observe a class or borrow lecture notes from experienced teachers and then after a period of first-hand experience full of ups and downs, they would gradually hammer-harden and accumulate their own teaching style, and achieve the teaching purpose by making full use of the practical knowledge. Document data of Amy's lesson plan presented below is the result of the practice integrating from the direction of education bureau, predecessors' experience and her own practical knowledge. See Table 6.1:

Table 6.1   Amy's lesson plan to teach
a listening and speaking class (Document, P2-2, 2016)

Unit 6 Topic 3 Section A *Which is the way to the hospital?*
1. Teaching Objective
1) Ss will be able to use some key words in a real conversation: alone, turn, crossing, meter, across; 2) Ss will be able to use the proposition words or proposition phrases to express location; 3) Ss will be able to apply the proposition words and phrases appropriately in a real conversation; 4) Ss will learn and use communicative skills in a real situation; 5) Establish awareness of helping others through role plays in the classroom activities.
2. Approach, Method and Techniques
Approach: Guided by interactive language teaching approach, teacher helps Ss learn words and expressions to tell directions. The teacher motivates Ss to learn in an active atmosphere through different activities. Method: Creating situations and contexts for Ss to practice dialogues or making conversations as if in a real-life condition. Techniques: Help Ss to learn and consolidate language points and skills through role play, individual/ group presentation or quiz.

continued

<table>
<tr><td colspan="3" align="center">Unit 6 Topic 3 Section A
Which is the way to the hospital?</td></tr>
<tr><td colspan="3">3. Procedure</td></tr>
<tr><td align="center">Steps</td><td align="center">Teacher's instructions</td><td align="center">Students' activities</td></tr>
<tr>
<td>Step 1
(Input)
Learning new words
and expressions(10')</td>
<td>1) Greetings.
2) Present new words and expressions about showing direction:
Go along…/ go up
Turn right/ turn left
Turn… at the…crossing
3) Ask Ss from different groups to act according to the teacher's order.</td>
<td>1) Greetings.
2) Ss learn different expressions about direction.
Ss give timely response to the teacher's instruction and orders to act and practice the expressions about showing direction.</td>
</tr>
<tr>
<td>Step 2
(Input)
Listening and
Speaking (15')</td>
<td>1) Play the recording three times.
2) Ask Ss to close their books and then listen to 1a and match the pictures with the correct sentences in 1b by looking PPT;
Open the books, read 1a and check the answers.
3) Listen to the recording, read after the speaker. Pay attention to the pronunciation and intonations.</td>
<td>1) Listen to the recording and take notes of the key words in the conversation.
2) Follow the teacher and learn the new words.
Repeat the actions.
3) Listen to 1a and match the pictures with the correct sentences in 1b.</td>
</tr>
<tr>
<td>Step 3
(Input)
Revision (15')</td>
<td>1) Analysis the conversations in 1a.
2) Ask Ss to summarize how many ways they can use to ask the direction.
3) Write Ss' answers on the blackboard.</td>
<td>1) Translate and take notes of language points.
2) Read the conversation and find out how to ask a way in three ways.</td>
</tr>
</table>

continued

Unit 6 Topic 3 Section A *Which is the way to the hospital?*		
3. Procedure		
Step 4 (Output) Group work (15')	1) Pair works. Four Ss in a group, practice the conversation in 1a. 2) Ask some groups of Ss to practice. 3) Provide Ss a map, and start from anywhere on the map; Make up new conversations with Ss; Show Ss how to walk to the destination.	1) Practice the conversation of 1a and then make a performance. 2) According to the map, make up a new conversation with partners. Then show it to the whole class.
Step 5 Consolidation (4')	Guide Ss to listen to the conversation (find the way to Jane's home).	Look at the English map in 2b and listen to the conversation and find the way to Jane's home.
Step 6 Summary (2')	1) Review the new words 2) Review the sentence pattern	
4. Homework		
1) Make up a new conversation about 2b. 2) Finish the exercise in exercise book.		

As shown in Table 6.1, Amy designed her listening lesson plan in a detailed and specific way. She planned to deliver the lesson in six steps. The plan represented her understanding of language teaching and her actual implementation of her beliefs. Amy recalled how she made the plan in the interview:

> *I had some very difficult times in my beginning years of teaching. The classroom in rural secondary school was remarkably different from the class in which I practiced my practicum. I learned how to teach as a baby learns to walk. In terms of lesson planning, the official lesson plan would be helpful for the beginning teachers that you didn't have to worry about the format or procedures to deliver the class. Time and efforts could be spent on designing student activities.*
>
> (Interview, P2-8, 2016)

As mentioned in Jenifer's case, all the English teachers are advised to use the same format of teaching plan to deliver the class. Novice teachers would benefit from the unified format of lesson plan, which is based on interactive language teaching approach, because it would assist them to adapt to the real classroom teaching as soon as possible. Although the unified format is required, teachers still have much flexibility for classroom teaching. Amy continued in the interview:

> *The official format may guide new teachers to deliver the lessons in the initial preparation stage, while you have to design many other activities by yourself. When it came to the design of classroom activities, the voice of my teachers in college was always on my mind. I learned many interactive teaching skills, therefore I copied what I had learned in college to my current classroom.*
>
> (Interview, P2-9, 2016)

It can be indicated from the interview that the construction process of the professional identity of novice teachers is strongly influenced by their past learning experience, which proves to be true in Amy's lesson plan for a listening and speaking class.

Being guided by the official format of lesson plan, Amy's listening and speaking class was divided into six steps which basically followed the interactive language teaching approach. The language knowledge was instructed through interactive activities such as role play, games, group activities. Teachers' understandings and beliefs in language teaching and learning will be embedded into their instructive practices in the classroom, and behind the pedagogical activities is their professional identity. Amy explained why she used many interactive activities in her lesson plan:

> *I regard language as a kind of tool which can be used in different situations and do with different objects. The most efficient way to use the tool is to learn it in a real context. Because in China, English is a foreign language and there's no environment for students, also for teachers to practice and improve their language skills. The classroom is the sole place where they can speak and think in English. In addition, because most of my students hadn't learned English before going to secondary school, it would be very natural for*

them to feel the pressure or being intimidated in the English class. Therefore, I think interactive games or other classroom activities would first reduce their anxiety and get the students engaged in the learning process. My students are very happy to learn in a relaxing atmosphere and by "operating the tool". Maybe this is why interactive approach would be a popular way to maintain learning motivation and encourage them to learn the subject.

(Interview, P2-10, 2016)

Amy explicitly inferred her belief on language learning in the interview as a kind of tool which could be best learned through the "operational activities". In the next section, one of her listening classes in which Amy's identity-in-practice will be illustrated in detail.

6.3.2   The classroom activities

In the previous sub-section, the researcher presented Amy's lesson plan and her interpretation for adopting the interactive approach as the theoretical guidance in planning her instructional practice. In this sub-section, the researcher will illustrate Amy's interactive classroom activities by describing a classroom video in which a listening and speaking class was taught.

Classroom activity is explained by Zheng (2005) as a kind of tasks and practice employed in the classroom through the organized and directed interactions of teachers, students and materials (p.79). The classroom activity is the instructional strategy used by teachers to implement their teaching philosophy and identity in the language teaching process. Activities can be delivered in various patterns and styles as projects, contents, interactive contents or tasks. Amy's classroom activities are listed in Table 6.2 before they are depicted and analyzed, following the same format of data displayed in Chapter 5. Episodes in the video footage are selected for analysis in detail.

Table 6.2   Amy's instructional activities in teaching a listening and speaking class

Types of activities	Contents of activities	Focus of activities
Learn new words and expressions.	Learn the words and phrases like "go along, turn right/ left".	Vocabulary Pronunciation

continued

Types of activities	Contents of activities	Focus of activities
Practice the words/phrases in telling directions.	Ss act the teacher's instruction.	Understand the meaning of words/phrases and Ss can act the teacher's instruction.
Listen to the recording and do the match exercise.	Fill in the blanks and match the content in recording to the illustration in the book.	Listening skills
Review and prepare for the pair work.	Ss review the expressions learned in previous stages.	Revision
Pair work.	Ss work in pairs to act the expressions in telling directions.	Speaking skills

Since the objective of this listening and speaking class is to help students to learn how to give directions, Amy took advantage of multi-media teaching method so as to make it easier for students to have access to academic materials. The electronic teaching plan and electronic courseware are characterized with audio and video presentation in teaching vocabulary and useful expressions, rich in content and varied in style. The learning process and class participation and interaction seem to improve classroom instruction efficiency extensively. During the break, Amy divided the students into eight groups with six members in each group. Moreover, in order to help students to do the group role play and pair work, Amy pinned some big colored paper cards on the floor, representing the location of the "first crossing", "the bridge", "the hospital" or other landmarks. Next, some of the key episodes are selected, described and discussed.

Episode 1

Amy started her class in a traditional way by projecting the phrases and key words about directions on the screen. She firstly explained the Chinese meaning of each word and phrase, then she taught the students how to pronounce them. After that, a girl and then a boy student were invited to the front to play as Amy instructed, "OK now, Zhang Xin, please go along the Xinhua Street and turn left!" The student did as what Amy ordered, walking along the aisle between desks. The boy student repeated the same action. When the two students demonstrated "turn left" and "turn right" to the class, Amy stressed the two phrases again by asking students to read out loud three times.

Episode 2

After the two students demonstrated action phrases like "go along", "turn left" and "turn right", Amy added more words into the expression to give directions. She added the new words "crossing" and combined it with different action phrases like "turn left" or "turn right" to make a full sentence. After she explained and pronounced these words and phrases several times, she continued to ask her students to perform her orders. This time a boy student volunteered to act it out, and he was invited to the front. Standing behind the boy, Amy gave orders: " Zhang Zhuo, please go along the Xinhua Street, and turn left at the second crossing…" The boy student went along the aisle as if he were going along the street and turned to the right direction as the teacher asked. Another three students were asked to repeat the same action.

Amy continued to encourage students to make longer and more complicated sentences by adding more words and phrases to express directions. She added more related words like "bridge", "restaurant", "post office", for example, a sentence like "Go along the No.6 street about 100 meters and turn left at the first crossing, then turn right in front of the restaurant, the post office is on your left. You can't miss it."

Episode 3

Amy highlighted the words and expressions on the blackboard while the students were demonstrating the direction. Then Amy's class moved to the next stage: listening skills. To begin with, she described three pictures in the textbook in English for the students. The pictures were three roadmap photos signaling directions for the tourists in the park, and the students were asked to listen to the recording and then match the pictures with corresponding recordings. Amy played each recording three times and after the class finished the gap filling and match exercise, Amy played the recording one more time. In order to expand and strengthen the language points, she wrote some key sentences in the conversation and asked the class to make new sentences based on the given models.

Episode 4

The students were given five minutes to review the key phrases and sentences used in the recording, and next they were required to act out those expression with their group members, in pairs to be specific. During the preparation, the class became noisy when every group practiced the sentences out aloud. Amy walked around the class monitoring and tutoring her students when they needed help. "Ok, now, time is up, so let's begin the group work. Just now we learned may words, phrases and expressions to tell the direction. Now it's the time to see if you can use them. We learn the language and we use it in real life. This is *xue yi zhi yong*! (learning for practice)［学以致用］. OK, the first group, please!"

Two boy students of the first pair went to the class podium and demonstrated their prepared conversations. One of the boys, maybe out of nervousness, forgot his words at the very beginning of their demonstration, hiding his mouth with his hand and laughed a lot, and the whole class was amused by his funny expression. Amy stopped him with smile and helped him to work out the sentence: "Excuse me, would you please tell me how can get to the park?" Having overcome many difficulties, the first pair of boy students finished their show and returned to their seats. Though their performance was full of mistakes and wrong pronunciations, other students applauded warmly to extend their encouragement. More groups went on the podium and practiced the expressions that would be frequently used in giving directions.

Back to the lesson plan, Amy intended to complete the listening and speaking class by six steps, in which various contents, tasks and activities were planned to be carried out. The video recording data shows that the class has been almost delivered in line with the lesson plan despite some minor discrepancies in the steps and actual activities. The classroom video data proves that the pedagogy that Amy applied in this listening and speaking class is not interactive approach, but is congruent to language teaching model posited by Byrne in the late 1970s. Byrne (1976) suggests a "Presentation—Practice—Production" model for the delivery of knowledge in the classroom. At the presentation stage, Amy instructed the vocabulary, drills and expressions to the students before moving to the listening section. The class entered into the practice stage immediately when Amy finished teaching the meaning and pronunciation of new expressions. Individual students were invited to act the expressions, so that the students were tested if they had learned the knowledge. The class went into the presentation stage again during which Amy taught the listening skills. The second presentation stage was carried out in a traditional way, Amy played the recording three times and students were asked to do the exercises in the book. Thanks to the adequate preparation made in the previous stage, students did the exercises quickly and with accuracy. As argued by Byrne, no real learning should be assumed to have taken place until the students are able to use the language for themselves (p.9). At the last production stage, Amy assisted the students to work in pairs and use the expressions that were firstly instructed by Amy and then reinforced by the demonstrations from listening to recordings. Following the Presentation—Practice—Production Model and by implementing different classroom activities, Amy completed her instruction of listening skills.

6.3.3   The teacher's and students' roles

In the previous section, the researcher carefully presented Amy's classroom practices through description of teacher-student interactions in a listening and speaking class. Although Amy intended to design the class in an interactive way, her class was actually carried out in a "Presentation—Practice—Production" way. The classroom video data also reveals that Amy has played specific roles at different stages of the teaching process, and in this section, her roles in teaching this listening and speaking class are elaborated.

At the presentation stage, Amy played the roles as a resource provider and informant. Amy rearranged the sequence of instruction according to her own understanding of language learning. She began her teaching from the instruction of vocabulary because she thought that it would be as clear and memorable as possible for her students to learn the new content. At this time, the teacher was an informant and resource provider and students played rather passive roles as processors and knowledge receptors.

During the practice stage, the teacher played roles as a controller, conductor and a monitor. When Amy completed the instruction of expressions about telling directions, she tried to devise and provide the maximum amount of practice for students to internalize the knowledge. In line with her arrangement, students worked firstly on their own and then in groups to practice the expressions of giving directions. At this time, the teacher played a role like a skillful conductor of an orchestra, giving each of the performers a chance to participate and monitoring their performance.

In a language classroom, the production of knowledge is of paramount importance, because learners have finally been able to produce conversations from their internalized knowledge. At the last stage of instruction, Amy was a manager, controller and also a facilitator. When different student groups went to the podium to perform their prepared conversations, Amy managed the time and arranged the sequence in order to guarantee the opportunity could be delivered to each group. When students made mistakes or were in need of help to express ideas in an appropriate way, Amy provided timely help to assist students to make a complete conversation. Different roles played by Amy and her students are summarized in Table 6.3:

Table 6.3   Summary of the teacher's and students' roles
in teaching and learning listening skills

Classroom activity	Pedagogy	Teacher's roles	Students' roles
Instruction of vocabulary and expression	Grammar-translation	· Resource provider · Informant · Organizer · Controller	· Knowledge receptors · Processors
Student practice of giving directions	Interactive approach	· Controller · Assistant	· Participants · Performers
Instruction of listening skills	Grammar-translation	· Resource provider · Informant · Organizer · Controller	· Knowledge receptors · Processors
Student group work	Interactive approach	· Manager · Controller · Facilitator	· Participants · Performers

In this section, Amy's lesson plan, classroom activities and corresponding roles played by the the teacher and students during the specific classroom interaction are presented. In this process, the picture of Amy's professional identity as a language teacher at her initial stage of teacher career has emerged from multiple perspectives. To conclude, for one thing, Amy's personal experiences like her language learning habit, education background and co-workers all have influenced her identity formation as a novice language teacher. For another, compared with personal experiences, her professional experiences including the work place environment, the peer coaching within the TRG and the demographical reality of her students are key factors that have influenced Amy's professional identity as a novice teacher.

Another distinctive feature has emerged from the data that Amy processes higher agentive quality in professional development. Such a quality could be identified in her early language learning years in the middle school where she could integrate personal talent of singing English songs with the subject knowledge on linguistics, and then her personal experiences in language learning with her classroom instructions on subject matter knowledge. Her agentive quality could also be identified when she started the teaching career as a language teacher in a rural middle school with high expectation but soon found that the school-based professional training was out of the question. She made use of all possible resources to learn from veteran teachers and other resources to expand her expertise and pedagogical competences.

Since the language teachers' identity is an ongoing process, when the National Teacher Training Plan has been launched, a new and significant opportunity has been provided for Amy to develop her professional expertise, and to develop new teachers' identity as well. In the next chapter, the researcher will present with sufficient interview data to illustrate Amy's identity construction process through the NTTP.

6.4   "The training does benefit my teaching" —Amy's experiences in attending the NTTP

When the NTTP was launched in the education sector of Jinghong city in 2015, Amy was selected as the backbone teacher (or model teacher) (*gu gan jiao shi*) [骨干教师] because of her notable achievements and dedicated attitude in teaching. Having participated in all the three modules in the NTTP through which Amy not only improved her pedagogical competences but also constructed new professional identity. In this section, the researcher will describe how her professional identity is enhanced, reshaped and transformed in this critical stage of her professional development.

6.4.1　The Trainer-Training Module

As aforementioned in Chapter 2, the Trainer-Training Module is one of the most effective ways to train the rural school teachers by using the resources in teachers' colleges and universities (normal universities). According to the top-down design of the nationwide teacher training program, the Trainer-Training Module in university usually lasts for 20 days, and the training contents generally fall into two categories, —courses for general education and courses for specific subjects. The courses on general education provide trainees with practical knowledge on curriculum design, classroom management and classroom-based research. The courses for specific subjects, such as math, Chinese and other major disciplines are tailored for the need of that subject. Taking English courses for example, teachers are trained to deepen their understanding of the subject matter knowledge, update existing pedagogy or observe teachers' classroom practice in the unban schools.

Together with Jenifer, Amy participated in the "Trainer's Training" which was organized in Yunnan Normal University in the autumn semester in 2015. Recalling her experience and comment for this period of training, Amy gave her general feedback as quoted below:

> *As I mentioned in the previous interview, I didn't received any professional training in my beginning days of teaching. I've been practicing the very traditional pedagogy inherently as what my college teachers did years ago. I've been longing for breathing more fresh air and expand my knowledge about teaching. I'm very grateful for the chance and feel lucky to be selected as a member in the teacher training programs like the NTTP, which offers teachers from rural schools such a good opportunity to see a bigger world.*
>
> (Interview, P2-12, 2016)

Amy regarded her opportunity to participate in the NTTP program as a once-in-a-lifetime chance to improve her professionalism and she reflected on a specific lecture that:

> *There were many lectures I found useful for my classroom teaching. Among the training courses, lectures on interactive group activity and the "Three Stages of Lesson Planning" were impressive. I used to do a lot of activities in my class but just based on my limited understanding about the interactive teaching approach, and based on some skills learned from elder teachers in my school. The lecture thoroughly changed my understanding about what interactive classroom activity was. When I returned to my class, I soon changed my practice and designed new activities. The training was very pragmatic and productive!*
>
> (Interview, P2-13, 2016)

It is a common practice and continuous attempts for the primary or secondary school teachers who work in the northwest or southwest remote areas to receive sustainable professional training. Therefore, it is understandable for Amy to feel fortunate to have the opportunity to improve her teaching competence. As one of the essential modules, the Trainer-Training Module aims to make the best use of the limited resources to broaden teachers' professional knowledge scope, improve their subject matter teaching skills, capability of classroom management and their own English language skills. In this view, it is also an unprecedented opportunity for teachers to construct new professional identity to become a successful and legitimate language teacher.

6.4.2   The Demonstration Module

The Demonstration Module is an innovative training module that constitutes the NTTP. It is not a component in the original plan (designed by the MOE), but a new module developed by the panel of experts supervising the implementation of the NTTP in Yunnan province. The Demonstration Module is a critical component in the NTTP in which the trainee teachers are transformed into teacher trainers. When the chosen core member teachers complete their training sessions in university and return to the secondary schools, they take over the mission to train their peer teachers who are not engaged in the NTTP program by offering demo classes. The "Teacher Trainers" are supposed to share their feedbacks on the training experience, and in addition, to display to other teachers the new teaching skills or pedagogical innovations that they have learned in university.

The Demonstration Module functions as the critical catalysis assisting the process that transforms trainee teachers into competent teacher trainers who can understand, implement and disseminate the curriculum innovations. It is a great challenge for a classroom teacher to become a qualified teacher trainer, for they have to make every endeavor in learning, digesting, experimenting, exercising so as to accomplish a well-planned and organized demo class. Here is the quotation from Amy's reflection on the Demonstration Module:

It is easy to sit in the classroom to learn those linguistic knowledges or to try some new teaching methods, and it is not that hard to experiment these new pedagogies in my own classroom, but it would be challenging enough for me to demonstrate what I have learned to the counterparts in other schools. You would be nervous, sleepless, sweaty and suffer from constant anxiety. Each time when I give the demonstration class, it takes me much time and efforts to prepare, and no matter how hard you have tried, you cannot make perfect.

(Interview, P2-14, 2016)

Upon reflecting her experience in delivering the demo class as required by the NTTP, Amy described it as both a mentoring experience and depressing event. The Demonstration Module is a stringent requirement for both novice and experienced trainee teachers in the NTTP program. However, it also functions like an education incubator in which teachers' subject matter knowledge is enhanced, with teaching beliefs remolded, and professional identity incubated. Amy's statements quoted as follows further prove the above viewpoints:

Although I've been frustrated and suffered a lot in preparing the demonstration, I have to acknowledge that it is also particularly rewarding. Firstly, just as I mentioned before, it's easy for you to learn, but it is hard for you to do. Presenting the demonstration class is actually to internalize the leaned knowledge and exercise them in a real situation. It is just the apprentices in a blacksmith's shop, —you first learn the craftsmanship, and then practice it before the experienced masters. Secondly, even though I have been placed under high pressure, I considered it as positive one, and after many rounds of practice and demonstration, the pressure makes me increasingly confident in classroom teaching.   (Interview, P2-15, 2016)

If the NTTP program might be regarded as a situated professional learning context, in Amy's case, the Demonstration Module is a place where apprentices are forged into experienced craftsmen. Apart from the stressful training job, the teacher trainers (mentors) would have to spend a lengthy time doing the preparation. Nevertheless, they would also benefit from substantial gains that are harvested from the challenging experience. Having completed the Trainer-Training Module, the trainees have been equipped with new subject matter knowledge and teaching skills. And thus, a platform for the implementation of integrated practical activity curriculum should be made for them to exercise their learned knowledge.

Therefore, the Demonstration Module is the right arena where apprentices are tested if they reach the benchmark to be qualified craftsmen. For the teachers who missed the opportunity to participate in the NTTP program or in the university training project, the Demonstration Module is a timely help to observe the new teaching methods and to mull how to contextualize the module in the classroom.

6.4.3   The Distance Education Module

The last two decades have witnessed the application of the Open and Distance Learning (ODL) in the field of language learning and teaching, as well as in the education of language teachers. Thanks to the advantages of the Internet technology, the ODL has been used as an effective means to train large numbers of teachers within a short period of time and in lower cost, so that the substantial gap of educational inequality between rural and urban areas can be bridged beyond the limit of space and time. When the Ministry of Education commenced the NTTP, the OLD was incorporated as one of the essential modules into a wider blueprint of the Distance Education Module.

As introduced in Chapter 2, the ODL module in the NTTP takes two forms, learning via the official distance education website and learning via the teachers' online community. The OLD module is actually a nationwide online learning platform which opens for all participants of the NTTP across China. All secondary school teachers in Jinghong city are required to complete various online learning courses every semester. Teachers get access to their online courses through different entries according to geographical areas and subjects. Moreover, they are also required to complete many other teaching related missions including watching the demonstration classes presented by the expert teachers from other cities, submitting personal reflections on the demo classes, or handing in their revised lesson plan based on their reflections. Despite the official distant education, the teachers' online community is a necessary supplement to the official one. The teachers' online learning group is based on the WeChat discussion group, a popular social network application used on every cell phone. The online discussion group which is organized by the *Jiao Yan Yuan* from the City Education Bureau is much more flexible in time and space. This, in turn, offers an interacting platform for teachers to discuss about any teaching related topics by using photos, animations, document files or even voice and video messages.

As quoted in Chapter 5 of Jenifer's case, teachers' professional identity is constructed in either the face-to-face or electronically mediated mode. Both the ODL and online Wechat discussion group provide a situated learning context for teachers to grow professionally and develop new professional identity as well, especially in the later one. Teachers' experience and comments on the official distance education platform and the WeChat discussion group diverge. Amy gave her opinion on the two forms of learning:

My learning experience on the distance education platform is rather boring, and teachers around me all complain about the Distance Education Module. I regard lack of interaction as the major reason for teachers' annoyance in doing this kind of compulsory task. When I was doing the online tasks, what I had to do is to watch the video, type in my reflections, and then answer the questions. Teachers seem to be treated like machines in learning the online courses and doing the assignments.

However, teachers show quite different faces in the WeChat discussion group. In that online group, we feel free to talk about any topics related to everyday teaching. It is convenient for teachers to discuss grammar knowledge, review teaching plans, share new ideas or tell their life stories. And occasionally some experts from universities were invited to join the online discussion. They first gave lectures by sending voice messages and the audience would ask questions or exchange reflections. Compared with the school-based peer coaching in TRG, the online Wechat discussion group, which is based on mobile phones, does facilitate teachers to learn and share professional knowledge free of the limit of time and space. (Interview, P2-16, 2016)

The Internet based approaches of teacher training provide another context in which teachers can enhance their professional development. Although with some inherent flaws the official Distance Education Module does not seem to be very attractive for teachers to learn online, the cellphone based social network service applications such as Wechat and QQ have became a supplement to the official teacher training approach, and they do help teachers to develop an online community of practice.

In section 5.5, the researcher presented Amy's experiences and reflections on the three major training modules provided by the NTTP. As a core trainee teacher, Amy considered her experience of being immersed in various professional training courses as unforgettable life experience, and her learning through the three major training modules as an educational incubator. The displayed and analyzed data indicates that the Tainer-Training Module has expanded Amy's interactive pedagogical knowledge and her broadened teaching skills have been tested and enhanced in the Demonstration Module. Although her learning experience in the official Distance Education Module was not as effective as that of the other two modules, the online discussion group worked as a more flexible supplement extending teachers' professional growth beyond time and space. The metaphor used by Amy regarding the professional trainings provided by the NTTP is like an available platform for the future professional development. Accordingly, it is also a situated learning context that prepares teachers to construct new professional identity. In the next section, ample data will be further explored to illustrate how Amy applies her internalized experiences into pedagogical practices in the language teaching classroom.

6.5 Amy's classroom practices in the post-NTTP period

"I hold mixed attitude towards the new model." (Amy, Interview, P2-3)

The secondary school English teachers who have done better in improving students' academic performance are selected as "backbone teachers" in the NTTP. With the expectation that after three years of consecutive training, their subject matter knowledge and pedagogical competence would be effectively enhanced. They are also expected to become more aware of their values and beliefs about language learning and teaching. Having gone through the three major training components, the trainee teachers would be prompted to draw comparisons with their past language teaching methods and the new approaches they learned through the NTTP. It is anticipated that they would become more aware of exercising new pedagogical practices and then adapt these pedagogical approaches, methodologies and strategies to their "real world". Their trials in applying the new teaching mode, skills or methods provide an appropriate window to explore their ongoing development of professional identity.

Following the same format of data displayed in Jenifer's case, in section 5.6, the researcher will analyze Amy's changed "identity-in-discourse" and "identity-in-practice" in her post-NTTP period by presenting multiple data about her lesson plan, classroom activities and roles during the teaching process.

6.5.1 The lesson plan

In this sub-section, document data is used to present Amy's improved lesson plan. The new lesson plan could be regarded as an adaptation to the official guidance, in which teachers are required to follow the "Three Stages and Seven Steps" teaching model. The "Three Stages and Seven Steps" teaching model, which has been introduced and discussed in Jenifer's case, can be regarded as either direct intervention or an explicit roadmap guiding or facilitating teachers' pedagogical practice in the classroom. In this sub-section, both the document data and interview data will be presented and discussed in order to probe into teachers' identity.

The lesson plan was designed for a reading skills class which was observed and video recorded during the researcher's fieldwork in Jinghong. It could be identified that Amy's lesson plan shared many features with those of Jenifer's. This was because from the fall semester in 2016, teachers from 13 secondary schools in Jinghong city were trained and required to use the new teaching model. Being guided by the new teaching model and integrating her prior training experience, Amy designed the lesson in a new way of three stages and seven steps. Amy's lesson plan for a reading class is shown in Table 6.4:

Table 6.4　Amy's lesson plan to teach a reading class (Document, P2-3, 2016)

Unit 4—Topic1—Section C		
Teach Reading Skills	Date: Dec 20th, 2016	Grade 7
Teaching Objective: to train Ss to summarize the main idea		
Topic	Amazing Science	
Key Sentences	1. That's why now we have planes. 2. Remember that no idea is too silly.	
Vocabulary	Come about, invention process, laugh at, share with	
Ability Objective	1. Identify the main idea of the passage. 2. Summarize the process of an invention.	
Culture and Emotion Objective	Stimulate Ss to think differently and innovate.	
Teaching Aid: Multimedia Courseware		
Teaching Method: The Communicative Approach		
Teaching Procedures		
Pre-Reading	Step 1	1) Watch the video and answer the questions. Q: What's the video about? (Ss may answer: <u>Invention</u>) Q: What can you see in the video? (Ss may answer: telephone, dust collector, car and so on.) 2) Could you tell me other inventions in your life? (Ss may answer: light bulb, electric fan …) 3) Learn the words: inventions.
While-Reading	Step 2	Task 1: Identify the main idea of the passage by scanning. What's the main idea of this passage? A. What is an invention? B. How to be an inventor? C. The importance of invention. D. How do inventions come about.

continued

Unit 4—Topic1—Section C		
Teaching Procedures		
While-Reading	Step 3	Task 2: Read Para. 1 and answer the question. Q: How do inventions come about? Ss may answer: Most of time, inventions happen because someone works to solve a problem. Sometimes inventions are the results of accidents. Task 3: Read the following paragraphs and put the sentences in the correct places. A. Draw your invention. B. Name your invention. C. Test your invention. D. Use your imagination. E. Plan and design your invention. Task 4: Read the passage again and underline the phrases and language points.

Post-Reading	Step 4	Task 5: Ask Ss to do vocabulary exercises.
		1) How many steps are needed to invent something?
		    A. Five. B. Six. C. Seven. D. Eight.
		2) The word "brainstorm" in the passage probably means_____
		    A. 头脑 B. 集思广益 C. 智力 D. 智囊团
		3) When great inventors were laughed at, they would_____.
		    A. give up B. ask for help C. be discouraged D. keep on trying
		4) —Do you know when the car_____? —In 1885.
		    A. invent B. invented C. is invented D. was invented
		5) Thomas Edison is a great _____(invent).
		6) Many important _____have changed our life. (invent)

Home Work: Reading for writing. If you were an inventor, what do you want to invent for your mother/father/friends …? If I were an inventor, I want to invent_____ because_____		

The document of teaching plan indicates that Amy makes the lesson plan in line with the official direction from the education bureau. Her instruction of reading skills was distinctively modularized into three major stages—pre-reading, while-reading and post-reading with four teaching steps. Moreover, different teaching activities/tasks were arranged for each step with the focus on training specific reading skills. Amy interpreted her intention for her teaching plan below:

I used to teach the reading class by following the interactive approach, but I changed a lot from my past practice. The current teaching plan is an integration of the knowledge I learned from the NTTP and the requirement demanded by the education bureau.

Although the interactive approach works well in my class, it is effective to foster listening and speaking skills. For a very long time, I had been wondering how to teach students the reading skills and what approaches and method could be more effective in improving the reading skills. Without clear answers to my question, I spent too much time in training students to enlarge their vocabulary by rote learning. I had tried very hard to train students to improve vocabulary but their performance in reading comprehension tests had been unsatisfying. My inappropriate beliefs and practices in teaching reading skills were transformed by the new integrated approach advocated by the NTTP.

The City Education Bureau has been active in disseminating the fruits of teacher professional development that the NTTP yielded. They went one step further to work with the curriculum experts and designed a "Three stages and Seven Steps" model. I have "mixed" feelings towards to the unified teaching model. For one thing, I believe that the new teaching model is a necessary measure to guarantee teaching quality, because there is a considerable gap in teaching competence between individual teachers; For another, the unified format of teaching plan sometimes limit teachers in their creativity. The rigid "pre-", "while-" and "post-" organization of class confines teachers in a fixed model. In my teaching, I would integrate my own design into the official model.

(Interview, P2-17, 2016)

As discussed in Jenifer's case, secondary school English teachers do not have much flexibility to plan their teaching as teachers in the tertiary level. Their teaching practice is limited to the framework in line with the textbook and regulated by the official directions stipulated by the local education bureau. This rigid system seems to be inattentive and not flexible enough, but particularly pragmatic for the teachers working in the rural and remote regions, who are less trained and inexperienced in pedagogical innovations.

Since the lesson plan manifests teachers' practiced beliefs and understandings on language teaching and learning, the classroom activities are the carriers to implement their practiced beliefs. In the next section, the observation data will be utilized to show

Amy's classroom practice in instruction of reading skills.

6.5.2　The classroom activities

The data displayed in this section is based on the researcher's classroom observation conducted during the fall semester in 2016. Two classes of Amy's reading skill instruction were observed and video recorded. In this section, the researcher will choose to present the more complete one carried out in line with the lesson plan the researcher described in the previous section. The observation data will be displayed through four classroom activity episodes with expectation to reveal Amy's upgraded concept about language teaching as well as her professional identity-in-discourse after the participation in the NTTP.

Episode 1

The class began with Amy's interpretation of the learning objectives including the scanning skill for the main idea of the passage. As designed in the lesson plan, the reading class started with a Q&A activity based on a short video clip about a great scientific invention. Before playing the video, Amy projected on the screen two questions, "What is the video about?" and "What inventions did you see in the video?" In addition, students were asked to take notes as much as possible about the inventions mentioned in the video while watching it. Then the students were required to retell the inventions in English, such as the washing machine, the vacuum cleaner, etc.

After watching the video, Amy asked several students to answer the questions projected on the screen. Students actively answered the questions, but frequently jabbered about the names of inventions. Seeing students getting stuck in vocabulary or pronunciation, Amy would offer timely help.

Episode 2

After video watching and the Q&A section, Amy stressed two key words "invention" and "inventor" mentioned in the video. By doing this, she began to instruct the knowledge of word formation. She explained that the two-noun form of words was derived from the root word, "invent". Then she wrote down three related words "invent" "invention" and "inventor" from left to right on the blackboard in order to show the word formation process more clearly. After that she gave two more examples of word formation process in order to enhance students' memory about it.

Because the rules of word formation were one of the important language points for middle school students, Amy stressed this knowledge by reiterating how the word "invention" was derived from "invent". Amy explained this language point by using examples which were commonly seen and closely related to everyday life of the students. For example, she projected a table with the headline "Inventions in our life" on the top, and then the contents of the table were classified into two categories as "invention" and "inventor". Under the "invention" category are photos like "Instant Noodle", "Pencil" and "Battery", and under the "inventor" category, people of these inventions were listed. The photos and the names of inventors appeared in turns and Amy used the photos of inventions and names of inventors to help students have a more profound understanding of the two words.

Episode 3

Having been stimulated by the aforementioned activities, students were well informed about the vocabulary and definitions of the word "invent" and its variant forms. Then, the class moved into the next section —the so-called "While-Reading" stage. The classroom activities in this section were mainly about text reading skills. Amy firstly introduced the reading skill of scanning and the strategies to do the scanning. Secondly, students were given three minutes to read the first and second sentences of each paragraph to capture the main idea of the passage. When students finished to read the passage according to Amy's direction, two students were picked to share their reading comprehension of the passage. In the third step, Amy asked students to draw a mind map in which the general structure could be illustrated. When students completed drawing the mind map, they were required to discuss with their deskmate to check if they did it in the right way. In the fourth step, students were trained to identify the main idea again by reading the second paragraph. When students were asked to read the longer paragraph expounding on how a great invention came about, again students were asked to use the mind map chart to present the process of invention. Students then were given eight minutes to finish the task before they joined their deskmate for peer assessment. At last, Amy checked and commented on some mind map works of the students.

Episode 4

In this reading class, the technique of scanning for main idea was firstly instructed and then enhanced by another two rounds of "hands-on" reading exercise. In order to assess students' scanning techniques, Amy presented four multiple choice exercises which were closely linked to the passage:

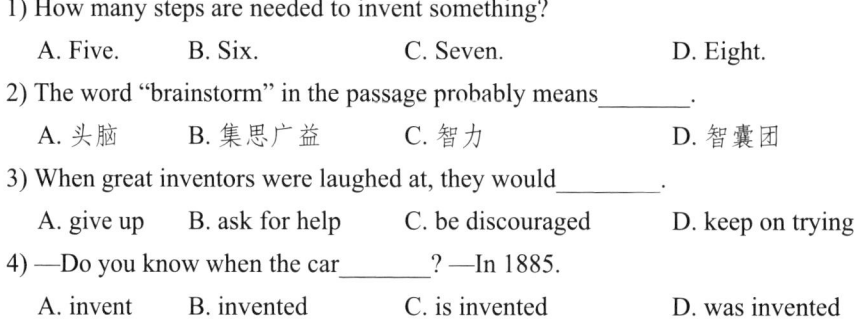

1) How many steps are needed to invent something?

    A. Five.   B. Six.   C. Seven.   D. Eight.

2) The word "brainstorm" in the passage probably means_____.

    A. 头脑   B. 集思广益   C. 智力   D. 智囊团

3) When great inventors were laughed at, they would_____.

    A. give up   B. ask for help   C. be discouraged   D. keep on trying

4) —Do you know when the car_____? —In 1885.

    A. invent   B. invented   C. is invented   D. was invented

The four multiple choice exercises are closely connected with contents of the passage, deliberately designed to assess reading comprehension ability of the students from different perspectives. The first question asked the detailed information, and the second tested the ability of word guessing from the context. The third question was from the original line of the text, aiming to test students' knowledge of phrase and usage of modal verb. The last question intended to test students' grammatical sense of "voice and tense".

Episode 5

Amy spent about 10 minutes explaining every test question carefully and patiently. With this done, she moved to assignment section, the last part of the reading class. Amy presented Doraemon as the after-class assignment, a popular cartoon figure who has the magic of inventing all kinds of playful things for kids. The homework was a writing task with the interlinked theme of the passage. To complete the assignment, students were supposed to write a short paragraph with imagination about inventing something for their families, such as an automatic cooking robot to help mothers prepare food. Despite the invention, students were required to give reasons to further prove why they wanted to create such an invention.

The first-hand observation of teachers' classroom practices provides direct insight into the context in which teachers' beliefs are implemented and professional identity is constructed. In section 6.5.2, Amy' s classroom practice has been illustrated by describing five episodes extracted from the classroom video. The observation data shows that Amy's classroom teaching model is teacher-centered, and for Amy, this is a very "effective and pragmatic way" of teaching. In the next section, the researcher will analyze the teacher's and students' roles in these activities, thus Amy's changed professional identity can be more evident.

6.5.3   The teacher's and students' roles

Comparatively speaking, there is a world of difference between the teacher's classroom roles Amy played before the NTTP and her change in the teacher's roles after the NTTP. Amy used to play various roles in classroom teaching but in her current teaching she intended to play a teacher-centered, monotonous role in her class. From the very beginning of the class to the end, Amy dominated the class as a resource provider, conductor, controller and facilitator. In the first activity of video-watching, Amy prepared the materials beforehand with clear intention. As described in Chapter 5, Jenifer used the students' video to attract students' attention and improve their motivation in learning the language. This technique pattern was copied in Amy's classroom to achieve the same goal. Therefore, in the video-watching activity the teacher played the role as a resource and information provider, and accordingly her students played the roles of audience and knowledge processors. In another two major instructive activities, teaching word formation and scanning skills, Amy used the traditional grammar translation pedagogy and played the roles of a resource and information provider, and an assessor. These roles were particularly clear when the teacher asked the students to complete word formation exercise. Amy's roles in the fourth and fifth activity did not change when she carried out the Q&A and gave assignments. In these two activities, the teacher played the role as the knowledge provider again and the students have been limited to the passive roles solely as knowledge processors. See Table 6.5:

161

Table 6.5   Summary of the teacher's and students' roles in a reading class

Classroom activity	Pedagogy	Teacher's roles	Students' roles
Watch the video clip	Interactive approach	· Resource provider · Informant · Organizer · Controller	· Audience · Knowledge processors
Give instruction of word formation	Grammar-translation	· Controller · Assessor	· Knowledge processors
Give instruction of reading skills	Grammar-translation	· Resource provider · Informant · Organizer · Controller	· Knowledge receptors · Processors
Complete the multiple choice	Grammar-translation	· Manager · Controller · Facilitator	· Participants · Performers
Give assignments	N/G	· Resource provider	· Knowledge processors

Together with the detailed description of Amy's classroom activity, the analysis of teacher's and students' roles makes it easier to better understand Amy's ongoing professional identity development. Compared with her classroom activities and roles before the NTTP, Amy's teaching concept has evolved from more teacher-centered pedagogy to students-centered module in accordance to the official directions.

In this section, the researcher analyzes the different roles played by the teacher and students in Amy's reading class. Based on the observation data, Amy's roles were basically the resource provider and controller and students remained to be knowledge receptors. Although the teacher's and students' roles were not as diverse as the roles in the class before the NTTP, Amy confirmed the effectiveness of the new model. In the next section, the researcher will continue to explore Amy's professional identity as a teacher researcher in terms of Amy's personal motivation, research practices and constraining factors.

6.6   Amy's reflection on doing classroom-based research

"Doing research keeps me in a constant status of learning."

(Amy, Interview, P2-18)

For the secondary school language teachers, active engagement in classroom-based research not only signals their maturing pedagogical competence but also marks the critical shift in their professional identity. In this section, the researcher will use interview data to interpret Amy's perceptions and practices in doing the classroom-based research. In this way, Amy's professional identity-in-practice, her identity as a teacher researcher in specific will be explored.

6.6.1   Amy's motivations for doing research

For many other secondary school language teachers, their motivations for doing teacher research might be keen competition among colleagues for academic promotion. In the case of Amy, however, the reason for her to participate in the classroom-based research is to keep her in a "constant status of learning" (Interview, P2-12, 2016). Amy explained her motivation to be engaged in research projects below:

The reason for me to be engaged in action research is simple. A year ago, one of the senior teachers was doing her classroom-based inquiry and I was asked to help her to do some basic work in collecting materials. I gained some rudimentary experiences from the case conducted by my senior colleague and this aroused my curiosity in doing research, because I saw that the results or findings from the inquiry did help solve some tricky problems in our daily teaching.

The young and inexperienced teachers, like me, can benefit substantially from either process of learning and doing research. More new and innovative ideas would generate when you are engaged in the research project, and the findings, discoveries, in turn, finally could be used to improve your classroom teaching practice. Doing research keeps me in a constant status of learning.

(Interview, P2-18, 2016)

The interview data shows no evidence of research obligation from institutional requirements. Amy was more motivated by her agency to be involved in the research activity. Secondary school language teachers seem to feel physically and mentally exhausted in daily teaching practice, which is why they appear to be reluctant or even rejected to join or contribute their efforts in doing research. However, Amy believed that she benefited much more from doing research and in doing so, and her career life seemed to be different from that of the others: she became more resourceful, responsible and resilient as a lifelong learner and educator.

6.6.2 Doing the classroom-based research

In this section, Amy's interpretation about doing research and the interview data are quoted to present Amy's practical reflections on doing the research. At the time she was interviewed, she was taking part in two research projects. This is what she commented on her experience in detail:

Up to date, I have been engaged in two different research projects. The first project was about vocabulary teaching and the other was how to improve students' learning motivation. My colleagues and I observed that in our daily classroom teaching most of the students learned new words by rote, and they saw learning vocabulary as a plague. In addition, the students performed poorly in reading and writing because of their poor spelling and limited storage of vocabulary. However, some other students did very well in learning vocabulary, as teachers we were curious about this phenomenon. In the TRG meetings, we discussed and tried to find out features of those students who could do well in weekly vocabulary tests, and later we planned to disseminate our findings. Before spreading the findings of good learning habits, an veteran teacher who has experience in doing research projects suggested starting a pilot study by using the questionnaire before our inquiry so that we could discover more reasons or features for the students' learning behavior on vocabulary learning. From then on, a small idea of inquiry grew into a research project. Of course, our endeavors to do the research cannot be compared with those researchers or experts in college or university in terms of quality and depth of inquiry, but the findings are pragmatic for our classroom teaching.

Based on knowledge and practices we learned from last project, from this semester, we initiated another project named "Happy Classroom". This research project intended to improve students' motivations in learning English. We planned to probe what and how teachers can do to create a more relaxing and joyful learning environment for language learning, not from teachers' perspective but from students'.   (Interview, P2-19, 2016)

Amy reported her experience in doing and planning two research projects and it could be noted that she completed the research in collaboration with other teachers and received help from senior colleagues. In fact, for secondary school teachers, it is impossible to conduct research projects on their own. More still, they would certainly encounter myriads of difficulties doing the research projects. In the next section, the researcher will explain personal and contextual factors hindering Amy from doing classroom-based research.

6.6.3   Personal and contextual constraints

Doing classroom-based research is much more challenging for the secondary school language teachers than those from the tertiary level. Amy claimed that her deficiency of research related knowledge base was the major hindrance to doing research:

Because we have not been well trained about any skills on doing research, it would be challenging for us to conduct research projects. For example, in my last project on improvement of vocabulary learning, I intended to use questionnaires to collect data, however, because of the inappropriate design of the questions, the whole project turned out to be invalid. It was a heavy blow to my confidence and enthusiasm for doing research. I conclude some of important factors that constrain teachers from doing research. Firstly, we are badly in need of theoretical guidance on the general principles, methodology, use of different data collection instruments. Secondly, knowledge about data collection and analysis procedure is of critical importance. What often happens to teacher researchers is that once the data has been collected, they would be lost in the messy data and have no idea of data analysis. Thirdly, in this information age, the information and communications technology knowledge is indispensable for doing research. Teacher researchers are sometimes desperate in their search for literature and use of relevant data analysis software. (Interview, P2-20, 2016)

The interview data shows that for Amy, the lack of research capacity is the major barrier that obstructs her research attempts. Amy summarized that direction in theory, data processing and ICT literacy were the major hindrances as well as the cutting-edge knowledge or know-how for secondary school teachers to assist classroom-based research.

In this section, the researcher recounts how Amy constructs her professional identity as a researcher through description of her attitude for doing classroom-based research, her attempts in doing research and some practical constrains in doing research. Amy regarded conducting research as a way that motivated her constantly to learn new knowledge and in turn, her classroom practice benefited from the results of her research projects. When conducting the research projects, Amy discovered that knowledge about the research theory, principles in data processing and use of ICT (Informatin and Communication Technology) tools were indispensable to teachers for accomplishing a research project.

6.7 Discussion and summary

This chapter presents data about the professional identity development of Amy, the second participant in this study. Efforts made in this chapter are to explore how Amy has developed her professional identity through earlier language learning experiences in middle school and college, her novice teaching practice before the NTTP, the experience in participating in the NTTP, her upgraded teaching practice after the NTTP, and her attempts in doing the classroom-based research.

Data collected from Amy's personal biography reveals that she has received complete education from primary school to college and enjoyed much more education resources. Amy began to learn English as a foreign language in her middle school and she became fascinated about singing English songs. Amy kept the hobby and integrated her hobby into classroom teaching. She taught students to sing English songs with expectation to enlarge their vocabulary and to improve their pronunciation skills. In addition, Amy discovered that teaching music and songs in class could arouse students' interest in learning the language. Amy's practice to incorporate personal hobbies and talents with her classroom teaching helped her to gain popularity among students and thus made her more confident in teaching them language knowledge.

The significant others played a critical role for Amy to choose language teaching job as a career. Her interaction in the middle school with the NGO volunteer, who was a native speaker prompted Amy to become an English teacher. Later her college education laid a significant foundation for Amy on the journey of becoming a language teacher. During the teacher preparation program in teachers' college, Amy demonstrated her agentive quality either in learning subject matter knowledge enthusiastically or in participating in many kinds of contests or students' activities, in order to gain experience and confidence in preparation for future teaching career.

It is common for the less-resourced rural secondary schools to sponsor or organize professional development schemes for their faculties. In her early period of teaching career as a novice teacher, Amy did not receive much workplace professional development. Instead, the TRG provided a significant context for Amy's professional growth. The TRG functioned as a community of practice, assisting teachers to construct professional identity from perception to practice. Since for a long time there had not been external training programs, Amy had been applying teaching methods she learned from her teachers in high school and in college. In addition, in this period of time as a novice language teacher, Amy's quality of teachers' agency should be noted as a distinctive feature in the development of professional identity. In an under-resourced institutional environment, Amy didn't wait but to learn and tried different teaching methods actively, and through learning of the instructional matters, such as planning and delivering lessons, managing the classroom and assessing students, Amy prepared herself to be a successful and legitimate language teacher.

For the secondary school language teachers in rural and remote areas, the NTTP training leaves a distinguishing mark in their professional learning and pedagogical practice. Participation in the NTTP helped to enhance Amy's self-efficacy as a frontline pedagogue. Activities in the training courses of the NTTP, such as lectures, coursework, observation of expert teachers' class, demonstration class and the WeChat online discussion group were all instant access for Amy to her subject matter knowledge and pedagogical expertise. The NTTP, as Amy commented, functioned as "a furnace and a launching pad" in her professional development and fundamental shift in her construction of professional identity.

The classroom observation data shows that together with the pedagogical knowledge learned in the NTTP, the new official teaching model has strongly affected Amy's classroom teaching in the post NTTP period. Amy shifted from her past interactive teaching to the "Three Stages and Seven Steps" teaching modle advocated by the education bureau. Amy soon adapted to the localized pedagogy and designed her lesson plan faithfully implementing the new model. The teacher-centered new model also changed the roles that the teacher and students played in the classroom. Amy played basically singular roles as a resource provider, informant, controller and an assessor, while students were more passive as knowledge receptors.

In the last section of this chapter, Amy's attempts in doing classroom-based action research is examined. Amy was firstly inspired by other teachers who conducted classroom-based research and then she began her own inquiry in collaboration with others. In the process of probing problems which emerged from her daily instruction, Amy encountered theoretical and practical problems which she expected to overcome by training in future.

In sum, based on multiple data resources, this chapter traces Amy's professional identity development from personal and professional dimensions. Moreover, the contextual factors affecting Amy's teacher identity construction, such as the school environment and local sociocultural context are also delineated.

Chapter 7 | The Case of Kelvin

Chapter 7 investigates the identity construction processes of Kelvin, the third focal participant of the present study. Participant classroom observation, semi-structured interview, documents and field notes are adopted as research instruments for data collection. As a non-English major graduate, Kelvin "accidentally" entered the profession of language teacher. Kelvin's case provides a special perspective to investigate the discursive and multifaceted nature of language teachers' identity.

Following the same format of data display used in Chapter 5 and Chapter 6, sections 7.1 and 7.2 present Kelvin's biographical profile and his workplace context. Section 7.3 describes Kelvin's pedagogical practice and roles in the classroom before he was engaged in the NTTP. Section 7.4 elaborates on Kelvin's learning experiences and his reflections on the different training modules in the NTTP. Section 7.5 reports his changed teaching practice after the NTTP. Section 7.6 presents Kelvin's reflections on doing classroom-based research.

7.1 Kelvin's biography

Kelvin has been teaching English subject in the border secondary school for eight years when he was interviewed and selected as one of the focal participants of this study. A notable difference that distinguishes Kelvin from other teachers is his educational background as a non-English language major—he studied Agriculture Science in university.

Kelvin is a local man whose family members are living about three hours ride from the border school where he teaches. Both his parents used to work for the local state-owned farm planting natural rubber trees. Workers of the farm often go deep into the mountain and sometimes they would take their children with them when working in the forest. Walking with his parents in the ocean of forests and playing by the babbling creeks were deeply embedded in Kelvin's memory of childhood.

As a bright and talented boy with optimistic characters, Kelvin did very well in both primary school and secondary school. Kelvin believed that he was gifted in learning language and he had a strong interest in learning English subject. However, his passion for English was strangled by one of his English teacher in high school. As Kelvin recalled:

> *I was good at learning English, for example, I was able to imitate the native speaker and pronounce the English words better than other children, and later I could speak sentences more fluently than other students. I achieved high scores in English in secondary school. Moreover, I had some talent for singing songs, not only Chinese songs but also English songs. I preferred to singing English songs. When I enjoyed the beautiful melodies, I also learned many English words and improved my pronunciation as well.*
>
> *But things changed like a nightmare when I entered high school. The English teacher at that time was so harsh with us that students frequently got physical punishment for making mistakes in assignments or for their mischief in class.*
>
> (Interview, P3-1, 2016)

As it was evidenced in Chapter 6 that Amy made the decision to take language teaching as her life-long career because of her interaction with a volunteer, the significant others played a ciritical role in Kelvin's case. Just because the negative influence of his high school English teacher, Kelvin lost his enthusiasm in learning English, he recalled that:

> *Many of my classmates were emotionally hurt by the English teacher and they finally gave up learning the subject. I also changed my attitude towards English subject once I was punished for not doing well in my homework. Time*

passed quickly and there came Gao Kao (the College Entrance Examination).
I made a decision that I would not choose English language studies or any
language related subjects as my major. I applied for the Southwest Forestry
University, and decided to study Forestry there.   (Interview, P3-2, 2016)

Kelvin worked very hard to pass Gao Kao and finally matriculated at the Southwest
Forestry University. In university, Kelvin majored in Botany and Plant Science and
trained diverse knowledge about biology and ecology as well. During his college life,
Kelvin's talent in language was revitalized. He improved his language competence by
taking part in different language learning societies, activities or contests. Kelvin recalled
that:

While I was busy working in the laboratory, I kept on learning English in
my spare time. For one thing, with sufficient language knowledge, I could read
English references published by researchers in Western countries. For another,
English had always been my favorite subject. I enjoyed learning that language
by participating in many English-related activities like oral English contest or
English study association. By doing this, I acquired much sense of achievement.
                                                      (Interview, P3-3, 2016)

Although Kelvin once gave up learning English subject in high school because of a
bad-tempered English teacher, his passion for English was reignited during college. The
flexible atmosphere in university provided Kelvin with much space to learn his major
knowledge as well as improving his English proficiency. When he was approaching the
end of four-year study in university in 2010, another significant event happened upon
Kelvin's graduation, which accidentally changed his choice of future career:

Upon graduation and in the job-hunting season, my life changed
drastically by bad news from my mother. She was diagnosed with cancer and
needed company and intense care. As the single child in my family, I had to
shoulder the responsibility and I decided to go back home to take care of my
mother. I gave up job offers in Kunming and from companies in other cities, and
went back to my mom. Fortunately, my mother recovered after a year of careful
treatment in Chengdu.   (Interview, P3-4, 2016)

Kelvin gave up his opportunities to live and work in big cities and went back to his hometown in Jinghong. In 2010, taking advantage of his English language competence, Kelvin took the Examination of Special Teaching Post in Schools of Rural and Remote Area (*te gang jiao shi*) [特岗教师] and was assigned as an English teacher to a secondary school in the southwestern border area close to Myanmar.

7.2　Kelvin's teaching context

Language teachers' identity is constructed and sustained to develop in both macro sociocultural environment and micro workplace teaching context. In this section, the external teaching context will be described from three perspectives: the school, the students and the Teaching Research Group (*jiao yan zu*) as the school-based professional development.

7.2.1　The school

The school which Kelvin was assigned to teach is located at the most populated and largest town in southern border area of Jinghong. Founded in 1974, aiming to provide formal education to the local ethnic communities, Dong Feng Middle School (pseudonym) grew up from two thatched hut classrooms and 15 pupils to a secondary school with 102 faculties and three grades. In 2016,

Photo 7.1　Dong Feng Middle School

there were 2,320 students from seven local ethnic communities such as Dai, Hani, Blang, Miao and children from some other less populated ethnic groups (Field notes, P3-1, 2016).

If sitting in any classroom inside the school, you can tell no difference between the border school in the ethnic regions and schools in hinterland. Most faculties are Han people and they are teaching the same textbooks and implementing educational policies that are basically identical to teachers' daily teaching practice in any other places of the province. However, located in the most southwestern border area which has been traditionally regarded as the center of Dai ethnic community, the school is shrouded by distinct ethnic cultures from outside. Among diverse sociocultural forces, the distinctive factor is the religious belief. Buddhism has been popular since the 14th century and was renewed in the 1980s in this area. Before the foundation of the People's Republic of China, Buddhist temples had been the major educational institution here to impart literacy knowledge and carry on local ethnic heritage culture. At present, every Dai village has its own Buddhist monastery, monks, and male novices. It has been a common practice for Dai parents to send their sons to local Theravada temples to study the Buddhist sutras in Dai script. Novices used to study in the temples from three or four years old and continued their Buddhist training and became monks when they were twenty years old. At present, the situation is more flexible. After attending the monastery for some years, male novices may choose to return to secular life, or go to regular schools while still maintaining their studies in the temples. Thus, many male novices can be seen in the classroom of Dong Feng Middle School, a scenario rarely seen in other schools in the country.

The second contextual factor that exerts great influence on teachers' classroom teaching is low parental investment, which can be accounted from local ethnic cultural and economic perspectives. Having been significantly influenced by the Buddhist beliefs, most Dai parents hold "natural" principle in educating their children. The parents hold that their children should grow up in a natural environment. Children should not be bothered or interfered by any external forces. If children can be taught in the Buddhist monastery, it is not very necessary for them to go to the normal schools. Moreover, as aforementioned in Chapter 5, the tropical climate in Xishuangbanna creates favorable natural environment for biological diversity. Local farmers have benefited considerably from doing timber business or growing tropical economic crops like natural rubber tree, pitaya or pineapple. The large scale of planting work necessitates labor force. Many parents keep their children out of school and let them work in their fields. The researcher's filed work shows that the average monthly cash income per household in this area may reach about 4,000 RMB (Field notes, P3-2, 2016). What's more, instead of working in the field themselves, many farming families begin to hire migrant workers coming outside Xishuangbanna to work for them. In this sense, the lower parental investment caused by their "natural education principles" and financially well-being can be construed as a significant barrier for teachers' classroom teaching. As the principal of Dong Feng Middle School remarked, "in other places outside Xishuangbanna, students leave school because of poverty, but here, students drop out of school for being well-off (Field notes, P3-3, 2016).

7.2.2 The students

Most students, making up about 40% out of the student body in Dong Feng Middle School, are from local Dai ethnic group. Although teachers there work very hard, the academic performance of the students is not satisfying. Taking students' performance in the final graduation test on July 3rd, 2017 as an example, 371 students from Grade 9 averaged 53.54 out of 100 as the full mark in English subject, ranked No.9 among 12 schools in Jinghong city (Document, P3-1, 2017). Apart from the lower parental support for education, students assemble some common characteristics with Dai students in urban schools as the researcher discussed in Chapter 5. Firstly, they are linguistically diverse. Since the class is composed of students from three to five ethnic groups, different ethnic languages are being used in the classroom, as Standard Chinese is their second language and English is virtually their third language. However, most of the faculties are Han people, and they don't speak in any of the local ethnic languages at all, thus the linguistic diversity is deliberately ignored by teachers. Secondly, because of the geographical uniqueness, most of the students are living with their families in natural tropical environment. They are pretty accustomed to playing outside in the forest or out-door environment. For most of ethnic students, studying in school makes them feel like being caged birds. Therefore, such disposition of ethnic students raises great challenge for teachers who only teach by rote learning or pedagogy of grammar translation. The polarization in academic achievement can be regarded as the third feature of the students. Although the motivation for learning subject (studying) in the walled school remains at a lower level, there are still some outstanding individuals who can do better by nature or through hard work. Thus, problems may arise due to the differences of students' academic competence.

7.2.3   The school-based professional development

Before the NTTP training, for most schools in the rural and border regions in Jinghong, the TRG had been the sole place where teachers could make concerted efforts to learn and achieve professional growth. According to in-class observation and interviews with teachers during the researcher's fieldwork, the Teaching and Research Group in Dong Feng Middle School was not as supportive as the TRG in other schools, like that in Green Leaf Middle School where Amy teaches. The TRG failed to offer positive support, which might be attributed to weak institutional support, limited pedagogical competence, and absence of the learning community.

In order to survive the official assessment, great attention has been paid to students' learning performance. Stiff rules and disciplines were made to regulate students' daily behavior and teachers were put under high pressure to prompt students to get higher scores. The school leaders didn't validate the professional development as an access for English teachers to their pedagogical competencies and thus as the way to improve students' achievements. The school leadership was unsupportive in organizing any activities about professional growth. In the interview, the principal accounted that:

> *As the principal of the school, we do care about students' academic achievements as well as teacher's professional development. However, if you intend to develop either short-term or long-term teacher training schemes, you'll need some professionals and he'd better be the member of management team. Unfortunate, I'm teaching physics and there is not a teacher in the management who is teaching the English subject. We know little about the nature of language leaning and teaching. For a very long time, I've been looking for prospective English teachers who would join in the leadership, yet they all seemed disinterested in doing so.*   (Interview, P3-5, 2017)

The principal's remarks revealed the difficulties that the management team was facing. Because the discrepancies between disciplines, the school management team could not initiate a tailored long-term plan for professional development of the language teachers. For the teachers themselves, they didn't have the interest to be involved in any additional management work at all.

In addition, teachers' limited pedagogical and linguistic competence might account for their inactiveness in school management and teaching and research activities. Teachers' average age in the English TRG reached to 40 (Field notes, P3-4, 2016), and the number of middle-aged teachers took up 60%, which indicated the the rather outmoded knowledge structure of teachers. This is evidenced in the researcher's participant classroom observation and interview with English teachers. In a group interview, a middle-aged female teacher confessed that:

> *Honestly speaking, from time to time I've been feeling terrible about my own subject matter knowledge. It has been 25 years since I left the teachers' school, and the language knowledge I learned 25 years ago is not compatible with students' need and popular pedagogies advocated by the bureau of education. I managed to improve my linguistic knowledge, such as spoken or writing skills, but, I finally gave up because of absence of either pressure and environment.*
>
> (Interview, P3-6, 2016)

Apart from ignorance for the professional development from school management and teachers' limited subject matter knowledge, absence of an active learning community is the third factor impeding the school-based professional development for this cohort of language teachers in Dong Feng Middle School. As Kelvin recalled his orientation years:

> *My colleagues seemed to be very busy. When I had a question in teaching, there wasn't anyone whom I could approach. Though I was confident in my subject matter knowledge and teaching competence, yet I was not sure if I was in the right track and got things right. Among the teachers in our jiao yan zu, there is only one who would offer help and open for discussion. I never forget those days when I passed her window (the teacher lives in the first floor and we are neighbors in the same apartment building), I tried to catch*

any possible opportunity consulting her about how to write the lesson plan…
Later, I gradually understood why those teachers were reluctant to share their
experience or offer possible help to young teachers, because they were quite
weak in linguistic knowledge and had no idea about what was better teaching.

(Interview, P3-7, 2016)

In this section, the researcher illustrates the socioeconomic and cultural background as well as the workplace context in which Kelvin teaches. From the description above, it can be seen that both the broader sociocultural background and workplace context are rather unfavorable for the professional growth for Kelvin's burgeoning professional identity. In the following section, the researcher will present Kelvin's classroom practice before the NTTP training through which Kelvin's emerging professional identity is explored.

7.3   Kelvin's classroom practices before attending the NTTP

"Teaching English is much different from learning it."

(Kelvin, Interview, P3-8)

In this section, drawing on classroom video and stimulate recall data, the researcher will describe Kelvin's classroom practices before he was trained in the NTTP. As a novice teacher who is not an English major, Kelvin is the only teacher in this study who has not received professional teacher education before entering the profession. Kelvin's pedagogical activities will be illustrated from multiple perspectives including how he plans the instruction of contents.

7.3.1   The lesson plan

The lesson plan is teachers' understanding of materials, implementation of beliefs, and enactment of teaching philosophy. The plan the researcher chose to describe was selected from one of Kelvin's grammar teaching practice before he participated in the

NTTP. The lesson plan underlines Kelvin's understanding on language teaching and learning, which shows that Kelvin's identity is transforming from a language learner to a novice language teacher. See Table 7.1:

Table 7.1   Kelvin's lesson plan for a grammar class (Document, P3-2, 2016)

Unit: 7	Topic 3	Section D
Grammar		
Teaching Objectives: To teach Ss the future passive voice.		
Teaching Aids: Multimedia courseware, LCD projector		
Teaching Procedures		

Step 1	1) Read out the word list.
	2) Introduce the objective of the lesson. Ask Ss following questions:
	  a. Do you like watching movies?
	  b. Have you ever watched a movie in the cinema?
	  c. How often do you go to cinema to watch movies?
	3) Discuss different types of movies with Ss, like science fictions or comics?
	4) Show Ss a movie poster with "will be shown on …(time)" on it.	

Step 2	1) Play the listening material in 1a. 2) Ask Ss questions about the conversation. 3) Ask Ss to read out the conversation first in groups then in pairs. Stress the phrases and key words.	
Step 3	1) Ss do the exercise on p.34, filling the blanks. 2) Read the exercises and then read the dialogue again. 3) Ask Ss to give answers to the questions and write the answers on the blackboard.	

Step 4	1) Review the grammar about passive voice.
	2) Introduce the grammar about future passive voice with the following sentences:
	  a. Traveling by spaceship will be realized in the future.
	  b. The work will be done in 2 days.
	  c. A new teaching building will be built.
	3) Highlight and explain the grammar point: Will be done
	4) Give more sentences as examples to show the usage of future passive voice.	

Step 5	1) Ask Ss in pairs to come to the front reading out the dialogue. 2) Give assignment: Read the dialogue and make sentences using the future passive voice.	

Kelvin's lesson plan represents his teacher-centered perception on language teaching. Meanwhile, the plan shows that Kelvin continues to use grammar translation as his teaching method to instruct the grammar knowledge. Kelvin explained his teaching beliefs in the interview:

> *Teaching English is very different from learning the language. Because I didn't learn many courses about language teaching approaches and methods, I just inherited the ways that were used by my middle-school teachers. At that time, I believed that language skills should be acquired by rote learning. Remembering vocabulary and reciting passages in the textbook were the duty of students. In terms of teaching language, I considered grammar-translation as the most effective method.* (Interview, P3-8, 2016)

Kelvin designed the grammar class based on his personal learning experience which was actually the method used by his middle-school English teachers. The plan indicates that for novice language teachers, the previous learning experience plays a significant role in their early teaching career and emerging professional identity as a language teacher. For Kelvin, who had limited English learning experience, this was particular true, for he had not been well trained in language teaching theories and pedagogy.

In order to present a full picture of identity construction, it is necessary to observe how the teacher implements the lesson plan. Therefore, in the next section, the researcher will present Kelvin's classroom practices of the grammar instruction class.

7.3.2   The classroom activities

The classroom activities the researcher chose to describe were based on a classroom video in which Kelvin instructed grammar knowledge about the future passive voice.

Episode 1

The learning objective of the grammar instruction class was to teach students the future passive voice. Kelvin didn't go directly to teach the grammar knowledge about tense or voice, but warmed up his class by presenting the poster of a popular movie. In his introduction of the movie, Kelvin repeatedly used the sentence "A science fiction movie will be shown in the cinema next week." in order to attract students' attention to the sentence structure. After the introduction, Kelvin asked students more questions about whether they liked watching movies or what type of movies they liked to watch. Students showed great interest in this topic and the discussion on the topic of movie lasted for several minutes. Kelvin ended their talk by writing the sentence "The new movie will be shown in the cinema next week." on the blackboard, and students were asked to read the sentence twice.

Episode 2

After students finished their discussion on the topic of movie, Kelvin asked them to listen to a dialogue between two speakers talking about their plan for fun. Two questions, "When will the movie be shown in the cinema?" and "What is the movie about?" were raised for the students before the audio recording was played. At the end of the dialogue, a sentence containing future passive voice was used and Kelvin played the sentence two more times. Two students were asked to answer his questions respectively and repeat the sentence. Kelvin then wrote down the sentence "The new movie will be shown in the cinema next week." he mentioned just now and the sentence "A wonderful movie will be shown tonight. Shall we go to see it?" in dialogue one on the blackboard. Kelvin firstly guided the class to find the similarity in the two sentences and then began his instruction on the future passive voice by demonstrating more examples.

Episode 3

The third section of this grammar class came to the assessment part. According to Kelvin's lesson plan, this section was designed to test if the students mastered the grammar knowledge of future passive voice. The assessment was achieved by doing exercises such as gap filling, multiple choices and sentence translation. The first three gap filling items were based on the passage in the textbook. Kelvin prepared additional sentences and made them as multiple choice and bilingual translation exercises.

Episode 4

Kelvin used role play as the student activity to conclude his grammar instruction. He firstly divided the class into groups which were formed by two deskmates, then the whole class was asked to read the dialogue in the textbook in loud voice. Later, a pair of students were invited to the front acting the dialogue in the textbook. At last, more pairs were asked to perform the dialogue. Every now and then, Kelvin helped the students if they made any mistakes.

In this section, the researcher illustrates Kelvin's grammar teaching practice through detailed description of four episodes extracted from the classroom video footage. Kelvin's classroom practice is basically in congruence with his plan. In the next section, the researcher will analyze the roles played by the teacher and students.

7.3.3　The teacher's and students' roles

In section 7.3.2, drawing on the video recording data, the researcher described four major episodes which represented some of the key steps that Kelvin delivered the grammar knowledge. In line with the lesson plan, Kelvin's instruction of the grammar class basically consisted four major parts: the preparation, grammar instruction, assessment and revision. In these teaching stages and activities, Kelvin and his students played diverse roles during the grammar class.

In the preparation stage, Kelvin played the roles as a motivator and informant, while the students played the roles as processors and participants. In the very beginning of the class, in order to attract students' interest, Kelvin presented a movie poster before his instruction on grammar knowledge. Then he extended the topic to the discussion of personal hobbies. The students were attracted by the poster and they obviously enjoyed the discussion. At this stage, Kelvin was the resource provider, informant and motivator, and his students were participants of Kelvin's teaching activity.

In the second stage of grammar instruction, Kelvin didn't teach the contents until the students became motivated. He used the dialogues in the listening material to repeat and stress the grammar knowledge which he would teach as the major objective. After playing the dialogue, Kelvin asked the students to repeat the conversation. In doing this, the knowledge was repeatedly "instilled" into the students. Therefore, in the second stage of teaching, Kelvin played the roles again as the resource provider, informant, controller and the careful manager while students were knowledge receptors and listeners.

In the assessment stage, Kelvin was the controller, grader and assessor of the class when he offered grammar exercises to test if the students understood the future passive voice. Both the document data of lesson plan and the video data of his classroom teaching indicate that Kelvin dominates this stage of instruction, and the students merely play the roles as knowledge processors.

Roles of the students changed in the last stage of this grammar instruction. They were the participants and team players as they worked in pairs to practice the grammar knowledge by repeating the conversation. At the same time, because they were asked to review the grammar knowledge learned in the class, the students also played the roles as knowledge receptors. Kelvin controlled, organized and managed the whole instruction; therefore, for the teacher's roles, he was the controller, organizer and manager in the last stage of instruction. Different roles played by the teacher and students are summarized in Table 7.2:

Table 7.2　Summary of the teacher's and students' roles in a grammar instruction

Classroom activity	Teacher's roles	Students' roles
Initialization	· Motivator · Resource provider	· Knowledge receptors · Processors
Instruction	· Resource provider · Facilitator · Careful manager	· Knowledge receptors · Listeners
Assessment	· Grader · Assessor	· Knowledge receptors · Processors
Revision	· Manager · Controller	· Participants · Team players

As introduced in section 7.1, Kelvin's education background is different from other trainee teachers in the NTTP training. Kelvin studied Botany in college and "accidentally" entered the profession of language teaching. Although Kelvin was confident in his teaching career, because of the institutional constraints and absence of external professional training, Kelvin learned to teach all by himself. Though he had been feeling sure about his teaching practice, he was uncertain if his classroom practices were running on the right track. In the interview, Kelvin reflected:

Learning the language is different from teaching the language. Even though I have been trying hard, I'm not sure that I'll be a qualified teacher. Before the NTTP, I had been applying the teaching methods used by my high

school or middle school teachers years ago. At the beginning years, I was worried whether I taught the students in the right way, but later I was assured and became confident after I observed how my colleague practiced in their classrooms. There were no differences between my ways and theirs.

(Interview, P3-9, 2016)

Kelvin adopted grammar-translation as the method in teaching English for years, but he gradually found that even with thorough preparation, it was hard to improve students' learning performance. If compared with the students from the same grade, his students could achieve higher scores in the test, but if compared with the learning performance of the students in other schools, the gap was remarkable. Kelvin noticed the problem and tried to analyze the reason. He reported in the interview:

I used to be confident with my teaching, but actually, that was a joke. As the old metaphor goes, I'm jus a jing di zhi wa〔井底之蛙〕(a frog living at the bottom of a well, referring to a person with a limited outlook). About a year ago, I was bitterly criticized by the TRG for my inappropriate way of teaching. Taking this grammar class as an example, I had believed that I was doing right; however, it was completely flawed from plan to implementation. Firstly, the teaching objectives were not explicit enough, though I intended to teach the grammar knowledge. Secondly, doing grammar exercise might be right but it was not very necessary to teach grammar through listening. Lastly, the class was totally teacher-centered but not student-centered, for I talked too much and dominated the whole teaching process [...]　　　(Interview, P3-10, 2016)

The interview reveals Kelvin's dubious perception on his teaching practice before he received the NTTP training. He was confident about his own language competence but adopted a skeptical attitude towards his pedagogical expertise. The uncertainty about his teaching practice stemmed from many reasons. Initially, his non-English major education background confined him to only applying his language learning experiences in teaching practice, which was rather limited and remarkably different from language teaching techniques. Furthermore, the absence of external training made no contribution to Kelvin's professional development. He was not well informed with the up-to-date approaches and methods in language teaching, just as Kelvin commented on himself as a "frog at the bottom of a well". At last, the peers or colleagues provided limited help for improving his teaching competence. There was no appropriate "role model" or "master" to follow or teachers' learning community to discuss with.

In section 7.3, the researcher presents Kelvin's practiced professional identity through the detailed description of his lesson plan and classroom practice illustrated by four teaching episodes from the videotaped grammar teaching class. The researcher then presents Kelvin's mixed teaching perceptions and briefly discusses the reason for his uncertainty about teaching practice. This uncertainty later grew into Kelvin's enthusiasm and motivation to explore more new and appropriate teaching methods for his class. In the next section, the researcher will continue to present Kelvin's learning experiences and his reflections on different training modules.

7.4 Kelvin's learning experiences in the NTTP

"Learning new things like the sponge absorbs water."

(Kelvin, Interview, P3-11)

Kelvin was selected as the "backborn teacher" in 2015 and finished part of his training coursework and modules provided by the Nation Teacher Training Plan when he was interviewed. Kelvin cherished the opportunity for the NTTP training as a path that led him to a broader horizon of professional development. In this section, the researcher will report Kelvin's experiences and reflections he has gained from his engagement of the ongoing training session. Attending the NTTP training marked a significant milestone in his teaching career for Kelvin was greatly improved from language ability to teaching competence. In this section, data and discussion will be presented in line with the format the researcher used in the preceding cases.

7.4.1 The Trainer-Training Module

As mentioned in Chapter 2, the Trainer-Training Module is one of the fundamental components in the NTTP training matrix. According to the top-downed syllabus of the training plan, this training module is usually carried out in colleges or universities and lasts for about 20 days. University lecturers and curriculum experts teach the trainees diverse coursework on language teaching approaches and linguistic knowledge. In the interview, Kelvin commented on his learning experiences that:

> *I've never imagined that the English language can be learned and taught in so many different ways! Twenty days of learning was worthy of many years of exploring by myself through working in the classroom! The training was really informative and inspiring!*

> *I took two lines of courses in the Trainer-Training Module. The first category of lectures was about current top-downed education policy such as the introduction to the "Key Competence-Oriented Education Reform"; the second category of coursework focused on specific language pedagogical techniques, such as collaborative learning, integrated learning, process writing, English phonics or reading through picture books, to name just a few. From different perspectives, these lectures or coursework informed me the direction ahead and enhanced my pedagogical expertise and competence. I learned new knowledge as a sponge absorbs water, and what I learned during the NTTP functioned like a "helping hand" which greatly assisted my classroom teaching.*

> (Interview, P3-11, 2016)

Learning new knowledge as "a sponge absorbs water", Kelvin quoted the telling metaphor to describe his learning experiences in the Trainer-Training Module of the NTTP program. As an English teacher without systematic education of linguistics, pedagogy and curriculum, additional training on professional expertise in language learning and teaching would be imperative. The training benefited Kelvin for his professional development and accelerated his becoming of a legitimate language teacher. With broadened theoretical horizon and enriched teaching expertise, Kelvin returned to his school and began to give open classes (*gong kai ke*) ［公开课］ as an enhancement of his learned knowledge. Kelvin's reflections on the Demonstration Module will be elaborated in the next section.

7.4.2 The Demonstration Module

According to the syllabus, every trainee teacher is required to give a demonstration/ open class for teachers who don't participate in the training in a rural school. It is a challenging task for the trainee teachers because they need to integrate the newly learned teaching approaches or specific methods with their teaching experience accumulated through daily pedagogical practice. But for Kelvin, he showed his confidence and excitement about giving the demonstration class:

> *The training sessions in the Normal University did inspire me to teach English using innovative methods, and the coursework ignited my passion to teach the subject. During my training sessions in university, I took two important courses — "process writing" and "collaborative language learning". Drawing on my own teaching experience and the techniques I learned from the training courses, especially the collaborative language learning, I designed the demonstration class. Before I gave the demonstration class, I practiced this new teaching method with my own students. My students responded positively to my new approach and I decided to continue and improve it in my future teaching. The demonstration class was rather successful and the teaching research officer complemented my demonstration and gave me positive feedback.* (Interview, P3-12, 2016)

Kelvin's case is an example showing that the Demonstration Module functions well as a catalyst prompting the trainee teachers to change their cognized knowledge into practiced competence, to integrate the new methods and their experiences into updated teaching practices. In addition to the training modules of teacher trainer and demonstration, distance education is another important component in the NTTP training program. Kelvin's reflections on the distance education and online learning community will be introduced and discussed in the coming section.

7.4.3 The Distance Education Module

The NTTP training program features its direct impact on teachers' linguistic proficiency and pedagogical competence. In addition, application of information technology is another innovative way in teacher education. Both the Internet-based distance education and the SNS-based (Social Network Service) online discussion group extend teachers' professional development beyond time and space. As described in both Jenifer's and Amy's case as well as in other interviews with the local teachers, all reveal that most teachers are inclined to hold a negative attitude toward the official distance education, which is flawed in its lack of interaction and unattractive contents. By contrast, teachers are active and the atmosphere is vibrant in the online discussion group. Kelvin had his own understandings about the distance education and SNS-based online discussion group. He quoted a metaphor to express his perceptions, "I consider the distance education as a television antenna on the roof, which is used to receive signals from the outside world" (Interview, P3-8, 2016). As Kelvin explained:

> *It is not convenient for teachers to go outside and sit in the classroom of other colleagues, observing or exchanging ideas with them. Moreover, because of geographical distance, it is almost impossible to communicate with expert teachers or professionals in pedagogy or curriculum. Thanks to the Internet and the development of information technology, teachers in the remote area can learn synchronically with teachers in every corner of the world.*
>
> (Interview, P3-13, 2016)

Kelvin compared his learning experience on the official distant learning platform with his engagement in the online discussion group and reflected that:

> *Though the contents of the official Distance Education Module are comparatively dull but it is still worthy of learning when you don't have any one to turn to or learn from. I enjoy the online discussion group very much, for it is much more convenient for us to learn and everything can be done just on the cellphone. I often pose various questions about grammar and teaching methods, and I always get reply from some unknown but warmhearted teachers in the online discussion group.*   (Interview, P3-14, 2016)

As Kelvin commented in his interview, it's hard for people who are living in the urban towns with abundant cultural and economic resources to imagine how much efforts a rural school teacher should make to achieve professional development. Owing to the fast development of modern technology, various online communication platforms and instant communication applications are being adopted to assist rural teachers in remote areas with their professional development.

In this section, the researcher draws the picture of Kelvin's learning experiences and reflections on his participation of different training modules provided by the NTTP. It is notable that Kelvin has used different metaphors to describe his identity or what the module could do for teachers' professional development. In the Trainer-Training Module, Kelvin compared him as a sponge learning language knowledge and teaching methods from external resources. He used the catalyst to describe the Demonstration Module as an intense context for the trainee teachers to change their identity from the ordinary frontline practitioner to the teacher trainer. Kelvin considered the distance education learning and online discussion as his antenna to extend his horizon beyond time and space.

In the next section, participant observation and in-depth interview data will be used to present Kelvin's classroom practices after the NTTP training, to explore his shift of identity-in-practice.

7.5   Kelvin's classroom practice in the post-NTTP period

"The new model makes me feel more professional."

(Kelvin, Interview, P3-17, 2016)

When Kelvin completed his 20 days of teacher trainer's training module in university and returned to his school, he demonstrated three open classes for the teachers in Dong Feng Middle School and in two other schools. He later took a series of lectures on teaching materials and classroom activity design. These training programs were part of external training designed for in-service teachers working in rural schools in remote regions. As introduced in Jenifer's and Amy's cases, from fall semester in 2016, the Municipal Bureau of Education launched a new teaching model which was tailored for teaching English in schools in Jinghong. All English teachers have been required to use the "Three Stages and Seven Steps" model to guide their classroom teaching. For Kelvin, he followed the new model as advocated by the bureau of education and changed his teaching by incorporating new teaching approach and methods he learned in the trainer's training module.

In the following section, drawing on a video recorded writing class, the researcher will present Kelvin's efforts in practicing his new perceptions. Following the same format of data display, the researcher will first present Kelvin's lesson plan and then episodes of this writing class, and at last the researcher will analyze different roles played by the teacher and students.

7.5.1   The lesson plan

The data presented in this section is generated from a video recorded writing class. In this subsection, the researcher will first display Kelvin's lesson plan as document data. It is notable that after his participation of different training modules under the NTTP, Kelvin's teaching practice is "becoming legitimate" (Interview, P3-4). He made a dramatic shift from his old grammar translation teaching method to more diversified way of teaching, which could be evidenced by his lesson plan and classroom recording. His lesson plan for a writing class is presented in Table 7.3:

Table 7.3   Kelvin's lesson plan for a writing class

Topic	A Pleasant Trip (Grade 8, Unit 3, Section D)
Skill	Writing Skill Instruction
Teaching Objectives	· Write about a trip based on the given material. · Writing through reading: practice the "integrated writing instruction".
Difficulties	Ss are able to compose a passage with complete structure in logic sequence and can use key words and sentence patterns. Ss are able to write different parts of the passage in collaboration with other students.
Teaching Aids	Multimedia courseware, LCD projector, Ss' video
Teaching Approach	Process Writing

continued

Topic		A Pleasant Trip (Grade 8, Unit 3, Section D)
Teaching Procedure		
Stage 1 Pre-writing	Step1 Warming- up and Brainstorm	Present the task and introduce the learning objectives. 1. Ss watch the electronic album of the teacher's traveling. 2. Brainstorm. (Ask some students to say out any words or phrases about traveling.) 3. Conclude the key words or phrases.
	Step2 Analysis of the Text	1. Present the letter of Bill written to Darren. Teacher and students analyze the text together. 2. List the key points we can write about our travel experiences. Use following points: Where/When/How long/How to get there with whom Things to do /The most interesting/funny thing
Stage 2 While-writing	Step 3 Group Writing	1. Group writing Encourage Ss to discuss how to write the travel experiences. (Four groups write the beginning and ending, eight groups write the body.) 2. Comment on the group's work and list the good points on the blackboard to make the outline. 3. Individual writing According to your group's discussion and other group's good opinions, write your own travel experiences.
Stage 3 Post-writing	Step 4 Peer Evaluation	Peer Checklist After reading my classmate's travel experiences, I know ★ where he/she went Yes/No ★ when he/she got there Yes/No ★ how he/she got there Yes/No ★ what he/she did Yes/No ★ how he/she felt Yes/No
	Step 5 Homework	Revising the passage: A Pleasant Trip

The plan of this writing class was notably different from his previous teaching practice of the same lesson. The lesson plan featured with its three major stages, the pre-writing, while-writing and post writing, and the teacher used five teaching steps to implement the teaching objective. The first stage was actually a lead-in in which the students were prepared with sufficient materials as the input. The teacher planned to show his photo album in order to arouse students' interest about the topic of travel experience. Then students would be asked to use their own words, such as "exiting, funny, impressive" to express personal feelings on their travel experience. At last, the teacher would use a mind map to summarize possible expressions that could be appropriately used to describe travel experience. In another step of the first stage, the teacher would continue to scaffold the students about how to develop their composition. A passage from the textbook was used as an example and it would be carefully analyzed from different perspectives such as diction, structure, grammar and logic. In the second teaching stage, students would work in groups and write in collaboration to compose one of the parts of their passages. Four students would work in a group writing about the lead-in part, body part or conclusion part of the passage. Students were required to develop their writing with reference of the model showed in preceding instruction. In the last stage, when every group finished their writing, their works would be reviewed by other groups. They were required to use the peer evaluation checklist to grade the writings.

In the interview, Kelvin commented on his application of the new teaching model in this writing class:

> *Before the NTTP training, I had explored for better teaching approach all by myself, and I was not very sure about the methods I used in my class. From the last semester, all English teachers were trained and required to use the new teaching model which divided the teaching process into three major stages and several steps. I considered the new teaching mode as a helping guideline and an efficient tool in making lesson plans, rearranging the contents and designing classroom activities. Now with the help of the new model, I'm becoming more confident in teaching.* (Interview, P3-15, 2016)

In addition to the application of new teaching model, Kelvin adopted "collaborative writing" as his attempt in using the "process writing" approach. He reflected in the interview:

> *Writing skill had been the headache in my teaching. I used to skip the writing task or just gave some examples for the students to imitate. I didn't*

know any concepts about scaffolding or process teaching until I learned them in the NTTP. Upon returning from my training session in the Normal University, I decided to make some breakthrough in my pedagogy. Therefore, I decided to try the "process writing" approach to train my students on their writing skills.
(Interview, P3-16, 2016)

The interview data suggests that both the national-level teacher training program and the local curriculum reform exert a great influence on teachers' classroom practice. The teaching plan also evidences teachers' improved perceptions on both general approach and specific methods in language teaching. In the next section, the researcher will continue to present how the plan is implemented by illustrating three episodes extracted from the classroom video.

7.5.2 Classroom activities

Based on the lesson plan, Kelvin carried out the writing class in three major steps, the scaffolding, collaborative writing and individual writing. In this section, the researcher will use three episodes extracted from the classroom video to show how Kelvin implements his reshaps teaching perceptions.

Episode 1

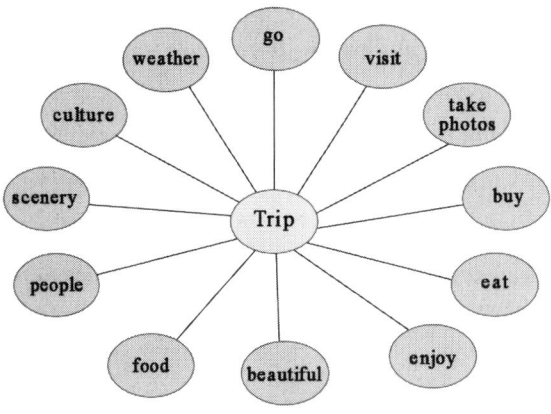

Figure 7.2　The PPT slide from Kelvin

According to the lesson plan, the first stage of the writing class was the scaffolding stage. After the greetings, Kelvin clarified the learning objectives and major contents of this writing class. Then Kelvin projected a photo collection showing photos he took on the trip to different places. Kelvin introduced each photo by repeatedly using different adjectives such as "interesting", "funny", "impressive" or "exciting" to describe the photos, expecting his students could remember those adjectives. After presenting the photo collection, Kelvin asked his students how they felt about these photos and their travel experiences, and several students were invited to share their travel experiences in simple English. At last, Kelvin presented a mind map to summarize the words that could be used in composition of travel experiences.

Kelvin explained each word in the mind map and instructed the students that they could compose their writing by using the words listed in the mind map.

Kelvin reflected in the interview:

> *The mind map is a very powerful teaching technique which I learned in the NTTP training lectures. The mind map can facilitate the teacher to present his or her intentions in a clear and logical way, meanwhile, the students can use the mind map to develop their ideas and then put their ideas into writing. This is a very good tool that makes my class efficient.*   (Interview, P3-17, 2016)

Episode 2

In the second stage, the writing class entered into the most critical phase. Although the students were clear about their tasks and were prepared with necessary vocabulary, they still needed to be informed about the structure with examples. In the beginning of the second stage, Kelvin continued to scaffold his students in detail by analyzing the passage from the textbook. He first outlined the structure and then highlighted the semantic functions of each sentence group. At last, he stressed on the grammar, especially about the tense used in every sentence.

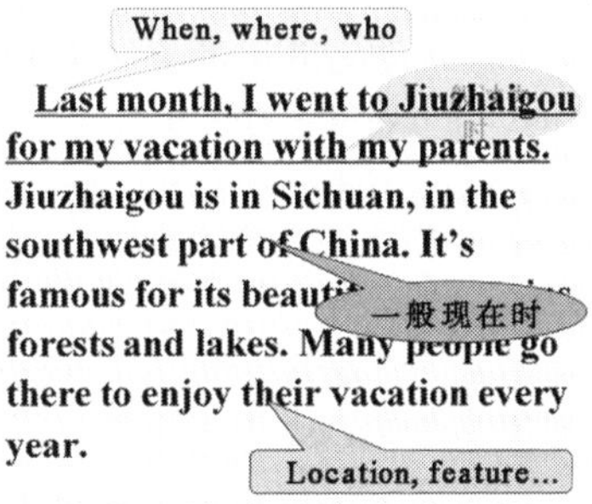

Figure 7.3   The PPT slide from Kelvin

Having been informed by the example on writing travel experiences, students began to compose their writing in groups. Since the students were grouped before the class, each group was assigned with different writing tasks. Some groups were required to write the beginning paragraph, and some groups were asked to write the body, and others were assigned to compose the conclusion.

Kelvin reflected on his practice of the "collaborative writing" techniques in the interview:

> *I learned a lot in my first attempt of using the "collaborative writing" method. I had never tried to teach writing skills in this way, but to kick a start would be very important. The "collaborative writing" is one of the components in the "process writing". I didn't do a good job in the time control and it was hard to monitor the writing process of each group. Maybe this is why the "individual writing" is indispensable for applying this method.*

> (Interview, P3-18, 2016)

Episode 3

When each group finished their composition of the assigned task, Kelvin collected their works and projected them on the screen. He marked out the mistakes and pointed out good sentences in their works. The last stage was the "individual writing", in which every student was required to compose a complete passage on travel experiences by using the vocabulary and structures learned in this class. The individual writing task was carried out until the end of the class.

Kelvin summarized this writing class in the interview:

> *Teaching writing skills had been a headache for me until I learned the approach of process writing and in specific, the collaborative writing method. Writing skills were critically important in terms of language proficiency, but I chose not to teach the writing skills on purpose or simplified this task by showing students some sample passages. My lack of responsibility was the result of my limited writing skills and shortage of appropriate teaching methods. In the NTTP training, I was inspired about some language teaching approaches and many specific teaching methods which would work well in my classroom teaching. I'll continue to learn and try my best to put them into my classroom*

teaching. In doing this, I believe that I can be a qualified language teacher.

(Interview, P3-19, 2016)

In this section, the researcher presents Kelvin's changed perceptions and teaching practices after the NTTP training through detailed description of the lesson plan and three episodes from one of his video-recorded writing classes. Compared with his perceptions on language teaching and classroom practices before the NTTP training, Kelvin made a remarkable improvement in pedagogical competence, which could be the result of two powerful factors, his active agency in learning new knowledge and the push from external training. Since Kelvin adopted new teaching methods, the roles played by the teacher and students changed accordingly. In the next section, the researcher will discuss the changed roles of the teacher and students respectively in this writing class.

7.5.3　The teacher's and students' roles

In this writing class, the teacher and students played more dynamic roles than they did before. The application of new teaching method allowed the teacher to take more diverse roles like a motivator, facilitator, monitor and assessor, while students were no longer passive knowledge receptors but active participants, partners and assessors.

In the first teaching stage, the teacher prepared the materials and controlled the teaching process, so he was the resource-provider and controller of the class. When the class entered into the second stage of group collaborative writing, students took the chief role in the class activity. When the teacher analyzed the sample writing, he was the resource-provider. The teacher's roles changed to a facilitator and monitor when students began to co-work and write their passages. In the second teaching stage, students were active and played the roles as partners and collaborators. In the last stage of teaching, students were still the center of the class since they had to work in groups again to assess and grade writings from other groups; therefore, they took the roles of assessors or graders, while the teacher was facilitating and monitoring the whole process. Different roles played by the teacher and students are summarized in Table 7.4:

Table 7.4　Summary of the teacher's and students' roles in the writing class

Classroom activity	Teacher's roles	Students' roles
Preparation	· Resource provider · Controller	· Knowledge receptors
Group collaborative writing	· Resource provider · Organizer · Facilitator · Monitor	· Knowledge receptors · Partners/collaborators
Peer evaluation	· Monitor · Facilitator · Assessor/grader	· Participants · Assessors/graders

In this section, the researcher summarizes the roles played by the teacher and students in this video recorded writing class. Kelvin's class shifted from teacher-centered to student-centered, in which their roles changed accordingly. The change of both the teacher's and students' roles indicates the change of Kelvin's teaching belief. He began to take more diverse positions in his classroom practice, thus the change of roles would contribute to his construction of new professional identity; as Kelvin commented on his growth, he was becoming more "legitimate".

7.6　Kelvin's attempts in doing the classroom-based research

"It is almost impossible for me to do it."

(Kelvin, Interview, P3-20, 2016)

In the final section, the researcher will report an aspect of professional identity as a teacher researcher. It is worth mentioning that despite the positive reflections from other teachers, like Jenifer and Amy who demonstrate strong motivation for their engagement in classroom-based research, Kelvin maintains somehow negative attitude toward doing classroom-based research. Based on his research experience, Kelvin compared the similarities and differences in doing research in natural science and applied linguistics:

I majored in Botany in university, and my understanding of doing research

in the field of natural science is totally different from doing research in applied linguistics, language learning and teaching in particular. Doing research in natural science, you must go to the filed or work in the lab observing, recording and calculating your data, because most research is quantitative. However, when it comes to research in applied linguistics or language teaching and learning, for example, the subjects you have to face are humanities, so you have to be skillful in observing the teacher, the students and the class, and you should be able to discover the reasons beneath the surface, which is the thing I'm not very good at.　　　　　　　　　　　　　　　　(Interview, P3-20, 2016)

Kelvin was very honest to acknowledge his weakness in doing research, and he continued to analyze the influencing factors that prevented teachers in rural schools from doing classroom-based research:

It is very difficult for rural teachers like me to conduct any research. Firstly, for doing the research, it takes a lot of time to read the literature and to write the paper. As a teacher in the rural school, it is nearly impossible for me to find time reading books, since we are occupied in tremendous student management work irrelevant to our own discipline. Secondly, most teachers in the rural school are very weak in both theory and practice in doing research. If one intends to conduct a research, it is difficult for him or her to have a co-researcher in the research team. So far, I haven't found any qualified or devoted teacher who are willing to conduct any classroom research together with me. Thirdly, apart from the lack of qualified research partner, I am also frustrated by my poor research resources. Working in the remote border schools means you are far away from the research center, where there are abundant research resources such as experts, professionals, lectures, conferences or references. We do need some professionals to instruct or direct rural teachers to conduct research projects. I hold rather pessimistic beliefs that without the help from experts or professionals from universities or other institutions, it would be extremely hard for rural teachers to conduct research projects.

(Interview, P3-21, 2016)

Kelvin's reflection on doing research reveals the status quo for rural middle school teachers to conduct research projects. Many reasons, such as weak research expertise and shortage of research resources are factors that demotivate teachers from doing research.

7.7 Discussion and summary

This chapter presents how Kelvin's teacher professional identity has been built through various of personal and professional experiences, as well as a wide range of influencing factors that affect his professional identity construction.

Kelvin's language learning experience is initially examined. Kelvin considered himself as gifted in language learning and he had been doing well in English subject. However, his interests in learning the language was disturbed by a stern English teacher who just demotivated students by physical punishments. Although Kelvin didn't choose English as his major, he continued to improve his language proficiency by participating in various contests and students' associations related with language learning.

Kelvin happened to enter the profession of language teaching and was assigned to a border school in 2010. Because of geographical remoteness, additional training outside the school was scarce, and the school-based professional development was limited to teacher meetings with the English TRG. Due to the absence of learning community, Kelvin learned to practice language teaching by himself and he inherited the teaching method used by his middle school teachers. Therefore, it is evident that the earlier language learning experience plays a pivotal role in teachers' emerging professional identity as language teachers.

Kelvin was offered an opportunity to join the NTTP which tremendously broadened his theoretical horizon in applied linguistics and significantly improved his pedagogical competence. Kelvin experienced all the three training modules which reshaped both his teaching competence and professional identity from different perspectives. The Trainer-Training Module equipped him the up-to-date language teaching approaches and methods; In the Demonstration Module, Kelvin's talent and passion in teaching were ignited and he made his effort to synthesize new teaching methods and his past teaching experiences. Different from other teachers' opinion, Kelvin considered the distance education as a powerful tool for teachers to get access to quality professional development resources. In terms of the Internet-based online discussion group, Kelvin regarded it as a pragmatic way to acquire peer support. Kelvin's reflections on his experience in the NTTP prove that the external training program, be it the national-level or school-based, signals another powerful catalyst for teachers to form new professional identities and renders teachers in the rural regions valuable opportunities to learn professional knowledge, as Kelvin metaphorically applied that he could learn new approaches and methods like "a sponge absorbing water".

In the last section of this chapter, Kelvin's reflections on doing teacher research are presented. Kelvin held rather negative attitude for his identity as a researcher. This might relate to his personal education background and his workplace learning environment. As Kelvin pointed out, there are three major factors preventing rural teachers from conducting research projects. Firstly, rural teachers are fully occupied by various student management chaos so time for reading reference would be very little. Secondly, distance keeps rural teachers from the center of research resources. Because of the geographical remoteness, rural teachers rarely can have access to curriculum professionals or pedagogical experts in university or research institutions. Last, as rural teachers are weak in research expertise, they need step by step instructions in conducting research projects.

Chapter 8 | Discussion

This study examines the trajectory of professional identity construction of three rural EFL teachers and offers abundant, in-depth and valuable findings. The previous three chapters, namely Chapter 5 (Jenifer), Chapter 6 (Amy), and Chapter 7 (Kelvin), have presented qualitative aspects of teachers' identity construction, as well as factors that exert influence on the development of their professional identity. In this section, based on the analyzed data and guided by the integrated theoretical framework established in Chapter 3, an overall summary of findings will be firstly provided. Then commonalities and discrepancies in the construction of professional identity between these participant teachers will be discussed in detail. At the end of this chapter, a tentative model of secondary school language teachers' identity formation will be proposed.

8.1　Summary of findings

Base on the observation and interview data, the research findings show that teachers' personal life experiences play a significant role in shaping teachers' professional identity. In teachers' earlier life experiences, critical events, significant others, teacher role models, personal hobbies, earlier language learning experiences have direct connection with the formation of teachers' professional identity.

From three cases, this study discovers that language teachers' identity is constructed by their professional experiences. Teachers' preservice learning experiences, reflective classroom practices, peer coaching activities within the school-based Teaching and Research Groups (TRGs), and external teacher training courses like the NTTP greatly strengthen teachers' professional self. In addition, the present study finds that teachers' engagement in the classroom-based research facilitates teachers' professional identity construction. However, for teachers in these three cases, their engagement in the research activity varies in motivations, perceptions and ways of participation.

The present study identifies three major tires of influencing factors that affect the case teachers' construction of professional identity. These influencing factors can be generally categorized into three levels: the micro-level, meso-level and macro-level. The local socio-economic situation and multiethnic cultural context are discovered as the macro-level factor that exerts influence on the formation process of teacher professional identity; institutional environment and different levels of professional training create the meso-level of influencing factors; besides teachers' personal biographies, their linguistic competences, teaching beliefs and agentive quality are posited as the micro-level of influencing factors. These influencing factors act as both formative elements and powerful variables that have much impact on the development of teachers' professional identity.

8.2　Commonalities and discrepancies in building LTI

The previous section generally summarized the findings discovered by the present study. Because of the ongoing and formative nature of the LTI, the trajectory of LTI development is traced over time. On the journey of building professional identity, the three case teachers showed different features in their construction of teachers' identity in different phases of professional development. In this section, their commonalities and discrepancies in construction of teachers' identity are compared and discussed in detail.

8.2.1　Creating LTI in personal biographies

As suggested by the previous studies, the construction of LTI should be viewed from the perspective of teachers' sociocultural and historical origins, as a history-in-person process. History is brought to the present through the minds and bodies of individuals, as they are addressed by external people, forces, and institutions and respond using the words and practices of others, representing history-in-person (Holland & Lave, 2009). In this study, the Theory of History-in-Person is used as a powerful theoretical framework in connecting teachers' past and present in the trajectory of professional identity formation. Thus, to understand professional identity construction, one's personal history and the present forces must be included in the interpretive frame.

Before the participants entered the teaching profession, their preservice education, language learning experience in particular, facilitated the formation of teachers' professional identity. The participant teachers' language learning experience influenced their instructional practice, teaching philosophy, and their teaching beliefs and perception about students. In addition, personal hobbies and previous teacher role models acted as formative elements and exerted an important and enduring influence on their teachers' identity formation.

According to the interview data, before entering the teaching profession, all the three case teachers learned English language in junior and senior middle school and then in university or teachers' college. However, the three teachers varied in their trajectory of language learning. In Jenifer's case, as other average students in China, Jenifer received basic education of rudimentary English language knowledge in her secondary and high school. But because of her unsatisfying performance in College Entrance Examination, Jenifer failed to go to university or college for further education. Jenifer continued to learn and acquired systematic subject matter knowledge about the language in a teacher education program in Jiangsu Institute of Education where she had also been trained to become an English teacher. In Amy's case, the identity formation as a language learner was more evident. Amy considered English as a pragmatic instrument to know the outside world and with such a deep-seated belief, she kept decent record in learning English subject when she studied in secondary school and high school. Amy's identity as language learner was strengthened when she matriculated at a teachers' college where she acquired comprehensive language related knowledge about linguistics, English history, Western culture and cross-cultural communication. Whereas in the case of Kelvin, the data infers to a different way for the construction of the identity as language learner. Unlike Jenifer and Amy who were English major graduates, Kelvin studied

Botany and Plant Science in university. Although Kelvin didn't choose English as his major, he was believed as a capable learner; as he asserted in the interview, he was "good at learning English and could achieve high score in the test".

The analyzed data indicates that personal hobbies affect the formation of teachers' identity as language learner. In Amy's and Kelvin's cases, both of the teachers reported that their interest in learning English language was aroused by their personal hobbies. For example, Amy mentioned that she benefited from her hobby of singing English songs, and she improved her English pronunciation, especially the liaison skills, through repeatedly imitating the lyrics in English songs. Kelvin shared the same hobby with Amy, he liked singing English songs and loved listening to music. In his interview, Kelvin also said that he expanded English knowledge, learning new words in particular, from singing English songs. From Amy's and Kelvin's cases, it is obvious that the language related personal hobbies can contribute to the construction of teachers' identity.

In all cases of the three teachers, it should be noted that the role model of previous language teachers and some "significant others" played important roles in the formation of teachers' identity in their language learning period. Some of the role models even had far reaching influence on teachers' choice of future career. Jenifer talked about her high school English teacher as "resourceful" and "humorous", and she inherited many language learning skills which she was still applying in her current instruction. Amy reported her short interaction with a native-speaking NGO volunteer whose friendly disposition and attractive teaching skills deeply impressed her and finally inspired her to become a language teacher. In Amy's case, the significant others exerted a vital influence on her identity construction. However, not all examples of teacher role model were positive. In Kelvin's story, his high school English teacher had a negative influence on his identity construction. According to Kelvin's narration, because of the teacher's imappropriate teaching manner and his hostile disposition and physical punishment, students had negative emotions towards the English subject. The learning experience in high school English class was described by Kelvin as a "nightmare". The negative image of teacher role model influenced Kelvin's choice of major for future study and profession.

Besides, the language learning experience had consequential influence on the teachers' professional identity construction when they entered the teaching profession. All the three participant teachers claimed that their language learning experience had a profound influence on their perceptions of language learning and teaching, which significantly affected their teaching practices in the classroom. Taking Jenifer's case as an example, many of her language learning skills were inspired by her high school English teacher, and her language teaching pedagogy was instructed by her teachers in the teacher training program. Jenifer learned these language learning and teaching skills and applied them in her current language teaching classroom. Nonetheless, Amy's earlier identity as a language learner influenced her subsequent teaching practices in another way. Amy applied her personal hobby of singing English song, which she took up in her language learning period, in her teaching. Based on her own language learning experience, Amy designed classroom activities teaching her students to sing English songs, and her pedagogical practice of teaching language through songs and music made her instruction more enjoyable for students.

The findings are consistent with discoveries in the literature concerning teachers' identity development (Borg, 2015; Donato & Darvin, 2017; Grossman & Stodolsky, 1994; Holland & Lave, 2001). The findings are also evidenced in an empirical study by Donato and Darvin (2017), which argues that teachers' instructional talk must be viewed from the perspective of their sociocultural and historical origins as history-in-person process. Findings in the present study also echo with Borg's argument that "prospective teachers' prior language learning experiences establish cognitions about learning and language learning which form the basis of their initial conceptualizations of L2 teaching" (Borg, 2015, p.62).

In this section, based on the analyzed data from previous chapters (Chapter 5, 6, and 7), teachers' identity construction in their language learning period has been summarized. Meanwhile, different factors that may possibly influence the identity formation of the participant teachers' identity as language learners, such as their personal hobbies, teacher role model and significant others are discussed carefully. In the next section, teachers' professional identity as practitioner, which is the second type of language teachers' identity will be summarized and discussed.

8.2.2　Developing LTI in professional experiences before the NTTP

As summarized in section 8.1, during teachers' early career in teaching profession before they took the NTTP, their language learning experiences had direct influence on creating teachers' language teaching beliefs and acted as essential components of their professional identity. In addition, the school environment, support from colleagues and school leadership, students, and local ethnic sociocultural context were constraining variables in creating their professional identity.

As indicated in the interview, observation and document data indicate that before the teachers participated in the NTTP, they held "independent" beliefs in language teaching. "Independent teaching beliefs" refer to teachers' original perceptions or stance of the function of English language and their pedagogical practice in imparting knowledge and skills of that language. However, their "independent" beliefs became "convergent" after being trained in the NTTP, and changes in their beliefs will be discussed in the next section. According to the interview data, Kelvin held a very traditional belief in language learning and teaching. Based on his own language learning experience, he used to believe that language competence should be acquired by rote learning and in terms of language teaching, for a long time he had held that grammar-translation would be the only pedagogy applied to teaching language knowledge. In contrast, thanks to her solid subject matter knowledge, Amy perceived that language was more instrumental when it could be used in doing things, so the best way for acquiring linguistic competence was to learn it in real contexts. Jenifer, who was a veteran teacher, had more pragmatic belief in her language instruction. Over twenty years of teaching experience enabled Jenifer to have a better understanding of the reality in the classroom. She had a constant belief that any subject, including English, should be taught from learners' perspective, and the teaching activities should be designed in consideration of the students.

The research findings demonstrate that teachers' knowledge base is also a powerful constraining factor that limits the construction of language teachers' identity before the NTTP. In this study, all the three case teachers reported that to a certain extent, they were deficient in either disciplinary or pedagogical content knowledge. Although Kelvin considered himself as a capable learner of English language and had an agency in learning to teach, because of his non-English major education background, he had limited disciplinary and pedagogical content knowledge, and a lack of both types of knowledge hindered him from becoming a legitimate language teacher and consequently constrained him in the development of professional identity. Kelvin reflected in the interview that he had been teaching like a "frog at the bottom of a well" (Interview, P3-10). Four years of professional learning in the teachers' college prepared Amy in both disciplinary knowledge and pedagogical knowledge. However, when she began to teach her class in a rural school, the classroom reality was remarkably different from the class in which she had been trained in the practicum. In her novice teacher period, Amy clearly found that she was in great need of updating her pedagogical content knowledge. Amy also confessed in her interview that she learned how to teach like "a baby learns to walk" (Interview, P2-8, 2016). Compared with two novice teachers, Jenifer was responsive to students and knowledgeable of the content. Yet, facing the frequent curriculum reform and increasingly higher requirement for language teachers, Jenifer sensed the tensions between her teaching competence status quo and the increasing demand of pedagogical expertise.

Supported by different levels of knowledge base and guided by their "independent" language teaching beliefs, the three participant teachers instructed language skills in different ways, and their professional identity was constructed through teachers' personalized classroom instruction. Before Kelvin took the training courses in the NTTP, Kelvin's classroom teaching had been rather "traditional", which was evidenced by his lesson plan, classroom activities and roles he played during the class. According to the documents and observational data collected from a grammar class, Kelvin's instruction was teacher-centered and the pedagogy he adopted was basically grammar-translation. In addition, the teacher's roles in the interaction with his students during the instruction were mainly a resource-provider and a controller, which again showed his dominating position during the instruction. Amy held the belief that language was an instrument and should be learned in real contexts. Such language teaching belief was reflected in her lesson plan, classroom activities and roles she played in her interaction with students in a listening class. Guided by the official format of lesson plan which was provided by the education bureau, Amy clearly stated that her teaching approach was "interactive" and her class was actually carried out in a "Presentation-Practice-Production" way. According to the classroom video, the listening class was divided into five steps and the contents were taught through interactive activities such as role play, games, group activities. Compared with Kelvin, Amy played more roles during her classroom interaction not only as a resource-provider, monitor and a controller but also as an informant, assistant and a facilitator. As an expert teacher, Jenifer had her critical perceptions on language teaching. Data reveals that Jenifer's instruction of a listening and speaking class is entirely distinct from that of other two novices in lesson plans and interactive activities. In Jenifer's lesson plan, the instruction of listening skill was divided into three phases, and she tried to conduct different student activities which she expected to meet the students' learning need. Moreover, her arrangement of activities was "flipped": the students had been required to prepare their collaborative tasks or individual presentations before they came to the class. When the class began, the students would deliver their works in turns and the teacher would just observe and assess their performance. Jenifer's classroom practice, which had been video-recorded, was in concert with her lesson plan. Different activities such as students' mini play, word match and bilingual translation were presented in line with the lesson plan. As for the teacher's roles, Jenifer took on different instructional roles according to student activities, such as a manager, controller, grader or an error corrector.

According to the data, the present study finds that some internal and external factors affect the construction of teachers' professional identity through their instructional practices before the NTTP. Firstly, past learning experiences were deeply embedded in their construction of professional identity. All the three teachers reported that when they began to teach, they relied heavily on their previous learning experience, as Amy claimed, she "copied" (P2-8, 2006) what she had learned in college to teach her current class. Secondly, teachers' beliefs and knowledge, either the disciplinary and pedagogical content knowledge, constrained their development of professional identity. Teachers' beliefs in language learning and teaching intrinsically connect with their classroom behavior as they make lesson plans and design students' activities. For example, in Kelvin's case, because Kelvin thought that rote learning was the way to acquire language skills; therefore, in his classroom practice, he chose to use grammar-translation, which was a rather traditional teaching approach. With regard to teachers' knowledge, again as vividly evidenced in Kelvin's case, it was a powerful restraining factor that affected teachers' professional identity development. Because of his non-English major education background, Kelvin had been weak in both disciplinary knowledge and pedagogical content knowledge. Therefore, it took him quite some time to look for appropriate teaching approach and methods in order to improve his teaching and students' performance. Kelvin traveled hard on the journey to become a legitimate language teacher. Thirdly, despite teachers' beliefs and knowledge, teachers' practice communities functioned as an external factor in affecting the construction of professional identity of the participant teachers. As reported by Amy, she felt lucky to work with groups of friendly and helpful colleagues in her school. In comparison, Kelvin's colleagues appeared indifferent and unfriendly and had little communication. The rather hostile environment frustrated Kelvin and became part of the reasons for his frequently-occurring idea of quitting from teaching profession. Obviously, teachers' relationship with colleagues of the same subject indeed influences their perception of their own professional identity (Beijaard, 1995).

In conclusion, through cross-case comparison, the three secondary school language teachers' formation of professional identity through their classroom practice is summerized and discussed. It is discovered that teachers' beliefs in language learning and teaching and their content knowledge base are the core elements in framing the professional identity. In addition, in the construction of professional identity, the institutional context and students are major influencing factors that facilitate or constrain the formation. In the next section, how teachers' professional identity is reshaped will be discussed.

8.2.3   The NTTP—powerful constituent in shaping LTI

The present study discovers that besides some occasional outside-school training courses, the external professional trainings, like the National Teacher Training Plan, enhance teachers' professional identity development. This is particularly evidenced in their support for teachers' knowledge base.

As reviewed and discussed in section 3.3.2, Richards and Farrell (2011) identify "disciplinary knowledge" and "pedagogical content knowledge" as two broad types of content knowledge relevant to language teachers. The findings of this study are concurrent with this discovery in literature. As introduced in Chapter 2, the NTTP is a nationwide in-service teaching training program constituting three major modules, namely Tainer-Training Module, Demonstration Module and Distance Education Module. From different perspectives and to a certain extent, the three training modules have broadened and strengthened teachers' disciplinary and pedagogical content knowledge. Taking Kelvin's case for example, he welcomed the training with great enthusiasm and he sponged all kinds of knowledge that could benefit his linguistic and pedagogical competence. As a young teacher without much professional training in language teaching, Kelvin had been struggling for effective teaching approach and methods for long. When provided with the opportunity, he cherished it a lot, as he acclaimed in the interview that the training "was informative and inspiring, twenty days of learning was worthy of many years of stumbling in the classroom" (Interview, P3-11, 2016). As mentioned in previous sections, though Kelvin was a quick learner and had talent in language learning, he was weak in pedagogical knowledge for language teaching. In the Trainer-Training Module, Kelvin took many hands-on lectures such as teaching of English phonics, reading through picture books, and process writing, which greatly strengthened his pedagogical expertise. Amy also reported her benefits gained from attending the Demonstration Module. In the interview, Amy recalled the experience when she gave the demonstration class in the presence of many colleagues and senior teachers, she described it as "trying and intimidating". Taking the demonstration class exerts great emotional pressure on novice teachers; however, it can also be a strong impetus for teachers' professional development. Amy compared the Demonstration Module to a "furnace" in which her "subject matter knowledge was enhanced, and teaching beliefs were remolded" (Interview, P2-13, 2016). The findings of this study also indicate that the NTTP has not only facilitated professional growth of novice teachers, but also helped senior teachers to update their subject matter knowledge and broadened their pedagogical horizon. As a senior teacher in school and the "backbone teacher" in the NTTP, Jenifer considered her learning experiences in the NTTP as a "turning point" on the road of professional development even she was approaching retirement. The

NTTP effectively enhanced her perception about language teaching, as Jenifer stated in the interview that "the lectures in the training furthered my understandings about the roles and positions I should take in the classroom, [...] what I learned from the training courses altered my beliefs as an English teacher" (Interview, P1-13, 2016).

As introduced in Chapter 2, the Distance Education Module in the NTTP takes two forms, learning via the official distance education website and learning via the SNS-based teachers' online community, and to different extent the two forms affect the professional identity construction. All the three case teachers agreed that the official distance education made less contribution to their professional learning during the NTTP. Teachers' negative feedback for the official distance learning sites might attribute to the unattractive contents and lack of interaction. As Amy pointed out, her learning experience on the distance education platform was rather "boring" and her colleagues reported the same comments. She regarded "lack of interaction as the major reason for teachers' annoyance in doing this kind of compulsory task" (Interview, P2-14, 2006) as the major flaw of the official online learning platform. With respect to the SNS-based online learning community, however, teachers showed quite optimistic attitude. Teachers' feedback for the SNS-based online learning community can be summarized by Kelvin's metaphor comparing the distance education to "a television antenna on the roof, which can be used to receive signals from the outside world" (Interview, P3-8, 2016). In addition, Kelvin enjoyed the discussion between teachers in the online learning community "because everything can be done just on the cell phone" and when he posed various questions about grammar and teaching method, he "always got reply from some unknown but warmhearted teachers in the online discussion group" (Interview, P3-15, 2016).

To summarize, it is clear to see that the additional professional training, especially the National Teacher Training Plan which is launched by the MOE (Minister of Education) and carried out by local universities, is instrumental in helping to upgrade the quality of teachers in the rural areas (Pawan et al., 2017). According to the analyzed data, the three training modules in the NTTP program have made contributions to the construction of teachers' professional identity from different perspectives. The Trainer-Training Module effectively expands teachers' horizon in their pedagogical content knowledge, while in the Distance Education Module, teachers not only receive additional knowledge for language learning and teaching, but also establish a learning community beyond the constraints of time and space. The additional training programs like the NTTP effectively improve teachers' disciplinary knowledge and pedagogical content knowledge which are two core constituents in constructing teachers' professional identity.

The next section will focus on discussing how teachers' professional identity is developed in teachers' changed beliefs and renewed classroom practices.

8.2.4 LTI negotiated in practicing competing pedagogies

As discussed in the preceding section, this study identifies the "Trainer-Training Module", "Demonstration Module" and "Distance Education Module" as three distinctive approaches in the NTTP that effectively affect the construction of teachers' professional identity. Based on the knowledge accumulated through years of classroom instruction, the three case teachers continued to experiment, negotiate and practice in their language teaching classroom with newly-equipped expertise upon returning to their own schools. In this period, the three teachers negotiated the old and new ways of teaching and continued to develop their professional identity. In this section, how the three case teachers' professional identity develops through classroom teaching in the phase after they have been trained in the NTTP will be summarized and discussed.

According to the interview data, Kelvin cherished his opportunity of being trained in the NTTP. He "sponged" pedagogical content knowledge provided by different modules in the NTTP and was active in the online teacher discussion group. When he completed the intensive training courses in university, Kelvin continued to take seminars or lectures and delivered open classes for his colleagues or teachers from other schools as required by the NTTP. Being guided by the upgraded language teaching beliefs, Kelvin began to try the new teaching model and different methods learned during the NTTP in his class. As shown in the document data of Kelvin's lesson plan (Document, P3-2, 2006), Kelvin began to adopt the "Three Stages and Seven Steps" teaching model which was required by the City Education Bureau and tried to use different pedagogical skills such as scaffolding and collaborative learning in his writing class. Kelvin reflected in the interview that before the NTTP, he was deficient in pedagogical content knowledge and had been in bad need of new knowledge to improve his classroom practice. After being trained in the NTTP, both the pedagogical content knowledge learned in the training course work and the official teaching model required by the education bureau functioned as the "helping hand" that assisted Kelvin to find effective teaching methods. Kelvin benefited from using the new model as he acknowledged in the interview "[…] with the help of the new model, I'm becoming more confident in teaching" (Interview, P3-16, 2016).

The training experience in the NTTP significantly influenced Kelvin's perceptions on language teaching, and accordingly changed his practices in the classroom. It is noteworthy that Kelvin's change in both beliefs and practices is his conformation to the local official requirement and national curriculum reform. Kelvin's change is also a direct result of his personal education background, workplace environment, scarce professional development resources and absence of teachers' community of practices, which are part of personal or professional factors affecting his construction of teachers' professional identity.

The findings demonstrate that after the NTTP, Amy has also conformed to the local official teaching requirement by using the officially suggested "Three Stages and Seven Steps" teaching model. However, Amy's belief and practices were twofold. For one thing, Amy participated in the same training modules as Kelvin did during the NTTP. By taking advantage of her broadened pedagogical content knowledge and supported by the new official teaching mode, Amy made considerable improvement in her classroom teaching, as she reflected in the interview "[…] my inappropriate beliefs and practices in teaching reading skills were transformed by the new integrated approach advocated by the NTTP" (Interview data P2-15). For another, before the NTTP training, Amy had the belief that language should be learned in a real context. In the guidance of such perceptions on language learning, she planned and implemented interactive activities simulating real contexts in her instruction of different language skills. After the NTTP, though Amy changed her teaching plan by integrating the approaches and the official model, she didn't abandon her own belief of language teaching. From the episodes of classroom video, it is evidenced that Amy has adopted the official model as a framework but still applied some interactive students' activities in her instruction of a reading class. The activities, apparently were designed according to her own belief of language teaching, which she had persisted before the NTTP.

It is not surprising to see Amy's two folded beliefs and practices in the period after the NTTP. Unlike Kelvin who lacked systematic preparation of becoming a language teacher and fully conformed to the official requirement, Amy had been well trained in her teacher preparation programs in college. Her past learning experience had a lasting influence on her future teaching practices. Therefore, when she positively responded to the local curriculum reform at a micro level and then national language policy change at the macro level, Amy partly maintained her own beliefs and practices in classroom instruction.

According to the data, commonalities are discovered between Amy and Jenifer in terms of their perceptions and practices in their teaching after they received professional training in the NTTP. As introduced in Chapter 5 and discussed in section 8.2 in this chapter, being a senior teacher with over 25 years of teaching experience, Jenifer accepted the unified teaching model advocated by the local educational authorities and the new theories, approaches, methods provided by the NTTP with enthusiasm. Jenifer acknowledged the contribution that the external training made to her professional development, as she commented in the interview that the training courses provided by the NTTP not only "broadened and strengthened my content knowledge about English language from both theory and practice perspectives" but also "changed my understandings about my roles and positions in my classroom", and the training courses "altered my beliefs as an English teacher…"(Interview, P1-13, 2016). Before the NTTP, Jenifer formed a constant belief which was derived from her many years of teaching in the frontline that teachers' classroom instruction should be "pragmatic" and "effective", and teachers should understand "students' learning ability and their performance status quo" (Interview, P1-10, 2016). According to the document data of Jenifer's lesson plan and the classroom video, after the NTTP, though Jenifer borrowed the "Three Stages and Seven Steps" teaching model as an overarching framework for her writing class and changed her instruction from "flipped" approach, she adhered to her personal teaching principle which was evidenced in her lesson plan and implementation of students classroom activities.

Based on the analyzed data, the present study finds that after being trained in the NTTP, the three case teachers have proceeded to build up their professional identity through their pedagogical practices but in different ways. Kelvin fully conformed to the new teaching model advocated by the City Education Bureau and actively experimented different teaching approaches or techniques in his classroom teaching; whereas, Amy and Jenifer shared some common features in their building of professional identity. In their classroom instruction, both of the teachers adopted the new teaching model as a framework in planning and classroom instruction, and tried new approaches or methods which they learned from the NTTP training. However, their disciplinary knowledge and pedagogical content knowledge still had powerful influence on Amy's and Jenifer's classroom instruction and the extent to which they conformed to the official requirement and curriculum reform.

In brief, teachers develop a personal understanding of teaching that incorporates beliefs, concepts, theories, and principles of teaching (Borg, 206). This understanding not only varies for every teacher, based on their differing backgrounds, characteristics and experiences, but also can be translated into future actions. According to the data, the three case teachers continued to develop their beliefs in language learning and teaching by integrating their past teaching experience and new pedagogical content knowledge. The participant teachers' integration of the knowledge learned in the past and present is a reflection of how one's identity as a teacher has evolved and influences teacher's thinking and classroom behavior in relation to a growing abstract system of knowledge and values against which to measure teaching performance (Pennington & Richards, 2016). This takes language teachers' identity beyond training (Richards, 1998), to a higher level of reflection that seeks to relate individual classroom actions and decision-making to each other and to higher principles (Pennington & Richards, 2016).

Construction of language teachers' professional identity is not only an ongoing process but also in multilayered context. In addition to the classroom instruction which is the major site the teachers' professional identity is built in, doing the classroom-based research is another important site recognized by the present study for teachers' professional identity construction. In the next chapter, how teachers' professional identity is developed and enhanced through doing action research will be discussed.

8.2.5　LTI enhanced by the classroom-based research

The present study discovers that teachers' engagement in the classroom-based research prompts teachers' professional identity construction. However, for the three case teachers, their engagement in the research activity varies in motivations, perceptions and ways of participation.

Findings in this study are in line with the literature that teacher research legitimates teaching practice in the classroom as a crucial site for teacher learning and identity construction (Johnson, Karen E., 2006; Pennington & Richards, 2016). In the words of Pennington and Richards (2016), language teachers are "like other teachers, should not only be familiar with the theoretical orientations of the field of language teaching and learning, but also be involved in constructing theory themselves" (p.19). As Sharkey (2004) points out, language teachers should be "active readers, users, and producer of theory" (p.281). In this vein, Johnson (2006) argues that "L2 teachers are users and creators of knowledge and theorize in their own right. Teacher research positions teachers as investigators of and interveners in their own practice while making their investigations and interventions, in essence their learning" (p.242).

As mentioned previously, the three participant teachers had different motivations to be engaged in the research activities. For example, Jenifer was doing two research projects when being selected as participant for the present study. Jenifer had dual motivations and her motivations were goal-oriented. For one thing, Jenifer had strong agency in learning new knowledge, as she expected "to learn from those who can do research" (Interview, P1-23, 2017); for another, because doing research and publishing papers were essential requirements for teachers in their application for higher title, like senior teachers, Jenifer must do research, publish paper and win awards in order to make progress in her profession. Doing research was part of her efforts of constructing the professional identity, as Jenifer claimed, "a higher title, I think, would not only be an evidence of my teaching competence but also a recognition for my 30 years of hard work […]" (Interview, P1-23, 2017). In terms of motivation, Amy and Kelvin shared some commonality. Doing research was not the original intention of the two young participants, they happened to be engaged in the research activity, as Amy reported, "the reason for me to be engaged in action research is simple. A year ago, one of the senior teachers was doing her classroom-based inquiry and I was asked to help her to do some basic work in collecting materials" (Interview, P2-16, 2016).

With respect to research, the present study concludes that the participants have relatively weak competence in conducting research, and their competences in doing research activities are retrained by many layers of personal and contextual factors. Firstly, the current teacher education program didn't prepare the teachers with essential knowledge that enabled them to conduct research independently. It proved to be true by Amy's statement that "because we have not been well trained about any skills on doing research, it would be challenging for teachers to conduct research projects" (Interview, P2-18, 2016). Secondly, the institutional context neither encouraged nor supported the teachers to conduct research. As Jenifer criticized, " […] middle school teachers are not encouraged to do research. Schools are pragmatic, even utilitarian in teachers' professional development. Because all schools are assessed by a set of indicators showing students' performance in tests, teachers have to follow and reach stringent requirements in helping students to make higher scores. […] In such 'score-driven' context, there is no academic environment for teachers to do research. Things are alike in both the in-school and out-of-school professional training programs. Time is usually spent on learning new education policies or practicing new pedagogical theories, because no specific contents are taught on research skills" (Interview, P1-24, 2016). Thirdly, based on the ethnographical observation, teaching in the remote rural schools, the three participant teachers were almost drowned in their daily teaching and student management chaos. It was truly difficult for them to squeeze extra time from their busy schedule to conduct any additional research, as Kelvin complained, "It is nearly impossible for me to find time reading books, since I will be occupied in tremendous student management works irrelevant to my own discipline" (Interview, P3-22, 2016). Moreover, it was also difficult for the rural teachers to get any possible access to the resources of research, as Kelvin reported, " […] Working in the remote border schools means you are far away from the research center, where there are abundant research resources such as experts, professionals, lectures, conferences or references. We do need some professionals to instruct or direct rural teachers to conduct research. I hold rather pessimistic beliefs that without the help from experts or professionals from universities or other institutions, it would be extremely hard for rural teachers to conduct research projects" (Interview, P3-22, 2016). Nevertheless, though having been frustrated by myriads of difficulties that confined their attempt in conducting research activities, the participant teachers benefited a lot from doing research, as Amy concluded, "For the young and inexperienced teachers, like me, we can benefit substantially from either process of learning and doing research. New and innovative ideas would generate when being engaged in the research project and the findings, discoveries, in turn, finally could be used to improve your classroom teaching practice. Doing research keeps me in a constant status of learning" (Interview, P2-16, 2016).

To summarize, the present study discovers that engagement in classroom-based research legitimates teachers' teaching practice and enhances their construction of professional identity, as Pennington and Richards (2016) maintain that identity is built cumulatively in sites of practices as not only a user but also a producer of both practical (pedagogical content) knowledge and theoretical (disciplinary knowledge) of the filed (p.16). The participant secondary EFL teachers, though being not competent enough in terms of conducting research, attempted to conduct classroom-based action research, and in turn, their efforts in doing research enhanced their conceptions on language learning and teaching.

8.3　Influencing factors on LTI construction

As evidenced in the finding chapters (Chapters 5, 6 and 7), the construction of the participant teachers' professional identity was shaped and reshaped by myriads of personal or professional, internal or external factors which could be generally categorized into three levels: micro-level, meso-level and macro-level. These influencing factors acted as formative elements and had profound effect on professional identity formation of the participant teachers.

8.3.1   The micro-level influencing factors

The first tier of influencing factors that affect the formation of language teachers' identity are associated with competences that help to create an "inside" identity as a language teacher. These competences stem from their personal biography, knowledge, beliefs, and agentive quality.

Personal Biography

The present study identifies that teachers' personal biography which includes family background, education experiences, teacher role models or significant others plays an important role in the formation of teachers' professional identity. As for the influence from teacher's family, Kelvin's case is a telling example. As introduced in Chapter 7, Kelvin entered the teaching profession "by accident". Kelvin studied Botanic Science in university and planned to find a job in a big city. However, the misfortune befalling in his family abruptly altered his career plan and made him a language teacher working in a remote rural school. Aside from family background, education experiences seemed to play a strong, mediating role in the formation of professional identity before their service. Conclusion can be drawn from the data that systematic and complete professional education background considerably benefit the participant teachers for their future teaching career. Take Amy for example. Taking advantage of her personal talent, Amy applied to study in a teachers' college and chose teaching English as her future career. As evidenced in the classroom video, her solid subject matter knowledge learned in college and pedagogy acquired in practicum facilitated her to build a professional identity. It was interesting to note that former teachers and significant others were seen as a "frame of reference" (Flores & Day, 2006) in their sense-making of teaching. To all three case teachers, the influence from previous teachers or significant others was apparent. For Amy, her dream of becoming an English teacher was ignited by her interaction with a kind native speaker who was a volunteer from an NGO program. Whereas Kelvin abandoned his idea of taking any teaching related professions because of his bad memory of an ill-tempered English teacher in middle school. Moreover, in Jenifer's case, her teaching approach before the NTTP had been significantly affected by her English teachers in high school and in teacher education program. The findings confirm earlier research (Flories & Day 2006; Knowles, 1992; Lortie, 1975) which argues that prior experiences seem to play a strong, mediating role in the identities which new teachers bring into their first school teaching experience.

Teachers' Knowledge

Based on Richards and Farrell's (2011) dichotomy of teachers' knowledge (disciplinary knowledge and pedagogical content knowledge), the present study regards teachers' knowledge base as one of the micro-level influencing factors that shape the teachers' professional identity. The data reveals that the knowledge base of the rural secondary school language teachers in Yunnan takes two distinctive features. Firstly, this cohort of teachers are commonly deficient in both types of knowledge; and secondly, teachers' prior knowledge base has enduring influence on their current instruction. Based on the ethnographic observation, the present study finds that the language teachers working in the rural or remote border schools in Yunnan are commonly frustrated by their insufficient knowledge about both English language and methods to teach the language. Interview data discovers that teachers might be confident in their pedagogical competence but weak in linguistic proficiency. As a school teacher reflected, "honestly speaking, I've been feeling terrible about my own English level" (Interview, P3-6). This could also be evidenced in Kelvin's case that he acknowledged his limited knowledge hindered his writing skill, "Writing skill is critically important […] but I often deliberately choose not to teach […] My irresponsibility is the result of my limited writing skill and shortage of appropriate teaching methods" (Interview, P3-6). As aforementioned, the knowledge that the teachers accumulated in preservice education period clearly influenced their future instructional practices. All the three case teachers reported that they incorporated disciplinary knowledge and pedagogical content knowledge (e.g. linguistic theories, Western culture, literature, or diverse language teaching approaches and methods) from their previous learning experience into to their current instruction.

Teachers' Beliefs

According to data of the present study, teachers' beliefs, like a compelling construct, influence the development process of teachers' professional identity. This finding is in concert with discoveries in literature examining the role of teachers' beliefs arguing that teachers' belief is a strong determinant of classroom practice (Deemer, 2004; Guskey, 1988; Murphy, 2004; Silva, 1999; Stein & Wang, 1988; Tan & Saw Lan, 2011). Examples in the three cases evidence that the participant teachers have built their professional identity through the negotiation of their past and changed beliefs in language learning and teaching. In Amy's story, the teacher held an instrumental view of the nature of English language, as Amy remarked, "I regard language as a kind of tool which can be used in different situations and do with different objects" (Interview, P2-9, 2016). Accordingly, guided by such language teaching belief, as showed in her lesson plan, many interactive students' activities were designed in order to create a real context for students to learn and practice. The teacher was satisfied with the result of her belief and practice, as Amy commented, "[…] my students were very happy to learn the knowledge in a relaxed atmosphere and by 'operating the tools'. Maybe this is why interactive approach would be a popular way to maintain learning motivation and encourage them to learn the subject" (Interview, P2-9, 2016). Kelvin's case is another example showing how teachers develop professional identity through negotiation of the past and changed teaching beliefs. In the interview after the NTTP, Kelvin commented, "Before the NTTP, I had explored for better teaching approach all by myself, I was not very sure whether the methods I used in my class were right. From the last semester, […] I considered the new teaching mode as a guideline and an efficient tool to help me in making lesson plan, rearranging the contents and designing classroom activities. Now with the help of the new model, I'm becoming more confident in teaching" (Interview, P3-16, 2016). Examples from the participant teachers show that the negotiation of the past and changed beliefs can be considered as one of the important sites for the teachers to develop their professional identity.

Teachers' Agency

As mentioned in Chapter 3, researchers agree that teachers' agency is important in professional identity formation (Beauchamp & Thomas, 2009; Beijaard et al., 2004; Parkison, 2008), and plays a critical role in sustaining teachers' professional development (Tao & Gao, 2017). The present study finds that agency is a propelling power for the construction of teachers' professional identity. According to the data, the three case teachers demonstrated their agentive quality in different time of professional development, namely language learning period, learning to teach in the NTTP and their active engagement in teacher research. The finding is basically in line with Maclellan's (2017) argument that agency is one of teachers' most important pedagogical resources, and the capacity to make principled choice, to take action and make that action happen (p.253).

In their language learning period, all the three case teachers showed their "inner power of learning". For example, in order to improve her subject matter knowledge, Jenifer looked for grammar books everywhere in the city in all manner of ways and waited for a long time for the books. Amy and Kelvin were not only active in learning language knowledge, but also passionate in taking various extra-curriculum activities such as English-speaking contest to practice their language proficiency. Although the three case teachers were relatively insufficient in both disciplinary and pedagogical knowledge, they showed earnestness and responsibility in classroom instruction. Just because of their outstanding teaching performance, they had been selected as the "backbone teachers" in the National Teacher Training Plan. During their training in the NTTP, they were all industrious in learning and disseminating the knowledge learned in the training program. Teachers' agency was also evident by their engagement in the classroom-based action research. Again, Jenifer is a telling example. Even though she was approaching her retirement, Jenifer was enthusiastic for teacher action research. Making time in her busy teaching work, she accepted the invitation to offer possible help in other teacher's research projects. With great interest in learning to do the research, Jenifer also began her own projects. As Jenifer noted in the interview, "[…] for one thing, I expect to solve some practical problems which have long hindered students in certain aspects from language learning; for another, I do wish to put my years of reflections on teaching into theory through doing the classroom-based action research" (Interview, P1-23).

In this section, micro-level influencing factors on the construction of teachers' professional identity are summarized and discussed. The micro-level or first tier of influencing factors is related to teachers' personal biography, knowledge, or beliefs. Since the professional identity is constructed in diverse milieu or contexts, in the next section, a wider context in which teachers' professional identity is shaped will be discussed.

8.3.2　The meso-level influencing factors

The present study finds that the construction of teachers' professional identity is challenged, impacted and reshaped by school context and professional training. These "outside" factors are regarded as crucial meso-level factors influencing teachers' professional identity development.

School Context

The institution, serving as the major context teachers work in, has been evidenced as an important source of factors influencing both teachers' teaching practice and their identity formation (Beijaard et al., 2004). In this study, the institutional factors may be interpreted from three perspectives: school context, students and parent investment, and peer teacher community.

As the working place where teachers spend most of their time, schools are an important milieu and domain for the formation and development of teachers' professional identity, as Lee points out, "schools have been considered as bounded containers in which professional identities of teachers are shaped by practices and social relations" (Lee et al., 2011, p.1). As for the influence, the geographical remoteness is the first aspect. Schools in which the participant teachers in this study work are located in rural or border regions in Xishuangbanna Prefecture in the southwest of China. The geographical remoteness hinders teachers from frequent communication with professionals from outside. As Kevin complained in the interview, "Teaching in the border school, it is not convenient for teachers to go outside [...] and because of geographical distance it is nearly impossible to communicate with expert teachers or professionals in pedagogy or curriculum" (Interview, P3-14). Limited support from school leaders is the second aspect, which is evidenced in remarks from the principal of Dong Feng Middle School. In his interview the principal regretted that "[...] if you intend to develop either short-term or long-term teacher training schemes, you'll need some professionals and he'd better be the members of management team. Unfortunately, no teacher in the management is teaching the English subject, because we know little about the nature of language learning and teaching" (Interview, P3-5). The remarks from the school principals reveal the half-heartedness in supporting teacher development. In addition, the "score-driven"

(Interview, P1-24) status quo in secondary schools still exists in China. Teachers' performance will be assessed not only by their competences in classroom instruction, but also by students' performance in examinations. In this sense, limited support from school management and "score-driven" based teacher performance evaluation system confine and influence teachers' sense-making of successful teacher, which accordingly influences their construction of professional identity.

Students and parents' investment is identified as an important factor that affects teacher professional identity construction. As Norton argues, if learners invest in a language, they do so with the understanding that they will acquire a wider range of symbolic and material resources, which will in turn increase the value of their cultural capital and social power (Darvin & Norton, 2015, p.37). The present study discovers that different levels of investment from students and parents affect teachers' sense-making to a different extent. In Jenifer's story, it was proposed that a possible reason for the lower student learning motivation might be partially attributed to the local economic well-being. In addition, ethnographic survey in the present study reveals that most parents in multiethnic regions in Xishuangbanna maintain a naturalistic belief in educating their children and consider that children should grow up in a natural environment. Such a loose and flexible parental belief in education together with lower learning motivation challenged teachers' classroom practice and efficacy, and accordingly influenced their construction of professional identity. However, in Amy's story, the data draws another picture of students and parental investment. The students in Green Leaf Middle School were less demographically and linguistically diversified than students in the schools in the central ethnic area (like the school in which Kelvin teaches). Students in Amy's school possessed comparatively higher motivation in learning school subjects. Higher parental investment in educating their children was evidenced in an interview with a mother, "[…] as a mother of my twin sons, I worked very hard in this coffee farm to support them to study in the school. I would offer any possible help for my sons to learn well, and I do expect them to go to university" (Field notes, P2-1). Encouraged by their parents, students in Amy's school were active in their classroom presentation, which is evidenced by observation data which also shows the teacher's active response to the students' enthusiasm in learning English language. In brief, different levels of student learning motivation and parental investment in education challenge or facilitate teachers' classroom practice, and also directly influence their construction of professional identity.

The colleagues can be influential in shaping teachers' professional identities (Beauchamp & Thomas, 2009). In this study, it has been found that the relationship with colleagues and peer teacher communities help to shape the way that the teachers perceive themselves and their professional identity formation. The acknowledgement and recognition of their competence which those colleagues provide not only one important source for their "positive self-esteem" (Gold, 1996, p.579) but also contribute to their job satisfaction and effective collaboration (Kelchermans & Ballet, 2002). Taking Kelvin as an example, Kelvin described his journey of becoming a language teacher as "a travel in the dark tunnel" (Interview, P3-7). Due to their insufficient language and teaching competence, the English teachers in Kelvin's school chose not to communicate with each other on the topic of teaching. As a novice teacher, Kelvin had received very little support from his colleagues. However, in Amy's case, she "considered her TRG members as a family" (Interview, P2-5). Amy learned from old teachers and was offered help in teaching-related affairs. Amy concluded her interaction with colleagues like this, "working in such a harmonious environment, everyone here in our group can learn and grow" (Interview, P2-5). Kelvin's and Amy's stories show that good collegial relationship helps novice teachers smoothly and successfully survive and develop into good and competent teachers, while hostile or negative work place environment hinders the process of self-reorganization. The study discovers that in spite of the conventional face-to-face peer teacher community in the school TRG, teachers are increasingly inclined to communicate via the SNS-based online discussion group, which enables teachers to be distant from one another to communicate beyond time and space. This has been elaborated in section 8.4.

Curriculum Reform-Based Professional Training

As mentioned in the previous section (8.4) in this chapter, it has been widely accepted that the construction of professional identity not only happens with teachers' interpretation and negotiation of meaning embedded within the context of the classroom, but also is facilitated and catalyzed at different levels of additional professional trainings outside the classroom. The professional training, or on-the-job training program in this study specifically refers to the National Teacher Training Plan (NTTP) which exerts systematic and significant influence on the professional development of rural teachers nationwide. Based on the data, the present study concludes that the NTTP has reconstructed the participant teachers' professional identity from different perspectives. The Trainer-Training Module effectively expanded the teachers' horizon in their pedagogical content knowledge, while the Distance Education Module facilitated the teachers not only to receive additional knowledge for language learning and teaching, but to establish a learning community beyond the constraint of time and space as well. And the Demonstration Module helped three case teachers to put their pedagogical knowledge learned in different training sessions into practical instructional experience. In brief, additional on-the-job training programs like the NTTP effectively improve teachers' disciplinary knowledge and pedagogical content knowledge which are two core constituents in constructing teachers' professional identity.

8.3.3　The macro-level influencing factors

Given the national policies on language, ethnicity, education and socioeconomic development, the present study identifies the national language policy, multiethnic culture and local socioeconomic development as the third-tier influencing factors, which affect teachers' construction of professional identity at the macro level.

As introduced in the research design, Xishuangbanna Dai Autonomous Prefecture, where this study was carried out, is located in the southernmost tip of Yunnan province. With a territory of 19,096 square kilometers and a population of 1,306,000, Xishuangbanna Dai Autonomous Prefecture is home to 13 officially identified ethnic groups, among which the Dai and Hani are major ethnic groups, speaking six different ethnic languages and more local dialects. As the only tropical rain forest nature reserve in China, the area has surprising biological diversity in the virgin forest. In religion, it is greatly influenced by Hinayana Buddhism of Southeast Asia.

In the past 30 years, China has experienced rapid changes in political, economic, educational, and language policies and practices. Thanks to the fast socioeconomic development and supporting development policies for ethnic regions, drastic social, cultural, economic and demographic changes have taken place in the ethnic community (Choi 2010, p. 173). As mentioned in Chapter 5, the tropical climate, fertile land, deforestation as well as favorite agricultural policies, farmers in Xishuangbanna have been growing rubber trees, banana trees and various tropical plants on an unprecedented scale. The tropical economic plants yield not only abundant produce but large seasonal cash income. According to fieldwork data, however, cash income usually would not be advisably deposited in banks or used to enlarge the production. Instead, most of the income might go for excessive or conspicuous consumption, with only a meager part spent on education. As remarked by the principal of Dong Feng Middle School, "[...] in other places outside Xishuangbanna, students leave school because of poverty, but here, students drop out of school for being well-off" (Interview, P3-4, 2016). The economic well-being led to students' low motivation and poor academic performance in school. The lower learner investment created more serious problems for teachers' classroom instruction, and the effect has been elaborated in Jenifer's chapter.

In addition, ethnic cultures exert influence on the school education from outside. Because of their religious beliefs, most parents in ethnic regions in Xishuangbanna possess a naturalistic conception of educating their children and consider that the children should grow up in a natural environment. Most parents hold a religious philosophy that children should not be forced to learn anything that they would not like. If the child hates going to school, for example, the parents would choose not to interfere or impose their own will or values on the child.

In this section, most external influencing factors that affect the professional identity construction are identified, summarized and discussed. In the next section, based on the discussion, a tentative model of secondary school language teachers' professional identity construction will be proposed.

8.4 A tentative model of secondary school language teachers' identity construction

In order to explicate the complex construction process of teachers' identity, as well as influencing factors that affect the process, different constructs such as teachers' knowledge, teachers' beliefs, etc. are organized in the following hypothetical model (Figure 8.1). This tentative model is framed by the analyses of data accumulated from finding chapters (Chapters 5, 6, 7) and discussion.

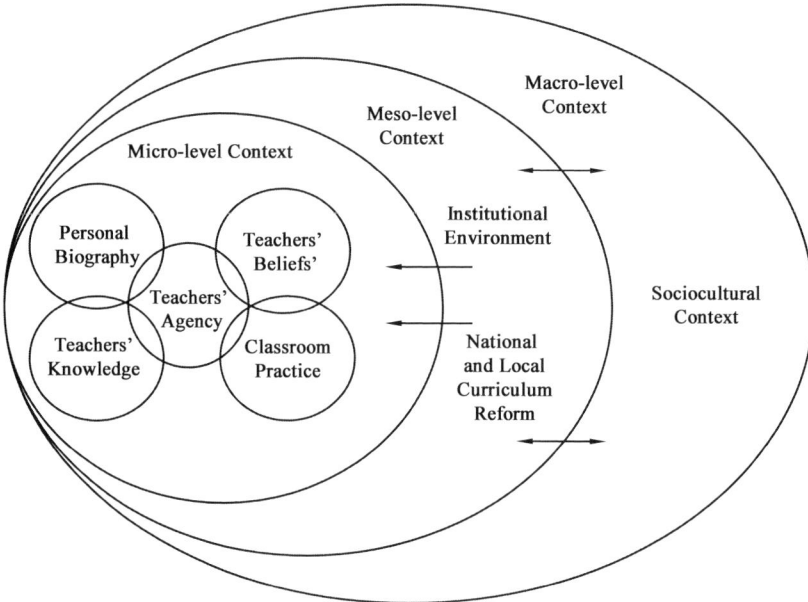

Figure 8.1　A tentative model of secondary school language teachers' professional identity construction

As can be seen in the figure, teachers' personal biography, knowledge, beliefs, agency and classroom practice constitute the micro-level context for the formation and development of teachers' professional identity. In this first tier of contextual factors, teachers' professional identity starts to take shape from the personal biography, including teachers' family background, past learning experience and impression of previous teachers' role models. When they start their teaching profession, these "precursor" elements subsequently adapt to teachers' instructional practices and then gradually develop into teachers' individualized disciplinary and pedagogical content knowledge. Guided by teachers' teaching beliefs, which have been formulated in teachers' past language learning and current language teaching experiences, such integrated knowledge base is practiced, contested, broadened or enriched through classroom behaviors over time. In the long accumulation of knowledge and experiences, teachers' agency plays a critical role. Teachers' agentive quality ignites and sustains their motivation and passion in acquiring new knowledge or expertise.

However, the external forces, such as the institutional context and on-the-job professional training program, identified as the second tier of influencing context in this research, have also been powerful forces on teachers' professional identity construction. For teachers, the school context has a strong and direct impact on teachers' performance. As Beijaard points out, the institution, serving as the major context teachers work in, has been evidenced as an important source of factors influencing both teachers' teaching practice and their identity formation (Beijaard et al., 2004). The on-the-job teacher education programs are considered by the present research as another site for the development of teachers' professional identity. The additional professional training programs offer valuable opportunities for the rural school language teachers to improve, broaden and enhance their teaching expertise.

At last, as shown in Figure 8.1, the most external influencing factor is the local socioeconomic context, which is discovered in this research as the third tier of contextual factor. The local socioeconomic context affects teachers' professional identity through national language policy, ethnic culture and local socioeconomic development. It is those complexities that constitute the process of teachers' professional identity. As argued above, it is suggested that the framework of these forces for teachers' professional identity illustrated in Figure 8.1 can serve as a tentative model of secondary school language teachers' professional identity for further relevant research studies.

8.5   Summary

To summarize the chapter, it has been found that the teachers' professional identity formation is "an ongoing process of integration of personal and professional sides" of becoming and being teachers (Beijaard et al., 2004, p.113). Both personal and professional sides are important for the teachers' professional identity formation. Teachers develop and form their "core" professional identities through their early language learning experiences, role models, and significant others or experiences, and these "core" identities are also socially formed and informed (Gee, 2001, p.99). Teachers' professional identity has been formed, developed, and reconstructed under three levels of professional contexts including the personal biographies, professional experiences and sociocultural context. The meso context of school leaders are more important and influential than other contexts. In the professional identity formation processes, teachers exercise their strong agency to pursue their goals with the constraints of the professional structures. When their goals are consistent with their structures, teachers smoothly acquire their goals; when the goals are inconsistent with their structures, teachers can exert agency and make compromise; however, when their agency is inconsistent with the structure of school leaders, their agency is constrained and even undermined and the teachers may choose to leave or sink into low morale.

Chapter 9 | Conclusion

This chapter presents the conclusion of the present study. To begin with, it summarizes the major findings which provide an answer to the research questions. Then it states the main contributions which have been made in this research area. Then, the significance of the present study is addressed, followed by the implications of the present study. The last section describes the limitations of the present study and introduces recommendations for future research.

9.1 The major findings of the study

This study has examined the teachers' professional identity formation of three secondary school EFL teachers and offered abundant, in-depth and valuable findings. This section presents the major findings of the study based on the following two research questions:

1) How is secondary school EFL teachers' professional identity shaped and developed by their personal and professional experience?

2) What are the possible factors that influence the teachers' professional identity construction in different phases of their professional development?

With reference to RQ1, the present study finds that teachers' personal biographies play a significant role in shaping teachers' professional identity. Before the three case teachers entered teaching profession, their preservice education, language learning experience in particular, influenced the teachers' formation of professional identity. The participant teachers' language learning experience influenced their instructional practices, teaching philosophy, teaching beliefs, and perceptions about students. In addition, personal hobbies and previous teacher role models also acted as formative elements and exerted enduring influence on their teachers' identity formation.

During the period before the teachers took the National Teacher Training Plan, their development of professional identity had been facilitated or constrained by past learning experience, teaching beliefs, workplace culture and local sociocultural context. The professional identity not only happened inside the school with their instructional practices, but also was facilitated by the professional training outside the classroom. Based on the data, the present study finds that besides some occasional outside-school trainings, the external professional training, like the National Teacher Training Plan, enhance teachers' professional identity development. This is particularly evidenced in its support for teachers' knowledge base. At last, being engaged in different teacher action research helped to enhance their professional identity construction. For the three case teachers, they gained research knowledge and skills from doing classroom-based research by their own or by joining other teacher's research projects. The experiences in doing action research further enhance teachers' professional selves.

With respect to RQ2, the present study identifies three major tires of influencing factors that affect the case teachers' construction of professional identity. These influencing factors can be generally categorized into three levels: the micro-level, meso-level and macro-level. The local socio-economic situation and ethnic cultural context are discovered as the macro-level factors that exert influence on the formation process of teachers' professional identity; institutional environment and different levels of professional trainings have created the meso-level of influencing factors; besides teachers' personal biographies, their linguistic competences, teaching beliefs and agentive quality are posited as the micro-level of influencing factors.

9.2 The major contributions of the study

In light of the previous literature, the present study aims to examine the professional identity development of three rural secondary school EFL teachers and how their professional identity has been affected by personal, professional, and contextual factors. This study has filled several important research gaps and the findings of this study help enhance the understanding of teachers' professional identity formation. This research contributes to current knowledge on language teachers' identity with the following features: 1) the combination of a relatively uncommon theoretical framework and methodology; 2) the selection of research participants who are teaching in multiethnic and multilingual sociocultural context; and 3) the identification of three tiers of influencing factors affecting the teachers' professional identity construction.

This study is the first one to date—to the researcher's knowledge—that explores the secondary school language teachers who are teaching in rural and multiethnic regions in China. As described in section 2.2, though China is advancing toward modernity at unprecedented speed and efficiency, gaps are existing between urban area and vast rural regions in terms of socioeconomic development. Rural schools are facing significant challenges in providing effective professional development opportunities for teachers because of geographic disadvantage, limited availability of resources, and the lack of available staff. The situation of lacking educational resources and opportunities is even challenging in the multiethnic regions. Having been introduced in section 2.4, there are 56 officially recognized ethnic groups living in these regions in China. Additionally, different ethnic groups are diverse in terms of history, culture, traditions, and language. The ethnic groups usually inhabit in some geographically remote regions. Geographical remoteness, together with being different from the Confucius culture, creates some unique problems for schools in rural ethnic areas. These schools face difficulties that other rural schools and teachers have, such as insufficient financial investment, shortage of competent teachers or lack of professional support. Schools and teachers in multiethnic regions have also been troubled with particular problems raised by multilingualism and ethnic cultures. Teachers working in rural ethnic schools have been experiencing various difficulties too. For one thing, rural teachers are comparatively weak in content knowledge; for another, most rural teachers have not been well supported in professional development. While existing literature has documented the challenges associated with teachers' professional development in rural areas, stressing the need to consider the rural context (Glover et al., 2016; Ping, 2013; Zhou & Xiong, 2017). Studies of teachers' professional development are not well represented in the rural education research literature, and little is known about the professional identity construction of rural teachers, particularly in comparison with teachers in urban areas and in higher education institutions. Therefore, this research is unique in terms of selection of participants, which chooses three rural school EFL teachers in Xishuangbanna Dai Autonomous Prefecture. Thus, this research contributes to filling the gap in the literature concerning the participant and research context aspects of teachers' identity construction studies.

The second contribution of this research is the combination of an integrated theoretical framework which is uncommon in other studies. In order to understand the dynamic construction of language teachers' identity, this study is guided by an integrated theoretical framework including the "Identity Formation Theory" (Wenger, 1998), "History-in-Person" (Holland & Lave, 2001), and "Identity-in-Discourse and Identity-in-Practice" (Varghese et al., 2005) as theoretical underpinnings. Firstly, Varghese's et al. "Identity-in-Discourse and Identity-in-Practice" theory aids the study to explore teachers' professional identity construction from "what teachers say" and "how teachers do". "Identity-in-Practice" and "Identity-in-Discourse" are the two facets of a coin, and each dimension plays a pivotal role in identity formation. Teachers' pedagogical perceptions and beliefs are evident in their instructional languages in the classroom and talks with colleagues, further in how teachers' pedagogical thoughts are enacted in their classroom activities. By interviewing teachers and observing their classroom behaviors, the researcher has gained an insight into the trajectory of professional identity construction.

Secondly, the present study employs the "History-in-Person" theory as another supporting theory. Development of professional identity is not only largely manifested through teachers' talk and practices but also should be traced in their personal life experiences. As Holland and Lave (2000) point out, History-in-Person represents the generative fashioning of individual identity and self-making through their relationship with local conflictual practice in the past and present (p.21). The "History-in-Person" theory is powerful in supporting the present study in connecting teachers' past and present in the trajectory of professional identity formation. Thus, to understand professional identity construction, one's personal history and the present forces must be included in the interpretive frame.

As the third constituent in the theoretical framework, Wenger's (1998) "Identity Formation" theory helps this study in exploring language teachers' identity formation and to be creative in theory application. In Wenger's theoretical framework, identity construction is reflected in terms of three modes of belonging: engagement, imagination, and alignment. Through engagement, individuals establish and maintain joint enterprises, negotiate meanings and establish relations with others; imagination moves beyond the physical limits of engagement by enabling individuals to create images of the world, and their place within it, across time and space; alignment translates into the membership of social communities, which constitutes one's identity formation as a form a competence—the competence of knowing who we are and who we are not.

This combination, however, has great potential for providing a broader interpretive framework than some of the commonly used methodologies in educational research.

The study makes a contribution to the understanding of language identity research by recognizing three essential but important levels of professional contexts, including macro, meso and micro contexts. The identification of the three-level professional contexts provides a holistic picture of EFL teachers' professional contexts in rural and multiethnic regions and achieves rich and deep understanding of influence on teachers' professional identity formation. Moreover, exploring the three-level contextual factors clearly discerns the most crucial and influential level of context on teachers' professional lives and identity formation in ethnic sociocultural contexts. The macro contexts of the local economic development and ethnic culture have influenced and impacted the teachers' professional lives and identities to a large extent; the meso-level, referring to institutional working environment and curriculum reform-based professional trainings, has powerfully improved the development of teachers' professional identity; while teachers' personal biography, teacher's knowledge, beliefs and teachers' agentive quality function as the micro-level influencing factors that directly affect the formation of teachers' identity.

Finally, few studies examine language teachers' identity construction by observing their classroom practices. By using different qualitative data collection instruments, the study gathered diversified and substantial qualitative data in order to understand teachers' professional identity formation and development. The findings have revealed that the teachers' professional identities are indeed manifested in their classroom practices (Coldron & Smith, 1999) and could be interpreted through classroom teaching practices, thus classroom teaching is a useful perspective to examine and understand teachers' professional identity formation and also provides a positive and empirical evidence for the mixture of multiple research instruments in the research about teachers' professional identity formation.

9.3　The significance and implications for practices

The study has provided abundant and valuable information and knowledge about professional identity construction of secondary EFL teachers who are teaching schools in the multiethnic, multicultural, and multilingual regions in Yunnan province. It has significance and implications for government policymakers, teacher educators, educational researchers and frontline teachers.

Firstly, the present study is significant for rural secondary school EFL teachers. This study examines professional identity formation of three rural secondary school EFL teachers, and their personal biographies, language learning and teaching beliefs and experience gained from professional training programs are valuable for frontline teachers.

Secondly, detailed comparison of teachers' classroom practice before and after their participation in the NTTP offers the teacher educators and school leaders a useful reminder to understand teachers' true response to the curriculum reform and professional training programs. The present study is particularly significant for educational researchers, for it provides a new perspective for other researchers to explore language teachers' professional identity.

Thirdly the present study is important for educational policymakers. This study selects rural EFL teachers working in multiethnic regions as focal participants, and describes how local socioeconomic situation and ethnic cultural characters indirectly affect teachers' teaching beliefs and pedagogical practices in the classroom. The data is particularly pragmatic for the policymakers.

9.4   Limitations and recommendations for further research

This study has certain limitations although it offers abundant and valuable findings and enriches the knowledge and understanding of the teachers' professional identity formation processes in rural schools.

The first limitation of this research lies in relatively small number of research samples. Due to the limited time and geographical remoteness, the researcher could not visit all 12 schools and approach all English teachers in Jinghong city when the researcher conducted the fieldwork. The study does not aim at making specific recommendations or generalizations about the exploration of teachers' identity. The objective of this study is rather to explore, describe, and interpret the intricate interconnectedness between personal, professional experiences and professional identity construction.

During the fieldwork in schools, the ethnographic observation was interrupted from time to time because of teachers' heavy workload. It is found that teachers' are not only busy with their own teaching but also are occupied by additional student management chaos. The fact somewhat constrains a continuous understanding of the teachers' lives and professional identity formation. The researcher has admitted that the prolonged engagement and persistent observation in the field could facilitate a deeper understanding of the school culture, and check for misinformation that stems from distortions introduced by the researcher or informants. Moveover, the data collection period which lasted for about a year may not have been sufficient for all participants to come to important changes in their perspectives. Thus, expanding the time frame of data collection would be advisable for future research.

Finally, this research project is carried out by one researcher, therefore any limitations and mistakes in the study are solely the researcher's responsibility. The study can be regarded as the researcher's first step in establishing his career as a professional researcher and future academic.

Appendix 1 | Interview Questions

Questions related to personal experiences:

1) Do you have any memorable experiences from your early childhood?

2) Do you have an important memory from middle school?

3) What significant experiences do you remember during your university studies?

4) How do you think these experiences influenced your views on teaching and learning?

5) Could you talk about your family members who have given you deep impressions?

6) Could you talk about your teachers who have given you deep impressions in middle school, high school and in university respectively?

7) How do you think these people who influenced your views on teaching and learning?

8) Do you have any language learning related hobbies? Do you think these personal hobbies may affect your language learning?

9) Did you enjoy learning English? (why or why not?)

10) What are your personal ways of learning English?

Questions related to professional experiences:

11) How long have you been teaching English?

12) Could you please talk about your practicum experiences?

13) How do you understand your students and their parents?

14) Can you summarize briefly your teaching beliefs?

15) In what way do you think language should be taught?

16) How do you prepare lessons?

17) How do you understand teacher education and teacher professional development?

18) Could you share your training experiences during the NTTP?

19) what are your reflections on the three training modules in the NTTP?

20) Do you see any change in your beliefs, perceptions, and perspectives in how you perceive language learning and teaching after attending the NTTP training courses?

21) What did you learn from your engagement in the classroom-based teacher research?

Questions related to institutional and sociocultural context:

22) How do you comment on your school and school leaders?

23) Do you think the school has provided teachers with sufficient support on professional development? What are your expectations?

24) How do you understand the people from local ethnic communities?

25) How did you feel about the local ethnic culture? Do you think the local ethnic culture has positive or negative influence on your teaching?

Appendix 2 | Sample of Transcription of Interview

<u>Interview with Jenifer:</u>

问：能否请您谈谈您在"国培"中的经历？

答：好的。"国培"中安排的课程其实挺多样化的。我记得曾经上过语音、课堂活动设计、二语写作这些课程，当然还有其他一些。这些课程对扩 [拓] 展提升我的专业知识有很大帮助。哦，对了，我还上 [听] 过一次关于教师行动研究的讲座，是关于如何开展基于课堂的教师行动研究的方法。除上过语言知识方面的课程外，我还听了一些讲座，比如中国传统文化和云南地区民族文化这样的讲座。"国培"为我们提供的这些课程不仅让我的专业知识得到了一定程度的扩展和提高，并且让我更深入地理解自己在课堂教学中的角色，"国培"中学到的这些知识，的确在一定程度上改变了我对英语教学的观念。

举个例子吧，我之前经常只是抱怨我的学生在学英语的时候很笨，却没有去潜心寻找其中的原因，帮助他们提升学习能力。这样的想法在"国培"学习后就变了，学生学不好，其实并不完全是他们的问题，其实是老师忽视、没有使用得当的教学方法。老师在课堂中的角色也应该更加多样化，而不能总是一个人在那里控制课堂，演独角戏，当复读机，只会重复教学内容。老师应该设计多样化的、有趣的课堂活动，甚至是与学生一起完成一些课堂活动，参与他们的创作过程。如果老师能够更好地理解学生，为他们的学习搭好"支架"，我想他们会爱上学英语，问题也会减少很多。

Question: Could you share your experiences in attending the NTTP training course?

Jenifer's response:

[…] contents of the training courses offered by university were quite diversified. I took courses like Phonetics, Designing Classroom Activity and Second Language Writing. Those lessons helped me a lot to enhance my subject matter knowledge. Moreover, I also took Action Research—a course focused on how to conduct classroom-based research. In addition to lessons about the language and research methods, I attended lectures on Traditional Chinese Culture and Ethnic Cultures in Yunnan. These courses provided by the NTTP not only broadened and strengthened my content knowledge about English language from both theory and practice perspectives but also changed my understandings about my roles and positions in my classroom, what I learned from the training courses altered my beliefs as an English teacher.

I used to complain a lot about my students for their clumsiness in learning languages but failed to find any appropriate ways to improve their performance. My beliefs in teaching and students changed after attending training in the NTTP that it is not students' fault to have problems in learning, but the teachers' ignorance of suitable or creative methods in teaching. Teachers should play diverse roles in the classroom instead of only being a classroom controller, organizer or knowledge resource provider, just like a monodrama player standing in the classroom or like a tape recorder repeating instructions over and over. Teachers should design some enjoyable tasks and even work with students to practice the tasks... if teachers know how to scaffold their students and to work with them, I'm sure that they will love this subject and make rapid progress.

References

Adamson, B. (2002). Barbarian as a foreign language: English in China's schools. *World Englishes, 21*(2), 231-243.

Adamson, B., & Feng, A. (2014). Models for trilingual education in the People's Republic of China. In D. Gorter, V. Zenots, & J. Cenoz (Eds.), *Minority Languages and Multilingual Education* (pp. 29-44). Dordrecht: Springer.

Adler, P. A., Adler, P., & Weiss, R. S. (1995). Learning from strangers: the art and method of qualitative interview studies. *Contemporary Sociology*, 24(3), 420-428.

Akkerman, S. F., & Meijer, P. C. (2011). A dialogical approach to conceptualizing teacher identity. *Teaching & Teacher Education, 27*(2), 308-319.

Alsup, J. (2006). *Teacher Identity Discourses: Negotiating Personal and Professional Spaces*. Mahway, N. J: Lawrence Erlbaum Associates.

Aneja, G. A. (2016). (Non) native speaker: rethinking (non) nativeness and teacher identity in TESOL teacher education. *TESOL Quarterly, 50*(3), 572-596.

Barkhuizen, G. (2017a). Investigating language tutor social inclusion identities. *The Modern Language Journal, 101*(S1), 61-75.

Barkhuizen, G. (2017b). *Reflections on Language Teacher Identity Research*. New York: Routledge

Beauchamp, C., & Thomas, L. (2009). Understanding teacher identity: an overview of issues in the literature and implications for teacher education. *Cambridge Journal of Education,* 39(2), 175-189.

Beauchamp, C., & Thomas, L. (2011). New teachers' identity shifts at the boundary of teacher education and initial practice. *International Journal of Educational Research, 50*(1), 6-13.

Beijaard, D., Meijer, P. C., & Verloop, N. (2004). Reconsidering research on teachers' professional identity. *Teaching and Teacher Education,* 20(2), 107-128.

Beijaard, D., Verloop, N., & Vermunt, J. D. (2000). Teachers' perceptions of professional identity: an exploratory study from a personal knowledge perspective. *Teaching and Teacher Education,* 16(7), 749-764.

Bergner, R. M., & Holmes, J. R. (2000). Self-concepts and self-concept change: a status dynamic approach. *Psychotherapy Theory Research & Practice,* 37(1), 36-44.

Block, D. (2007). *Second Language Identities.* New York: Continuum.

Block, D. (2015). Becoming a language teacher: constraints and negotiation in the emergence of new identities. *Bellaterra Journal of Teaching & Learning Language & Literature,* 8(3), 9-15.

Bolton, K. (2003). *Chinese Englishes: A Sociolinguistic History.* Cambridge University Press.

Borg, M. (2001). Teachers' beliefs. *ELT Journal,* 55(2), 186-188.

Borg, S. (2006). *Teacher Cognition and Language Education: Research and Practice.* London: Continuum.

Bromme, R. (1991). Wissenstypen und professionelles selbstver standniss: types of knowledge and professional self-concept. *Zeitschrift fur Pa,* 25(37), 769-785.

Bukor, E. (2015). Exploring teacher identity from a holistic perspective: reconstructing and reconnecting personal and professional selves. *Teachers and Teaching,* 21(3), 305-327.

Bullough, R. V. (1997). Becoming a teacher: Self and the social location of teacher education. In B. Biddle, T. Good, & I. Goodson (Eds.), *International Handbook of Teachers and Teaching.* Dordrecht: Kluwer Academic Publishers.

Burns, A. (1999). *Collaborative Action Research for English Language Teachers.* Cambridge: Cambridge University Press.

Cammarata, L., & Tedick, D. J. (2012). Balancing content and language in instruction: The experience of immersion teachers. *Modern Language Journal,* 96(2), 251–269.

Chesnut, C. (2015). "But I'm a language teacher!" —Dual immersion teacher identities in a complex policy context. *Mid-Western Educational Researcher,* 27(4), 339-362.

Cheung, Y. L. (2015). Teacher identity in ELT/TESOL In Y. L. Cheung, S. B. Said, & K. Park (Eds.), *Advances and Current Trends in Language Teacher Identity Research* (pp. 175-185). New York: Routledge

Cheung, Y. L., Said, S. B., & Park, K. (2015). *Advances and Current Trends in Language*

Teacher Identity Research. New York: Routledge.

Cohen, J. L. (2010). Getting recognised: Teachers negotiating professional identities as learners through talk. *Teaching & Teacher Education, 26*(3), 473-481.

Cohen, J. L., Manion, L., & Morrison, K. (2000). *Research Methods in Education*. London: Routledge.

Coldron, J., & Smith, R. (1999). Active location in teachers' construction of their professional identities. *Journal of Curriculum studies, 31*(6), 711-726.

Cooper, K., & Olson, M. (1996). The multiple "I's" of teacher identity. In M. Kompf, D. Dworet, & R. Boak (Eds.), *Changing Research and Practice* (pp. 78-89). London: Falmer Press.

Creswell, J. W. (2007). *Qualitative Inquiry & Research Design: Choosing Among Five Approaches* (2nd ed.). Thousand Oaks, CA: Sage

Danielewicz, J. (2001). *Teaching Selves. Identity, Pedagogy, and Teacher Education*. New York: SUNY.

Darvin, R., & Norton, B. (2015). Identity and a model of investment in applied linguistics. *Annual Review of Applied Linguistics, 35*(35), 36-56.

Day, C., & Kington, A. (2008). Identity, well-being and effectiveness: the emotional contexts of teaching. *Pedagogy Culture & Society, 16*(1), 7-23.

Day, C., Sammons, P., Stobart, G., Kington, A., & Gu, Q. (2007). *Teachers Matter. Connecting Lives, Work and Effectiveness*. New York: McGraw Hill.

del Rosal, K., Conry, J., & Wu, S. (2017). Exploring the fluid online identities of language teachers and adolescent language learners. *Computer Assisted Language Learning, 30*(5), 390-408.

Denzin, N. K., & Lincoln, Y. S. (2003). Introduction: the discipline and practice of qualitative research. In N. K. Denzin & Y. S. Lincoln (Eds.), *Strategies of Qualitative Inquiry* (pp. 1-45). Thousand Oaks: Sage.

Donato, R. (2016). Becoming a language teaching professional: what's identity got to do with it? In G. Barkhuizen (Ed.), *Reflections on Language Teacher Identity Research* (pp. 24-30). New York: Routledge.

Donato, R., & Davin, K. J. (2017). The genesis of classroom discursive practices as history-in-person processes. *Language Teaching Research*.

Duff, P. A., & Uchida, Y. (1997). The negotiation of teachers' sociocultural identities and practices in postsecondary EFL classrooms. *TESOL Quarterly,* 31(3), 451-486.

Dworet, D. (1996). Teachers' identities: overview. In M. Kompf, W. R. Bond, D. Dworet, & R. T. Boak (Eds.), *Changing Research and Practice: Teachers Professionalism, Identities and Knowledge* (pp. 67-68). London: The Falmer Press.

Elliott, A., & du Gay, P. (2009). *Identity in Question*. SAGE Publications.

Erikson, E. H. (1968). *Identity: Youth and Crisis*. New York: W.W. Norton.

Farrell, T. S. C. (2011). Exploring the professional role identities of experienced ESL teachers through reflective practice. *System,* 39(1), 54-62.

Fichtner, F., & Chapman, K. (2011). The cultural identities of foreign language teachers. *An Electronical Journal for Foreign and Second Language Educators,* 3(1), 116–140.

Flores, M. A., & Day, C. (2006). Contexts which shape and reshape new teachers' identities: A multi-perspective study. *Teaching and Teacher Education,* 22(2), 219-232.

Franzak, J. K. (2002). Developing a teacher identity: the impact of critical friends practice on the student teacher. *English Education,* 34(4), 258-280.

Freeman, D. (1993). Renaming experience/reconstructing practice: developing new understandings of teaching. *Teaching and Teacher Education,* 9(21), 485-497.

Gall, M. D., Gall, J. P., & Borg, W. T. (2003). *Educational Research*. New York: Pearson Education.

Gao, X. (2014). Shifting constructions of role models for English learners in China. *Changing English,* 21(3), 223-234.

Gass, S. M., & Mackey, A. (2000). *Stimulated Recall Methodology in Second Language Research*. Mahwah, New Jersey: Lawrence Erlbaum Associates, Publishers.

Gayton, A. M. (2016). Perceptions about the dominance of English as a global language: impact on foreign-language teachers' professional identity. *Journal of Language Identity & Education,* 15(4), 230-244.

Gee, J. P. (1996). *Social Linguistics and Literacies: Ideology in Discourse* (2nd ed.). London: Taylor & Francis.

Gee, J. P. (2000). Identity as an analytic lens for research in Education. *Review of Research in Education,* 25, 99-125.

Gil, J., & Adamson, B. (2011). The English language in China: a sociolinguistic profile. *World*

Englishes, 21(2), 231-243.

Glasersfeld, E. V. (1995). *Radical Constructivism: A Way of Knowing and Learning.* Bristol: Falmer Press.

Glover, T. A., Nugent, G. C., Chumney, F. L., Ihlo, T., Shapiro, E. S., Guard, K., . . . Bovaird, J. (2016). Investigating rural teachers' professional development, instructional knowledge, and classroom Practice. *Journal of Research in Rural Education,*31(3), 1-16.

Graddol, D. (2006). *English next.* London, UK: British Council.

Gu, Y. (1996). Steering a middle course: educational dilemmas in managing tertiary foreign language education in China. In P. Storey, V. Berry, D. Bunton, & P. Hoare (Eds.), *Issues in Language in Education* (pp. 145-151). Hong Kong: Hong Kong Intitute of Education.

Hall, L. A., Johnson, A. S., Juzwik, M. M., Wortham, S. E. F., & Mosley, M. (2010). Teacher identity in the context of literacy teaching: three explorations of classroom positioning and interaction in secondary schools. *Teaching and Teacher Education,* 26(2), 234-243.

Han, I. (2016). Conceptualisation of English teachers' professional identity and comprehension of its dynamics. *Teachers & Teaching Theory & Practice,* 23, 1-21.

Herrero, C. (2016). The film in language teaching association (FILTA): A multilingual community of practice. *ELT Journal,* 70(2), 190-199.

Higgins, C., & Sandhu, P. (2014). Researching identity through narrative approaches. In M. Bigelow & J. Ennserkananen (Eds.), *The Routledge Handbook of Educational Linguistics* (pp. 50-61). New York: Routledge.

Hoffman-Kipp, P. (2008). Actualizing democracy: the praxis of teacher identity construction. *Teacher Education Quarterly,* 35(3), 151-164.

Holland, D., & Lachicotte, W. (2007). Vygotsky, Mead, and the new sociocultural studies of identity. In H. Daniels, M. Cole, & J. V. Wertsch (Eds.), *Cambridge Companion to Vygotsky* (pp. 101-135). Cambridge: Cambridge University Press.

Holland, D., Lachicotte, W., Skinner, D., & Cain, C. (1998). *Agency and Identity in Cultural Worlds.* Cambridge: Harvard University Press.

Holland, D., & Lave, J. (2001). History in person: an introduction. In D. Holland & J. Lave (Eds.), *History in Person: Enduring Struggles, Contentious Practice, Intimate Identities* (pp. 3-33). Santa Fe, NM: School of American Research Press.

Holland, D., & Lave, J. (2009). *Social Practice Theory and the Historical Production of persons*. Osaka: Center for Human Activity Theory of Kansai University.

Holt-Reynolds, D. (1992). Personal history-based beliefs as relevant prior knowledge in course work. *American Educational Research Journal, 29*(2), 325-349.

Hu, D. (2007). *Trilingual Education of Members from Ethnic Groups in Yunnan*. Kunming: Yunnan University Press.

Hu, G. W. (2002). Potential cultural resistance to pedagogical imports: the case of communicative language teaching in China. *Language Culture & Curriculum,* 15(2), 93-105.

Izadinia, M. (2013). A review of research on student teachers' professional identity. *British Educational Research Journal,* 39(4), 694-713.

Jackson, L. G. (2006). Shaping a borderland professional identity: funds of knowledge of a bilingual education teacher. *Teacher Education & Practice,* 19, 131-148.

Jiang, Y. (2017). *A Study on Professional Development of Teachers of English as a Foreign Language in Institutions of Higher Education in Western China*. Berlin: Springer.

Jimenez-Silva, M., & Olson, K. (2012). A Community of practice in teacher education: insights and perceptions. *International Journal of Teaching & Learning in Higher Education,* 24, 335-348.

Johnson, K. E. (1992). The relationship between teachers' beliefs and practices during literacy instruction for non-native speakers of English. *Journal of Reading Behavior, 24*(1), 83-108.

Johnson, K. E. (2006). The sociocultural turn and its challenges for second language teacher education. *TESOL Quarterly,* 40(1), 235-257.

Johnston, B., Pawan, F., & Mahan-Taylor, R. (2005). The professional development of working ESL/EFL teachers: A pilot study. In D. J. Tedick (Ed.), *Second Language Teacher Education: International Perspectives* (pp. 53-57). Mahwah, N. J: Lawrence Erlbaum Associates.

Kagan, D. M., Dennis, M. B., Igou, M., Moore, P., & Sparks, K. (1993). The experience of being a teacher in residence. *American Educational Research Journal,* 30(2), 426-443.

Kanno, Y., & Stuart, C. (2011). Learning to become a second language teacher: Identities-in-Practice. *The Modern Language Journal,* 95(2), 236-252.

Kelchtermans, G. (1994). Biographical methods in the study of teachers' professional development. In I. Carlgren, G. Handal, & S. Vagge (Eds.), *Teacher Minds and Action in Varied Contexts: Research on Teachers' Thinking and Practice* (pp. 93-108). London: Falmer Press.

Kim, H. K. (2011). Native speakerism affecting nonnative English teachers' identity formation. *English Teaching,* 66(4), 53-71.

Kim, J. I., & Kim, M. (2016). Three Korean heritage language teachers' identities, their identification of their students, and their instructional practices. *Journal of Language Identity and Education,* 15(6), 361-375.

Kincheloe, J. L. (2003). Critical ontology: vision of selfhood and curriculum. *Journal of Curriculum Theorizing*, 47-64.

Knowles, G. J. (1992). Models for understanding pre-service and beginning teachers' biographies: illustrations from case studies. In I. F. Goodson (Ed.), *Studying Teachers' Lives* (pp. 99-152). London: Routledge.

Kumaravadivelu, B. (2012). *Language Teacher Education for a Global Society: A Modular Model for Knowing, Analyzing, Recognizing, Doing, and Seeing.* London: Routledge.

Kwo, O. W. Y., & Intrator, S. M. (2004). Uncovering the inner power of teachers' lives: towards a learning profession. *International Journal of Educational Research,* 41(4–5), 281-291.

Lam, A. S. L. (2002). English in education in China: policy changes and learners' experiences. *World Englishes,* 21(2), 245-256.

Lamote, C., & Engels, N. (2010). The development of student teachers' professional identity. *European Journal of Teacher Education,* 33(1), 3-18.

Lasky, S. (2005). A sociocultural approach to understanding teacher identity, agency and professional vulnerability in a context of secondary school reform. *Teaching and Teacher Education,* 21(8), 899-916.

Lave, J., & Wenger, E. (1991). *Situated Learning: Legitimate Peripheral Participation.* Cambridge: Cambridge University Press.

Leavy, P. (2017). *Research Design: Quantitative, Qualitative, Mixed Methods, Arts-Based, and Community-Based Participatory Research Approaches.* New York: Guilford Publications.

Lee, I. (2013). Becoming a writing teacher: using "identity" as an analytic lens to understand EFL writing teachers' development. *Journal of Second Language Writing,* 22(3), 330-345.

Lee, J. C.-K., Huang, Y. X.-H., Law, E. H.-F., & Wang, M.-H. (2013). Professional identities and emotions of teachers in the context of curriculum reform: a Chinese perspective. *Asia-Pacific Journal of Teacher Education,* 41(3), 271-287.

Li, M., & Baldauf, R. (2011). Beyond the curriculum: a Chinese example of issues constraining effective English language teaching. *TESOL Quarterly,* 45(4), 793–803.

Lichtman, M. (2006). *Qualitative Research in Education: A User's Guide.* Thousand Oaks, CA: Sage.

Lincoln, Y. S., & Guba, E. G. (1985). *Naturalistic Inquiry.* Beverly Hills: Sage Publications.

Liu, N., Lin, C. K., & Wiley, T. G. (2016). Learner views on English and English language teaching in China. *International Multilingual Research Journal,* 10(2), 137-157.

Liu, Y. (2009). Teachers' identities in personal narratives identities in personal narratives. In J. L. Bianco, J. Orton, & G. Yihong (Eds.), *China and English: Dilemmas of Identity* (pp. 255-267). Bristol, UK: Multilingual Matters.

Liu, Y. (2012). Review of research on language teacher identity from narrative perspective. *Foreign Language and Their Teaching,* 262(01), 11-15.

Liu, Y., & Xu, Y. (2011). Inclusion or exclusion?: a narrative inquiry of a language teacher's identity experience in the "new work order" of competing pedagogies. *Teaching and Teacher Education,* 27(3), 589-597.

Liu, Y., & Xu, Y. (2013). The trajectory of learning in a teacher community of practice: a narrative inquiry of a language teacher's identity in the workplace. *Research Papers in Education,* 28(2), 176-195.

Maclean, R., & White, S. (2007). Video reflection and the formation of teacher identity in a team of pre-service and experienced teachers. *Reflective Practice,* 8(1), 47-60.

Martel, J. (2015). Learning to teach a foreign language: identity negotiation and conceptualizations of pedagogical progress. *Foreign Language Annals,* 48(3), 394-412.

Martel, J. (2017). Identity, innovation, and learning to teach a foreign/second language. In G. Barkhuizen (Ed.), *Reflections on Language Teacher Identity Research* (pp. 222-227). New York: Routledge.

Martel, J., & Wang, A. (2014). Language teacher identity In M. Bigelow & J. Ennserkananen (Eds.), *The Routledge Handbook of Educational Linguistics* (pp. 289-300). New York: Routledge.

Martin, A. D., & Strom, K. J. (2016). Toward a linguistically responsive teacher identity: an empirical review of the literature. *International Multilingual Research Journal,* 10, 1-15.

Marton, F., Dall'alba, G., & Beattie, E. (1993). Conceptions of learning. *International Journal of Educational Research,* 19(2), 227-300.

Maxwell, J. A. (2004). Using qualitative methods for causal explanation. *Field Methods,* 16(3), 243-264.

Mccormick, C. B., & Pressley, M. (1997). *Educational Psychology: Learning, Instruction, Assessment.* London: Longman.

Mead, M. (1934). *Mind, Self and Society.* Chicago: The University of Chicago Press.

Meighan, R., & Meighan, J. (1990). Alternative roles for learners with particular reference on learner as democratic explorer in teacher education courses. *The School Field,* 1(1), 61-77.

Menard-Warwick, J. (2008). The cultural and intercultural identities of transnational English teachers: two case studies from the Americas. *TESOL Quarterly,* 42(4), 617-640.

Menard-Warwick, J. (2011). Chilean English teacher identity and popular culture: three generations. *International Journal of Bilingual Education and Bilingualism,* 14(3), 261-277.

Merriam, B. (2009). *Qualitative Research: A Guide to Design and Implementation.* San Francisco, CA Jossey Bass.

Merriam, S. B. (1997). *Qualitative Research and Case Study Applications in Education: Revised and Expanded from Case Study Research in Education.* San Francisco: Jossey-Bass Publishers.

Merriam, S. B. (1998). *Qualitative Research and Case Study Applications in Education.* San Francisco: Jossey-Bass Publishers.

Miles, M. B., & Huberman, A. M. (1994). *Qualitative Data Analysis: An Expanded Sourcebook.* Thousand Oaks, CA: Sage.

Miller, J. (2009). Teacher identity. In A. Burns & J. C. Richards (Eds.), *The Cambridge Guide to Second Language Teacher Education* (pp. 172-181). New York: Cambridge University Press.

Mills, A. J., Durepos, G., & Wiebe, E. (2010). *Encyclopedia of Case Study Research.* Thousand Oaks, CA: SAGE.

MOE. (2009). *The National Teacher Training Project for Primary and Secondary School*

Teachers in 2009. Ministry of Education of the People's Republic of China, retrieved from http://old.moe.gov.cn/publicfiles/business/htmlfiles/moe/s3088/201001/81500.html (in Chinese).

MOE. (2010). *Notification on the Implementation of the National Primary and Secondary School Teacher Ttraining Program.* Ministry of Education of the People's Republic of China, retrieved from http://www.gov.cn/zwgk/2010-06/30/content_1642031.htm (in Chinese).

MOE. (2011). *An Opinion on Strengthening Primary and Secondary School Teacher Training.* Ministry of Education of the People's Republic of China, retrieved from http://www.moe.edu.cn/publicfiles/business/htmlfiles/moe/s4559/201101/114220.html (in Chinese).

Moore, A., Edwards, G., Halpin, D., & George, R. (2002). Compliance, resistance and pragmatism: The (re)construction of schoolteacher identities in a period of intensive educational reform. *British Educational Research Journal,* 28(4), 551-565.

Motha, S. (2006). Racializing ESOL teacher identities in U.S. K-12 Public Schools. *TESOL Quarterly,* 40(3), 495-518.

Nguyen, C. D. (2017). Creating spaces for constructing practice and identity: innovations of teachers of English language to young learners in Vietnam. *Research Papers in Education,* 32(1), 1-15.

Nunan, D. (2003). The impact of English as a global language on educational policies and practices in the Asia-Pacific region. *TESOL Quarterly,* 37(4), 589–613.

Oda, M. (2017). Reflecting on my flight path. In G. Barkhuizen (Ed.), *Reflections on Language Teacher Identity Research* (pp. 222-227). New York: Routledge.

Olsen, B. (2003). Life themes: inter-relation of personal and programmatic experience(s) as beginning teacher knowledge construction. Paper presented at the Annual Meeting of the American Educational Research Association, Chicago.

Olsen, B. (2008). Introducing teacher identity and this volume. *Teacher Education Quarterly,* 35(3), 3-6.

Oyserman, D., Elmore, K., & Smith, G. (2012). Self, self-concept, and identity. In M. R. Leary & J. P. Tangney (Eds.). *Handbook of Self and Identity* (2nd ed., pp. 69-104). New York: The Guilford Press.

Pajares, M. F. (1992). Teachers' beliefs and educational research: cleaning up a messy construct. *Review of Educational Research,* 63(3), 307-332.

Palmer, P. J. (1998). *The Courage to Teach: Exploring the Inner Landscape of a Teacher's Life.* San Francisco, CA: Jossey-Bass Inc., Publishers.

Park, G. (2012). "I am never afraid of being recognized as an NNES": one teacher's journey in claiming and embracing her nonnative-speaker identity. *TESOL Quarterly,* 46(1), 127–151.

Parkison, P. (2008). Space for performing teacher identity: through the lens of Kafka and Hegel. *Teachers and Teaching,* 14(1), 51-60.

Patton, M. (1990). *Qualitative Evaluation and Research Methods.* Beverly Hills, CA: Sage.

Patton, M. (2002). *Qualitative Research and Evaluation Methods* (3rd ed.). Thousand Oaks, CA: Sage

Pavlenko, A. (2003). "I never knew i was a bilingual": reimagining teacher identities in TESOL. *Journal of Language, Identity & Education,* 2(4), 251-268.

Pawan, F., Fan, W., & Miao, P. (2017). *Teacher Training and Professional Development of Chinese English Language Teachers: Changing from Fish to Dragon.* New York: Routledge.

Pennington, M. C. (1989). Faculty development for language programs. In R. K. Johnson (Ed.), *The Second Language Curriculum* (pp. 91-110). New York: Cambridge University.

Pennington, M. C., & Richards, J. C. (2016). Teacher identity in language teaching: Integrating personal, contextual, and professional factors. *Relc Journal,* 47(1), 5-23.

Ping, W. (2013). Perspectives on English teacher development in rural primary schools in China. *Journal of Pedagogy,* 4(2), 208-219.

Qi, G. Y., & Wang, Y. (2017). Investigating the building of a WeChat-based community of practice for language teachers' professional development. *Innovation in Language Learning and Teaching,* (3), 1-17.

Reis, D. S. (2011). Non-native English-speaking teachers (NNESTs) and professional legitimacy: a sociocultural theoretical perspective on identity transformation. *International Journal of the Sociology of Language,* 2011(208), 139-160.

Richards, J. (2012). Competence and performance in language teaching. In A. Burns & J. Richards (Eds.), *The Cambridge Guide to Pedagogy and Practice in Second Language Teaching* (pp. 46-59). New York: Cambridge University Press.

Richards, J., & Farrell, T. (2011). The nature of teacher learning. In J. Richards & T. Farrell (Eds.), *Practice Teaching: A Reflective Approach* (pp. 15-30). New York: Cambridge University Press.

Richards, J. C. (1998). *Beyond Training: Perspectives on Language Teacher Education*. New York: Cambridge University Press.

Richards, J. C. (2010). Competence and performance in language teaching. *REFLC Journal*, 41(2), 101-122.

Richards, J. C., & Lockhart, C. (1994). *Reflective Teaching in Second Language Classrooms*. New York: Cambridge University Press.

Richardson, V., Anders, P., Tidwell, D., & Lloyd, C. (1991). The relationship between teachers' beliefs and practices in reading comprehension instruction. *American Educational Research Journal*, 28(3), 559-586.

Rodgers, C., & Scott, K. H. (2008). The development of the personal self and professional identity in learning to teach. *Handbook of Research on Teacher Education*, 732-755.

Ross, H. (1992). Foreign language education as a barometer of modernization. In R. Hayhoe (Ed.), *Education and Modernisation: The Chinese experience* (pp. 239-254). Oxford: Pergamon.

Rossman, G. B., & Rallis, S. F. (2003). *Learning in the Field: An Introduction to Qualitative Research*. Thousand Oaks, CA: Sage.

Salinas, D. (2017). *EFL Teacher Identity: Impact of Macro and Micro Contextual Factors in Education Reform Frame in Chile,* 7(6), 1-11.

Samuel, M., & Stephens, D. (2000). Critical dialogues with self: developing teacher identities and roles—a case study of South African student teachers. *International Journal of Educational Research,* 33(5), 475-491.

Sfard, A., & Prusak, A. (2005). Telling identities: In search of an analytic tool for investigating learning as a culturally shaped activity. *Educational Researcher,* 34(4), 14-22.

Sharkey, J. (2004). ESOL teachers' knowledge of context as critical mediator in curriculum development. *TESOL Quarterly,* 38(2), 279–299.

Smith, R. G. (2007). Developing professional identities and knowledge: Becoming primary teachers. *Teachers and Teaching: Theory and Practice,* 13(4), 377-397.

Smith, R. G. (2007). Developing professional identities and knowledge: becoming primary teachers. *Teachers & Teaching,* 13(4), 377-397.

Strauss, A., & Corbin, J. (1998). *Basics of Qualitative Research: Procedures and Techniques for Developing Grounded Theory*. Thousand Oaks. CA: Sage.

Sugrue, C. (1997). Student teachers' lay theories and teaching identities: their implications for professional development. *European Journal of Teacher Education,* 20(3), 213-225.

Sutherland, L., Howard, S. K., & Markauskaite, L. (2010). Professional identity creation: examining the development of beginning preservice teachers' understanding of their work as teachers. *Teaching and Teacher Education,* 26(3), 455-465.

Torresrocha, J. C. (2017). High school EFL teachers' identity and their emotions towards language requirements. *Profile Issues in Teachers Professional Development,* 19(2), 41-55.

Trang, T. T. T., & Baldauf, R. B. J. (2007). Demotivation: Understanding resistance to English language learning—the case of Vietnamese students. *Journal of Asia TEFL,* 4(1), 79-105.

Trent, J. (2010). Teacher education as identity construction: Insights from action research. *Journal of Education for Teaching International Research and Pedagogy,* 36(2), 153-168.

Trent, J. (2012). The discursive positioning of teachers: native-speaking English teachers and educational discourse in Hong Kong. *TESOL Quarterly,* 46(1), 104-126.

Trent, J. (2013). From learner to teacher: practice, language, and identity in a teaching practicum. *Asia-Pacific Journal of Teacher Education,* 41(4), 426-440.

Trent, J., & Gao, X. (2009). "At least I'm the type of teacher I want to be": second-career English language teachers' identity formation in Hong Kong secondary schools. *Asia-Pacific Journal of Teacher Education,* 37(3), 253-270.

Tsui, A. B. M. (2007). Complexities of identity formation: a narrative inquiry of an EFL Teacher. *TESOL Quarterly,* 41(4), 657-680.

Tsung, L. (2010). *Minority Languages, Education and Communities in China* (Vol. 23). Basingstoke: Palgrave Macmillan.

Ubaque, D. F., & Castaneda-Pena, H. (2017). Teacher research: uncovering professional identities and trajectories of teacher researchers through narrative research—a Colombia case. *International Education Studies,* 10(3), 35-45.

Varghese, M. (2006). Bilingual teachers-in-the-making in urban-town. *Journal of Multilingual and Multicultural Development,* 27(3), 211-224.

Varghese, M., Morgan, B., Johnston, B., & Johnson, K. A. (2005). Theorizing language teacher identity: three perspectives and beyond. *Journal of Language, Identity & Education,* 4(1), 21-44.

Volkmann, M. J., & Anderson, M. A. (1998). Creating professional identity: dilemmas and metaphors of a first-year chemistry teacher. *Science Education,* 82(82), 293-310.

Wang, L.-Y., & Lin, T.-B. (2014). Exploring the identity of pre-service NNESTs in Taiwan: a social relationally approach. *English Teaching Practice & Critique,* 13(3), 5-29.

Weedon, C. (1987). *Feminist Practice and Poststructuralist Theory.* Oxford, UK: Blackwell.

Wenger, E. (1998). *Communities of Practice: Learning, Meaning, and Identity.* New York: Cambridge University Press.

Wolcott, H. F. (1994). *Transforming Qualitative Data: Description, Analysis, and Interpretation.* Thousand Oaks, CA: Sage.

Wolff, D., & De Costa, P. I. (2017). Expanding the language teacher identity landscape: an investigation of the emotions and strategies of a NNEST. *Modern Language Journal,* 101(S1), 76-90.

Xu, Y. (2017). Becoming a researcher: a journey of inquiry. In G. Barkhuizen (Ed.), *Reflections on Language Teacher Identity Research* (pp. 120-125). New York: Routledge.

Xun, Y., & Zheng, X. (2014). A review of the studies on EFL teachers' identity in the past decade. *Modern Foreign Languages,* 37(01), 118-126.

Yan, H. B., Wei, F., & Li, M. B. (2013). The situation and development approach for the specialization of teacher training. *Xiandai Yuancheng Jiaoyu Yanjiu (Modern Distance Education Research),* 5(6), 43-50.

Yang, J. (2005). English as a third language among China's ethnic groups. *International Journal of Bilingual Education & Bilingualism,* 8(6), 552-567.

Yazan, B. (2017). "It just made me look at language in a different way": ESOL teacher candidates' identity negotiation through teacher education coursework. *Linguistics and Education,* 40, 38-49.

Yin, R. K. (2003). *Case Study Research: Design and Methods* (3rd ed.). Thousand Oaks: Sage.

Yin, R. K. (2011). *Qualitative Research from Start to Finish.* New York: The Guilford Press.

Yin, R. K. (2014). *Case Study Research Design and Methods* (5th ed.). Thousand Oaks, CA: Sage.

You, C., & Dörnyei, Z. (2016). Language learning motivation in China: results of a large-scale stratified survey. *Applied Linguistics,* 37(4), 495-519.

You, H. (2016). Constructing district professional identity, exploring new models of teacher development. *Journal of Curriculum and Instruction,* 34(5), 91-93.

Yuan, E. R. (2016). The dark side of mentoring on pre-service language teachers' identity formation. *Teaching & Teacher Education,* 55, 188-197.

Yuan, R. (2016). Understanding higher education-based teacher educators' identities in Hong Kong: a sociocultural linguistic perspective. *Asia-Pacific Journal of Teacher Education,* 44(4), 1-22.

Yuan, R., & Burns, A. (2017). Teacher identity development through action research: a Chinese experience. *Teachers & Teaching Theory and Practice,* 23(6), 1-21.

Yuan, R., & Lee, I. (2015). The cognitive, social and emotional processes of teacher identity construction in a pre-service teacher education programme. *Research Papers in Education,* 30(4), 469-491.

Zeichner, K., & Gore, J. (1990). Teacher socialization. In Houston, Haberan, & J. Sikula (Eds.), *Handbook of Research on Teacher Education* (pp. 329-348). New York: MacMillan.

Zembylas, M. (2003). Emotions and teacher identity: a post-structural perspective. *Teachers and Teaching,* 9(3), 213-238.

Zhang, L., & Zhang, D. (2015). Identity matters: an ethnography of two non-native English-speaking teachers (NNESTs) struggling for legitimate professional participation. In Y. L. Cheung, S. B. Said, & K. Park (Eds.), *Advances and Current Trends in Language Teacher Identity Research* (pp. 116-131). New York: Routledge.

Zhou, Y., & Xiong, Y. (2017). Live broadcast classroom: a feasible solution for Chinese rural weak education. *International Journal of Distance Education Technologies,* 15(3), 31-46.

Note: All qualitative interview data are transcribed, analyzed and categorized to generate themes. Interview data showed in each chapter or section is quoted from the interview transcript. Due to the maximum number of pages, interview transcripts are not listed in the appendix.